ISBN 978-0-331-43468-2
PIBN 11123469

THE AMERICAN ELEVATOR AND GRAIN TRADE.

Entered as second-class matter June 26, 1885, at the Post Office at Chicago, Illinois, under Act of March 3rd, 1879.

A MONTHLY JOURNAL DEVOTED TO THE ELEVATOR AND GRAIN INTERESTS.

PUBLISHED BY MITCHELL BROS. & CO. | VOL. XXIX. | CHICAGO, ILLINOIS, JUNE 15, 1911. | No. 12. | ONE DOLLAR PER ANNUM. SINGLE COPIES, TEN CENTS.

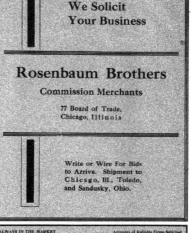

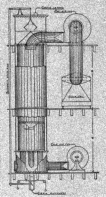

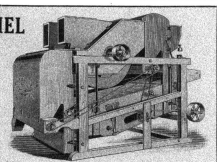

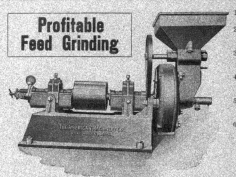

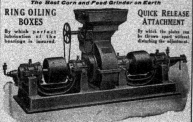

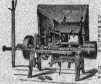

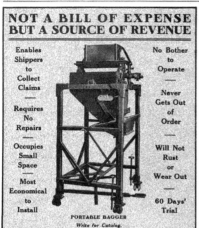

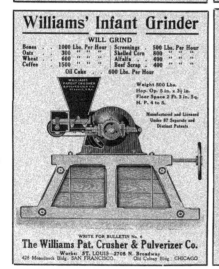

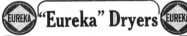

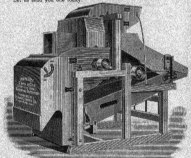

The American Elevator and Grain Trade

A MONTHLY JOURNAL DEVOTED TO THE ELEVATOR AND GRAIN INTERESTS.

VOL. XXIX. CHICAGO, ILLINOIS, JUNE 15, 1911. No. 12.

DENVER ELEVATOR COMPANY.

Colorado is not yet, strictly speaking, a grain surplus state. There is some shipment of flour into western Kansas and Texas; but for the most part the state eats up, in one form or another, about all the grain she produces "and then some," which is bought in western Kansas and Nebraska. Denver elevators are, therefore, more interested in the local consumption of grain and in the intrastate trade as distributors than in working state-grown grain forward to consuming markets in other states. This local trade is not only heavy enough to require elevators of considerable size to carry stocks adequate to meet the demand under all circumstances, but their equipment must be predecated on the necessity of cleaning and sacking.

The elevator of the picture, belonging to the Denver Elevator Co. and located at Twenty-second and Wewatta Streets, has bin capacity for 300,000 bushels, with a warehouse and basement each 55x125 ft. in size. While the elevator is small compared with Chicago houses, say, its equipment has been designed to meet exactly the requirements of the Colorado trade, which emphasize the feature of cleanliness of the grain. At Colorado rates of freight buyers cannot afford to transport into the interior offals of grain; and the result is that probably no state in the Union consumes more consistently clean grain than Colorado. How far the policy of the present manager of the Denver Elevator Co. influenced the trade to this general state policy cannot here be said; but certain it is that when one heavy dealer makes a point of clean grain and follows that policy habitually, his competitors must do likewise or quit the game. The characteristic shipments of this company (wholesale only) under the "Delco" trade mark, are (1) Mixed chop, ground oats, corn and barley, all recleaned; (2) "Chick Crax," fine cracked corn, rescreened; (3) Cracked Wheat, rescreened; and (4) Cracked Corn, rescreened. And guaranty of quality accompanies each pack.

ELEVATOR A, OF THE DENVER ELEVATOR CO., DENVER, COLORADO.

The Washington state inspection department has taken a new lease of life under the law passed by the last legislature, which authorizes the department to weigh as well as inspect grain at the Sound terminals.

The Hungarian Ministry of Agriculture has reorganized the statistical service, and, as required by the new system, forty-five official district surveyors have been appointed who must travel at least twice monthly through all parts of the district under their surveyance, in order to be able to check by personal observation the reports of the agricultural reporters; and only after such examination will a general report on the district, with the surveyor's remarks, be sent to the Ministry. The first report compiled by this new method was issued on June 1; the first quantitative estimates for wheat and rye will be issued on July 1.—Corn Trade News.

THE INTERNATIONAL INSTITUTE.

The General Assembly of the International Institute of Agriculture closed at Rome on May 20 its annual meeting. There were forty-nine agricultural countries represented by delegates. Although friends of the Institute in America have had great difficulty in holding the interest of the administration in the Institute sufficiently to obtain a recommendation for an appropriation for the expenses of the delegation from the United States and annual contribution (about $10,000), our delegation at the late meeting are said to have taken a "prominent part in the discussions and won all the points they sought. The discussions were vigorous but cordial, and the final conclusions unanimous.

"The Assembly decided urgently to request the governments adhering to the principles of the Institute to send to the Institute estimates of yields and conditions pertaining to the principal crops for the three months preceding the harvest and selected the American system, or 'single-numerical' statement,' for these reports. The Assembly also voted for the inauguration of a system of commercial and price statistics of exports and imports; recommending the Campbell system of dry farming, the organization of a permanent commission for the study of plant diseases; and a department of agricultural meteorology, which will probably be modeled on the American system.

"Delegates to the Assembly appeared generally to acknowledge that the United States was further advanced than any other country in all things relating to agriculture, and the American delegates expressed themselves as being impressed with the thorough and practical work of the Institute. The next Assembly will be held in 1913."

[For the "American Elevator and Grain Trade."]

AMERICAN GRAIN INSPECTION.

BY WILLIAM WELSH.

The discussion now in progress as a result of the embargo placed upon the shipments of corn from the port of Philadelphia by the Liverpool Chamber of Commerce, has attracted attention throughout the whole country, and particularly at the grain centers, Chicago, Buffalo, and New York. The railroads and shipping interests centering in Philadelphia are alike aroused and have both called upon the Commercial Exchange that controls the inspection at this port to make a rigid investigation. It means loss of business for both, if the embargo is not removed. It should be understood that the corn of which complaint has been made did not originate in Philadelphia. It had been subjected to inspection at other points, was unloaded from cars, passed through the elevators here direct to ship and without any long period of storage, possibly not more than five to ten days. It was of course inspected on arrival, and again delivered to ship. This particular corn of which complaint has been made was, we are informed, shipped in January and February, so that the critical period for corn had not been reached.

It should be understood that every receiving and shipping point of importance has its own standards and system of inspection. The exporter of grain from Philadelphia, New York or Baltimore buys his corn or wheat at Western points and must accept their certificates of inspection as final, when forwarded with bills of lading and sight drafts. It therefore becomes evident that it is not alone the inspectors in Philadelphia, or at other shipping points, who are responsible for grain arriving in Europe out of condition.

The inspectors at the seaboard are naturally influenced by the Western inspection and very loath to inflict loss upon the shippers at their respective ports. This, of course, is no justification for passing grain not up to the standard, but it affords a clue to a possible laxity, under such conditions. And it should be the chief aim of the investigation now in progress in Philadelphia to determine whether there has been such laxity or collusion with the shippers.

Let it be understood also that the millers, grain merchants and consumers who do a purely home trade are just as much interested in a just and rigid inspection of grain in this country as are European importers. Our exports of grain are but a small proportion of the grain received and shipped to the various sections of the country. And the mill.

ers and grain merchants who handle grain for milling and for home consumption are entitled to a full measure of protection from loose methods of inspection. We know from experience, as well as from personal investigation, that frequent losses are sustained by both the above classes by reason of grain arriving out of condition or mixed with inferior grain, causing great waste in cleaning.

With a knowledge of conditions that exist in our elevators it is not difficult to understand why this is so. Elevators at one time were supposed to exist for storage purposes only. Instead of that they are most largely used now for the manipulation and grading of grain. In Philadelphia, for instance, wheat is graded No. 1 and No. 2, steamer No. 2, and rejected A and B. Of the first there is not one car in a hundred immediately after harvest; the bulk of the winter wheat will be of the latter three grades. The steamer grade is supposed to be equal in quality to No. 2, but not sufficiently dry to stand a voyage by sail. Rejected A and B are too damp to grade "steamer," or not sufficiently clean, or with too much foreign substance, such as garlic, cheat or rye. The difference in price of these three latter grades when received, as compared with No. 2, is: for "steamer," 2c to 3c per bushel; for rejected A, 6c to 8c; and for rejected B, 10c to 12c. The shipper of the grain from interior points must take his chance and bear the losses on this steamer and rejected wheat. No miller or grain merchant would make this difference in buying from the farmers, except in extreme cases as to the conditions. What follows? These steamer and rejected grades are so handled in the elevators that they are eventually used in mixing with other No. 2 wheat and sold to millers or shippers as No. 2 and at the market price for that grade. There are of course certain charges for this work in the elevators, but these charges are small when compared with the difference in price made when received. The receiver makes the profit at the seaboard. In the West, we understand, those who own and control the elevators are not infrequently the owners of the grain, and therefore make the profit. Certain it is that no one ever heard, in Philadelphia at least, of a sale of wheat from the elevators of the rejected grades at the lower prices. The same is true of corn to a more limited extent as to prices. There is no No. 2 and steamer corn, No. 3 and No. 4 and rejected. The corn received at the shipping ports is practically all Western and comes in under Western inspection. The rejected corn received in the elevators, together with the No. 3 and 4, goes out as No. 2 or steamer after drying, perhaps, and cleaning.

It must be evident from this brief review of conditions prevailing at the seaboard elevators that a great responsibility rests upon the inspectors, and equally so at such receiving points as Chicago and Buffalo. Whatever defects may be said to exist in our present system of inspection, there has unquestionably been a great improvement during the past twenty-five years in handling and shipping grain from the West. The writer has handled millions of bushels of Western corn and wheat that arrived and was rejected because of its condition on arrival. Our elevators had then no such facilities as now exist for handling grain out of condition. It was not unusual for corn to arrive so much damaged that the price realized but little more than paid the freight. In such cases it could only be used after cooling and drying for mixing and distilling purposes. The West learned so many costly lessons in this respect that it is now the rule to ship only when shelled direct from crib, and, when any doubt arises as to its keeping qualities, to dry before shipment.

Notwithstanding these precautions, there is still considerable corn that arrives at interior points and at the seaboard in poor condition, particularly during the spring and summer months. Much of this is said to be "elevator" corn that has passed through a period of storage and been manipulated and mixed to pass inspection.

The question would therefore seem to be, how can our system of inspection be so improved and made uniform as to relieve the inspectors from being parties to this manipulating and mixing of grain? Or, why should not grain once rejected by the inspectors retain its grade or character and be sold on its merits by sample, even after being improved in the elevators? In the case of wheat, the millers would certainly prefer to do their own mixing and thus secure it at prices corresponding to its grade or quality. The principal defect in our present system of inspection is the fact that the standards at the numerous receiving and shipping points are not uniform. No. 2 wheat in Philadelphia will not grade No. 2 in New York. This has been tried over and over again; and yet it is claimed that Philadelphia No. 2 commands the same price in the European markets as that of New York. The same is true of Baltimore inspection. Their No. 2 will not grade No. 2 in Philadelphia. Whether this is a result of jealousy is an open question; but it certainly should be possible for the inspectors at these three Atlantic ports to get together and adopt uniform standards.

It is claimed by many who have had large experience in the handling and inspection of grain that a National system of grain inspection is the only remedy. For several years past an inspection

E. J. WATSON,
Commissioner of Agriculture, South Carolina.

bill has been introduced into Congress, but it has been opposed largely by the elevator interests, and has failed of passage. The various exchanges that control the inspection in their respective districts are also opposed to it, on the ground, in some cases, that it would cut down the emoluments that they now derive from the inspection. At one time in Philadelphia the inspection department was in the hands of an independent inspector who collected the fees and became personally responsible for any claims arising at home or abroad. During the existence of that system the export business of Philadelphia grew rapidly, until the Commercial Exchange concluded that this independent inspector, elected by themselves and working in co-operation with its own grain committee, was making too much money. He was offered a salary but declined it, and another was chosen to take his place. For the past two or three years the receipts of the inspection department have not been sufficient to pay the salaries and expenses. It must be added that the falling off in exports generally has contributed to this, but this is not the whole trouble. This independent inspector was in touch with the elevators and inspectors in the West; he made tours among them, and influenced large purchases and shipments through Philadelphia, after personal examination of the grain in Western elevators.

Do not these results indicate a solution of our present inspection problem? If not National inspection, then there must be uniform standards and co-operation among the inspectors of the whole country to maintain them. Loose inspection never pays in the long run, either for home trade or export. It is not unusual for grain merchants and shippers to say, when making purchases, "We are afraid of the inspection at this or that point," thus discriminating against it. The results of the investigation in Philadelphia will be looked forward to with interest; and whatever the result, it is to be hoped that the necessity of greater co-operation and more uniform methods of inspection will follow, and particularly that the elevators' interest in inspection shall cease to be the dominating factor, as it is unfortunately now.

AÇID CORN IN SOUTH CAROLINA.

Agricultural Commissioner E. J. Watson of South Carolina, who is also *ex-officio* charged with the execution of the pure food and feed laws of that state, has introduced a new spike in the cogs of the machinery that has been working "queer" corn into his state. In view of the samples of "No. 2 Corn," so certified by certain markets for local shippers to South Carolina buyers, which it was the privilege of this writer to examine during a recent visit of Commissioner Watson to Chicago, it was apparent that something besides "moisture content" must be set up as a defense against the commercial movement of such abominable stuff. The adjective is used advisedly. One can hardly conceive any lawful use to which such corn could be put—dry, of course, having less than 13 per cent of moisture when inspected, but with barely one per cent of sound grain, not contaminated by mould and dirt and the admixture of broken kernels; ear corn with hardly a sound kernel per ear. Yet Ohio river gateways inspected out such rotten stuff as "No. 2 Corn."

Now Mr. Watson has adopted as the basis of his estimation of the soundness of corn shipped into his state, in which he is sustained by the letter of South Carolina law, the principle behind the laws on the same subject in force in Austria, where he has studied the spoiled corn problem *in situ*. This may be briefy stated by quoting from Bulletin 199 B. P. I., Agr. Dept., entitled "The Determination of the Deterioration of Maize, with Incidental Reference to Pellagra," by O. F. Black and C. L. Alsberg, in which they say:

> The possibility that spoiled corn may possess poisonous qualities seems to have passed unnoticed in this country. Indeed, it is found that with the exception of [some works named in the Bulletin] upon the proteins, little work has been done on the chemistry of corn. Most investigators have contented themselves with the determination of protein, carbohydrate fat, and ash. Some have also studied certain of the simpler constants of these groups of substances. The attempt to disentangle the mixture of complex substances of which the corn seed, like any other living thing, is composed has hardly begun. The investigators of southern Europe who had in the alleged connection between pellagra and corn a great incentive to undertake this work have not done so. In southern Europe, however, much attention has been paid to the toxicity of spoiled corn, if not to the chemistry, and the relevant litreature is very large.

The authors of the Bulletin, therefore, took up for examination the work of the Italian and Austrian government experts with a view to presenting to Americans those methods of examining and determining the quality of corn and corn meal. Abroad the suspected corn is examined by skilled government experts, but in this country, owing to different conditions of control, a simpler method is called for to determine whether such products are fit for human food. Such a test is thought by Messrs. Black and Alsberg to be "the determination of the acidity in corn," upon which much stress is laid in both Italy and Austria as highly important. Commissioner Watson holds to the same view, and now applies the acidity test to suspected corn called to his attention, when such test seems necessary. On this point Messrs Black and Alsberg say:

> In this work the acid test has been found the most reliable means of distinguishing good from bad corn. All corn is somewhat acid, not necessarily to the taste, but to chemical reagents. Since the spoiling of corn is due to fermentation processes in which acids are among the products, the extent to which this deterioration has progressed can be measured by the amount of acid present. It becomes necessary then only to fix a standard of acidity

above which corn should be considered unfit for food.

It is desired at this point to avoid creating a misunderstanding. It is desired most carefully to avoid producing the impression that all fermented, heated, moldy or otherwise spoiled corn is necessarily dangerous to man. This would hardly be in accord with the facts. It is, however, quite generally believed by the majority of investigators that much of this sort of corn is injurious. As long as no more definite information exists, it seems the sane and conservative course to bar as far as possible damaged corn from human consumption.

It is not necessary to go into the methods for the determination of acidity; grain dealers are rarely chemists and few have as yet found it necessary to employ them or to maintain laboratories. Moreover, for the purposes of business, it is not necessary. So long as corn shippers to South Carolina grade their corn honestly to the standards of the Grain Dealers' National Association Grade Rules, they will have no trouble with Com'r Watson.

It is because shippers have not heeded the warnings to this effect sent out from Columbia by Com'r Watson that he has accumulated, as he says, a "warehouse full of damaged corn to be burned" and brought shippers from Ohio River and other gateways from the West to the Southeast to a realization that "something is doing" in South Carolina. The published reports of corn seizures by him have been exaggerated, however, in that they have conveyed the impression that Com'r Watson has been inclined to be arbitrary. As to this he writes us:

It is not my purpose to take advantage of any man, or firm, or section of the country, but our people are going to have protection from rotten corn, no matter what the cost. The law has been on the statute books for a year; and I have taken the most extreme pains to acquaint the trade with its requirements. I believe, and in fact have every reason to believe, that the majority of the members of the Grain Dealers' National Association welcome the inauguration of the exact system of inspection and examination that we have put into effect in this state. I am sure, too, beyond any reasonable doubt, that in the long run every member of the Association will not only favor it but urge their states to adopt it, for the reason that it must of necessity put the dishonest and cut-throat competitor out of the business. The object of the law is to give protection to the clean, honest dealer and with him we never have any trouble. There are some concerns, however, that for so long have been accustomed to their monopoly of unprotected states for use as a dumping ground for rotten products that they resent any one's interfering with that class of business by the state in its sovereign capacity, and it is from such, and such alone, that we have heard the howl. I knew it would come, and have been ready to meet it anywhere, at any time and in any manner. I can assure you of this, however, that it will have no avail in this particular case.

In view of Com'r Watson's attitude and the seizures he has made in the recent past, at the request of shippers, he met representatives of various markets at Nashville on May 29. Among those living outside of Nashville, there were present representatives of Zorn & Co., A. Brandeis & Co., and Callahan & Co., of Louisville, of the Henderson Elevator Co. of Henderson, Ky., R. L. Powell of Cairo, Ill., and Sec'y John F. Courcier of the National Association.

Mr. Watson was called on for a statement; but he had hardly begun what he may have intended as an address on the subject matter, when all formality was dissipated by a whirlwind of questions by shippers who wanted to know what they would have to do to keep out of trouble!

We may here, perhaps, summarize the results of this brisk and interesting examination by quoting certain statements by Com'r Watson in a letter dated May 17, addressed to a South Carolina commission house whose Ohio River clients had had corn seized as unsalable under the law, thus covering the same ground:

You told them exactly the truth. If they send corn into this state of grades No. 1, 2 or 3, they will have no trouble with the authorities in South Carolina. Somebody out in the Middle West, probably one of the same houses that have been shipping into this state the worst refuse that it has ever been our fortune to examine, and who has had that class of stuff confiscated, is undoubtedly systematically lying to the trade in that section; and I am not surprised that reputable houses have doubt as to whether to ship into South Carolina or not.

As you know, the law in this state does not permit of the sale of whole grains so damaged as to be dangerous. This law has been on the statute books of this state just one year, and the greater portion of the year we have endeavored through every possible channel to impressing upon shippers of corn into this territory, that it must be sound and pure, and must grade at least a No. 3, according to the Grain Dealers' National Association standards. At first it was difficult to determine when corn was so damaged as to be dangerous, and as long as there was the slightest element of doubt in reaching this determination, I did not attempt the confiscation of any goods, but warned the shippers repeatedly. After most careful investigation—and our laboratories had been established and placed in the hands of as competent men as can be found in this country—I put into the laboratories the complete method of exact determination which by scientific investigation had been in use in both Austria and Italy for a number of years. This method determines exactly and to the satisfaction of any court or jury when corn is dangerous as contemplated by the law, and in no instance has a genuine No. 2 or No. 3 which has been examined been found to be in that condition. This season we have found, seized, confiscated and destroyed a considerable quantity of the worst stuff I have ever seen in my life; and as long as I am in charge of this work, I propose to do the same thing with every pound of it that we can possibly find through our inspection force. I am fully determined to rule this rotten stuff out of the state of South Carolina, no matter whom it affects. There are a great many houses, I am sorry to say, who don't want to understand what we are doing and why, and don't seem to care how often they try to run in this kind of stuff. I am determined, however, to throw the fullest possible protection around the honest dealer and put him on a basis with every other competitor. No confiscation is authorized from this office until a careful examination of the samples has been made in the laboratories, and when the reports come to me they come in such form that I know just exactly what I am doing. . . .

Furthermore, if I can have any influence elsewhere, knowing what I do of the great damage being done to live stock and people in the South, I am going to do everything in my power to see the same system of examination and tests put into effect in all of the states that have heretofore been the systematic dumping ground. In the enforcement of this law one man stands the same chance as another. In some instances some of these houses have thought me so innocent as to be frightened by threats to withdraw from the market in South Carolina, unless they could ship stuff unfit for fertilizer even, which they sent out under a No. 2 contract.

The gist of the whole thing, as brought out at Nashville, was that if those shipping grain into South Carolina would honestly inspect their grain according to the "Grades of Grain" promulgated by the Grain Dealers' National Association, they would have no trouble. Just as the meeting was about to adjourn, Com'r Watson's chemist, Mr. Summers, addressed the committee, and in substance said: "In order that you may have a more definite and practical idea of what the acidity test means, I would say that all the tests we have made have run right along with the inspections made under the Rules in this blue book (holding in his hand a copy of the Grades of Grain promulgated by the Grain Dealers' National Association), and the conclusion is, that if you will take the pains to grade your grain according to these Rules, you will experience no difficulty in getting along with the acidity test."

Mr. Watson explained that the moisture content had nothing to do with the acidity test. As we understand it, however, that statement does not imply that the moisture test will not be applied in South Carolina, but that it will be supplemented by the acidity test, if need be, since most of the really rotten corn reaches South Carolina containing comparatively little moisture.

L. P. Brown, who executes the Tennessee pure food laws, expressed the probability that he would adopt Mr. Watson's methods for estimating the value of corn and corn meal in Tennessee.

The agreement of the grain handlers at Portland, Ore., with the shippers, for pay of 40c per hour, having expired by limitation after one year, the men now demand another advance of 5c per hour.

A settlement of the losses in the Perry C. Smith Grain Co. at Kansas City was effected on May 20, payment being made by the Mo. Pacific Ry., owner of the Kansas-Missouri Elevator, and J. Sidney Smith, father of Perry C. Smith, head of the embarrassed company. The Mo. Pacific paid $140,000 and J. Sidney Smith about $100,000.

[For the "American Elevator and Grain Trade."]

AS IT WAS THIRTY YEARS AGO.

BY DANIEL McALISTER.

On entering an elevator car in the Union National Bank building here at Columbus, O., recently, I was accosted by a sturdy, middle-aged and rather dapper looking gentleman thus:

"Well, I declare, if here isn't my old friend, Dan McAlister."

It was Joseph W. McCord, the present secretary and treasurer of Grain Dealers' Association here, with whom Time seems to have dealt so kindly that I failed to recognize in him my long-ago competitor in business.

He had been reading "The American Elevator and Grain Trade," so he said, and added that he had something in his office he thought I would like to see.

When we got there, he took from a drawer in one of his desks an old book of records, in which we found the minutes of the Association's first meeting, reading as follows:

PUT-IN-BAY, OHIO, July 1, 1880.

The grain dealers of Ohio met here today in general convention, for the purpose of organizing an association for the better protection of interests connected with the grain trade, and for the correction of abuses that have crept in, and are detrimental alike to the producer and the shipper of cereals.

The convention assembled at 10 o'clock a. m., with about ninety members present. The name of Col. S. H. Hunt was presented as temporary chairman, by John G. Ridenauer of Columbus, and was received with applause. Mr. Hunt was made temporary chairman, and Mr. L. C. Newsom, of Columbus, temporary secretary.

On motion of Mr. E. Lawson, the chairman appointed the following gentlemen a committee on permanent organization: E. Lawson, S. E. De Woolf and W. H. Banister.

The chair also appointed a committee of four on rules and order of business as follows: D. A. Johns, T. E. Barry, S. G. Fulton and R. B. Cowling.

After a short recess, the committee on permanent organization reported the following named gentlemen to act as the association's officers for the term of one year:

President, S. H. Hunt, Upper Sandusky.

Vice-Presidents (ten)—Boyd, Myers, Findley, Tracy, Ulrich, Derst, Fulton, Cowling, Thomas and Strong.

Secretary, L. C. Newsom, Columbus, Ohio.

Treasurer, John G. Ridenauer, also of Columbus.

The committee on Rules and Order of Business reported:

First, the organization shall be known as "The Grain Dealers Association of Ohio." Then follows ten sections of rules and eight points of order in business, as follows: First, Membership; second, Transportation; third, Contracts with farmers; Fourth, Loaning bags to farmers; Fifth, Grading of grain when purchased; Sixth, Weights of grain and seeds; seventh, Storage of grain for farmers; eighth, Condition of grain cars.

After adopting the foregoing reports and signing the roll of membership, the association recessed until 2 o'clock p. m.

AFTERNOON SESSION.

The following resolution was adopted in reference to transportation:

Resolved, That whilst it is not the desire of this convention to dictate the policies of railroad companies throughout the country, yet it is our earnest desire and request that the managers of the freight business so arrange their rates that there be but two changes each year; one for summer and one as a winter rate.

The following was also adopted:

Resolved, That a committee of five be appointed by the president to confer with the different railroad lines relative to establishing a stated time for changing rates on grain to the Seaboard; and the following committee appointed: W. H. Banister, S. H. White, L. C. Newsom, B. T. York and James Hamilton.

"Loaning of Bags to Farmers" was informally discussed and postponed until next meeting.

The grading of grain, weights of grain and seeds, storage of grain, and condition of box cars were all freely discussed, but no action taken.

The following resolution was then adopted:

"Resolved, That when we adjourn we do so to meet at Columbus, Ohio, on the 19th day of January, 1881."

And the convention adjourned.

Abstract of minutes, meeting Jan. 19, 1881, at Columbus, Ohio.

Convention called to order, 2 p. m., by S. H. Hunt, president.

First business, the unsettled bag question. Mr.

Whitehurst, of Canal Winchester, offered the following:

Resolved, That we, the members of this association, discontinue the furnishing of bags to farmers under all circumstances, and that we do so under the pledge and penalty of our honor.

Lost; 53 to 5.

The committee on railroads appointed at the last meeting not having reported were discharged and a new one appointed in its stead as follows: Daniel McAlister, I. L. Talbott, S. H. White, David Boyd and O. T. Brown. They were instructed to report at next meeting.

The following was adopted:

Resolved, That we, the grain dealers of Ohio, will hereafter discriminate against any Eastern elevator company found guilty of cutting in weights; and that each dealer will report to the next meeting any knowledge he may have of such cutting in weights.

Mr. Cowling introduced the following, which was adopted:

Resolved, That in justice to all buyers and sellers of corn, the Ohio legislature be requested to make the weight of a bushel of ear corn seventy pounds for the year round; and that our secretary draw up a petition to that effect.

The following preamble and resolution were voted down:

Whereas, Within the last few years a number of Eastern commission houses have established "agencies" throughout our state, along with other dealers who have located themselves in offices (without the expense of carrying on a warehouse), and who go scouring the country ready to BUY when grain is in active demand or an advance likely to occur, but who are "out of the market" when trade is dull or a decline is liable to take place, at which times they recommend "consignments" only, thereby causing many losses to regular dealers while they, themselves are "raking in" the profits; therefore, be it

Resolved, That it is not to the advantage of the warehouse men of Ohio to patronize or to encourage such dealers in any way.

Lost, by a vote of 43 to 6.

A vote of thanks was then tendered to the Ohio State Journal, the Columbus Evening Dispatch and the Columbus Times for favorable mentions; also to the City Council of Columbus for the use of their Chamber of Commerce rooms.

There being no other business of importance before the convention, a motion was made and adopted to adjourn; and to meet again at Put-in Bay, Ohio, on the third Wednesday in June, 1881.

L. C. NEWSOM, Sec'y.

Minutes of the association's meetings following after the above seem to have been kept elsewhere, or to have been lost, although the association has held its meetings regularly every year and sometimes twice a year through all the THIRTY intervening years; and many an outing to the lakes and streams throughout the state has been had, bringing the members together, mixing social pleasures with the regular work they had to do.

The next meeting is to be held at Cedar Point, Ohio, on June 21 and 22, 1911. I find the following record of a recent meeting, held in Piqua, Ohio, March 16, just past:

"At a meeting of the governing board, Grain Dealers' Association, held in Piqua, Ohio, March 16, the time and place for our next annual meeting was considered. Unless for sufficient reasons that may develop later, the thirty-second annual meeting of the association will be held at Cedar Point, Ohio, on Wednesday and Thursday, June 21 and 22, 1911.

"The members of the board were unanimous in their belief that we should make this meeting more of a social affair than heretofore, devoting the afternoon and evening of both days to entertainment and pleasure; and that every possible effort should be made to secure as large an attendance of ladies and children of members as possible.

"Due notice of the meeting, with full details of proposed program, will be given hereafter."

JOSEPH W. MCCORD, Sec'y.

Your correspondent prophesies for the dealers and their families, a happy and enjoyable time.

ERIE ELEVATOR AT JERSEY CITY.

The Erie Railroad Co. has purchased of the Erie Elevator Co., of which the D. O. Mills estate owned a controlling interest, the elevator properties at Jersey City, in accordance with a contract made thirty years ago, which obligated the Railroad Co. to make this purchase upon six months' notice. The railroad now proposes to lease the property to the Armour grain interests who have been negotiating for the exclusive use of the properties.

The lease has, however, hung fire, owing to the fact that the Interstate Commerce Commission to whom the question was referred may decide that the Erie Railroad Co. cannot haul grain for the Armour interests and at the same time lease to it the exclusive right to use the elevator at its terminal in Jersey City. The point raised is that the Armours would be able thus to shut out competing grain shippers over the Erie. A decision on this point is expected from the Interstate Commerce Commission shortly. If the decision is adverse, the Erie Railroad will be compelled to keep the elevator open to all comers or else sell it outright to the Armours.

There has been a great reduction in grain shipments to Jersey City during the last ten years, a reduction which made practically useless a big elevator on the Brooklyn water front, and this fact will be urged as a reason why the Commission should permit the Armours to lease the elevator.

IN THE ALFALFA.

As most men are imitators, or learn by object lessons, at least, acquire knowledge most easily objectively rather than subjectively, the most ef-

D. R. RISSER.

ficient teacher of agriculture is the experiment station and the demonstrator. What the farmer can see growing he can understand and believe in, and, if new and apparently profitable, is willing to investigate *in situ*. The elevator man, therefore, who owns a farm and is progressive enough to "demonstrate" a new crop or new methods or new seeds has special claims to recognition as a public spirited citizen and to "distinguished consideration" as a clever business man.

The picture is one of an Ohio elevator man examining his alfalfa, which looks pretty good at this distance. But it will doubtless yield the grower, D. R. Risser of Vaughnsville, Ohio, something more than the profit on the crop itself. For Mr. Risser operates elevators on the N. O., L. E. & W., and C., H. & D. Railways and handles grain, hay, seeds, feed and all sorts of things that farmers sell and buy for use on their farms, and as alfalfa is not a common forage plant of Ohio as yet, this "demonstration" of this valuable grass can hardly fail to bring Mr. Risser's name, and incidentally his business also, to the favorable attention of just the men whose good will and interest it is to his advantage to cultivate.

Mr. Risser's elevator specialties in grain are recleaned yellow shelled corn and good milling wheat; but he handles so many articles for grain farmers, dairymen and poultry growers as well as fencing and building supplies, that he issues a regular catalogue, which he finds it profitable to circulate freely in his territory.

F. B. Maclennen of the Manitoba Elevator Commission has resigned.

[For the "American Elevator and Grain Trade."]

THE CHICAGO BOARD OF TRADE: ITS USES AND ABUSES.

VII.

BY JULIAN KUNE.

After the Board had moved back into the reconstructed Chamber of Commerce Building, its prosperity more than kept pace with the prosperity of reconstructed Chicago. The ruling spirit of the day, which found its expression in the words of "I will," had become also the watchword and the battle cry of the members of the Board. Trusts and combinations, outside of the Standard Oil Company, had hardly been heard of as yet; Chicago's industries were in their formative period; and their growth was steady and healthy. Some members of the Board ran private wires into their offices, not for the purpose of controlling the grain trade, but merely to facilitate and expedite their growing business. "Live and let live" had not become as yet an obsolete motto to the owners of private wires.

MEMBERSHIPS REACH HIGHEST VALUE.

The number of memberships as well as their value reached their highest levels in 1881. There were then on the rolls of the Board 1936 members, of whom 74 had been admitted by initiation prior to the advance of the initiation fee from $1,000 to $2,500, and 69 were admitted just prior to the fee having been advanced from $2,500 to $5,000. The value of memberships kept advancing steadily, until one or two had been sold at $5,000 and several at between $4,000 and $4,700. Notwithstanding that the annual dues had been reduced to $20, there was still money enough in the treasury to cover all expenses. The years 1881 to 1883 inclusive were the halcyon days of the Chicago Board of Trade; but, as is often the case, great prosperity engenders greed; and so it was with some of the members of the Board. They were not satisfied with having a good and healthy trade, but incited by the pernicious examples set to them by Wall Street, they introduced into the Board some of the features of "high finance" in the shape of corners and manipulations of the grain trade. It was these days of manipulations of Chicago's grain markets that gained for the Chicago Board of Trade an unenviable reputation which, however, in many cases, was an unjust imputation, as the Board always contained scores of members who did only a legitimate grain trade.

PROPOSITION TO ERECT A NEW BUILDING.

As early as 1877 the question of procuring more room for the Board of Trade was agitated. At the annual meeting of 1884 steps were taken by the board of directors to purchase ground and erect a new building at the south end of LaSalle Street; and a proposition to that effect was submitted to the members at the annual meeting of 1881.

It was natural that the Board, prospering as it did, should wish to exchange its swaddling clothes for something more befitting its advanced and dignified position. Hence a board of real estate managers, composed of a president and four other members, was elected, two of whom were to be elected every two years on the first Monday in March. This board was authorized to accept plans and estimates for the construction of the new Board of Trade Building, to borrow money, arrange for a deed of trust, and to issue bonds. Of the Board's assets $40,000 was appropriated for a site on which to build.

Inasmuch as great responsibilities were placed on the shoulders of the real estate managers, I will name the gentlemen composing that body, to wit: Mr. Nelson E. Blake, as president of the Board, was ex-officio chairman; D. W. Irwin, Charles Counselman, John R. Bensley, William Dickinson, and A. S. Worthington, secretary.

The new building is the one the Board now occupies. It stands in Jackson Boulevard, between LaSalle and Sherman Streets. It has a frontage of 173¾ feet on Jackson Boulevard and 205 feet on LaSalle Street. Its height is 160 feet. The dimensions of the exchange hall are 152 by 161 feet, and the hall is 50 feet high. Its total cost was $1,730,000, a much larger sum than was anticipated.

It not only absorbed the total cash assets of the Board, but saddled upon the corporation an onerous debt in the form of debenture bonds to the amount of $1,250,000. But the worst feature of all was that the Board of Trade, in consideration of its being released from its contract with the Chamber of Commerce, which had to run yet nearly ninety years, surrendered its Chamber of Commerce stock, for which it had originally paid $78,792.32. In plainer language, the Board threw away a valuable asset which, at the time it surrendered the same to the Chamber of Commerce, was worth very near $200,000.

DEDICATION OF THE NEW BOARD OF TRADE HALL.

Although the new hall was not opened for business until May 1, the dedication took place on April 29, 1885. The dedication was a brilliant affair. Delegations from the various exchanges of this country and Canada, as well as some from across the sea, were present. All the rooms were thrown open and illuminated, while the echoes of the strains of music floated through the building, as the hundreds of visitors strolled from room to room admiring the frescoes on the walls and ceilings.

Promptly at eight o'clock the meeting was called to order by President Nelson E. Blake. Mr. John R. Bensley, in behalf of the board of real estate managers, delivered the keys of the building to the president, who, in accepting them, briefly responded, after which the orator of the occasion, Mr. Emory A. Storrs, was introduced. After giving a glowing historical account of the Board's activities since 1848, he delivered a eulogistic oration on the manifold benefits derived from boards of trade in general and the Chicago Board of Trade in particular. He showed how through the efforts of the Chicago Board of Trade the shipments of flour from 1848 to 1884 had increased nine fold, the shipments of wheat ten fold, the shipments of corn eleven fold, and the shipment of oats over 527 fold. Mr. Storrs further illuminated his arguments with quotations from legal lights, thus trying to prove that speculation, if carried on within reasonable bounds, is a great help instead of a detriment to commerce. He said that Lord Kenyon, England's Chief Justice in the eighteenth century, attempted to regulate the grain trade by adjudging all speculative transactions as void, but he could not enforce his opinion long, as the country raised a great outcry against it.

The thirty-eighth annual meeting took place on January 4, 1886, in the call room, which later was turned into a smoking, or visitors', room. Mr. A. M. Wright had been elected president and Mr. Geo. F. Stone, secretary. Memberships had dropped during January of this year from $3,300 to $2,100. It certainly was a surprise to the members of the Board to see the value of membership privileges drop instead of being enhanced after moving into the palatial quarters. The raising of the annual dues from $20 to $75 had something to do with it.

This depreciation of membership values could not have been ascribed to commercial inactivity, for the volume of the Board's business kept on growing larger than ever. The cause must have been the feeling of mistrust which had been engendered among members who were outside the charmed circle of private-wire and elevator men, to see the corporation loaded down with such a heavy debt for a building which from the start showed very poor construction and which was reared on inadequate foundations. It was not long before the tower, which was neither esthetic nor useful at any time, had to be razed at an expense of over $25,000.

ONE CAUSE OF DECLINE IN MEMBERSHIP VALUES.

Change in business methods undoubtedly had much to do with the discouraging condition in which the Board found itself after it moved into the new building. From day to day the strictly commission business in breadstuffs became less and less. The more opulent houses inaugurated the purchasing business, by sending out daily bids by postal cards. The smaller receivers of grain, who were not inclined to speculate, were thus crowded out; and at the present time most of the grain received on the floor of the Board is purchased in the country by representatives of local elevator proprietors or those who own elevators in the country.

I have no fear of contradiction when I assert that the present business of the Board could be done more profitably if the number of memberships were limited to eight hundred, or a thousand at the outside, instead of the Board having on its rolls over 1,700, half of whom can barely make a living.

The Board has for some time past pursued the policy of reducing the surplus memberships by buying them in. Thus far it has not met with the success anticipated. The members are taxed annually for an additional $50 for the purpose of creating a fund wherewith to buy memberships, but the value of them has not been affected by the purchases made. The additional taxation of $50 besides the annual dues of $75 is a heavy burden upon many members.

CONCLUSION.

I have earnestly endeavored to give an impartial and fair historical sketch of the institution with which I was continuously identified over a third of a century. I have watched with an almost filial affection its rise to prosperity, and if I have perchance criticised its policies too harshly I did so from pure motives. I look upon the Chicago Board of Trade as my business alma mater. I severed my connection with the Board in 1909; but I still entertain the same belief in its usefulness, which once a great philosopher said of commerce in general: "Commerce tends to wear off prejudices which maintain distinction and animosity between nations. It softens and polishes the manners of men. It unites them by one of the strongest of all ties: the desire of supplying their mutual wants. It disposes them to peace by establishing in every state an order of citizens bound by their interests to be the guardians of the public tranquility."

OFFICES OF THE ORVILLE-SIMPSON COMPANY.

The complete plant of the Orville-Simpson Company of Cincinnati, Ohio, in so far as exterior of the buildings is concerned, was shown in a recent issue of our journal. A full write-up, however, should include the very convenient offices of the new works; and these are shown herewith.

In the plans, as outlined by Mr. Simpson, arrangements were made for plenty of light and room, and these have been amply secured. Taking into consideration both windows and skylights, there are over 1,500 square feet of glass surface admitting light to the offices.

The floors are marbleized fibre, while the wood work is finished in the style of old English. The private office of President Simpson is shown at extreme right of the picture. Next comes the cashier's office, which is separated from the head salesman's office by the hall way leading to the shops. Then comes the superintendent's office, with the drafting room just in the rear; while shown in the left front is the office manager's and stenographer's desks, making a very complete and convenient business office.

OFFICES OF THE ORVILLE-SIMPSON COMPANY AT CINCINNATI, OHIO.

NEW COMMITTEES.

The agricultural committees of Congress have been announced, as follows:

Senate.—Henry E. Burnham of New Hampshire, Francis E. Warren of Wyoming, George C. Perkins of California, Simon Guggenheim of Colorado, Carroll S. Page of Vermont, Coe I. Crawford of South Dakota, William O. Bradley of Kentucky, William Lorimer of Illinois, and Asa J. Grouna of North Dakota, Republicans; and John H. Bankhead of Alabama, Thomas P. Gore of Oklahoma, George E. Chamberlain of Oregon, Ellison D. Smith of South Carolina, Le Roy Percy of Mississippi, Joseph M. Terrell of Georgia, and Luke Lea of Tennessee, Democrats.

House.—John Lamb of Virginia, Asbury F. Lever of South Carolina, Jack Beall of Texas, Augustus O. Stanley of Kentucky, Gordon Lee of Georgia, Ezekiel S. Candler, Jr., of Mississippi, J. Thomas Heflin of Alabama, James T. McDermott of Illinois, Robert C. Wickliffe of Louisiana, John A. Maguire of Nebraska, George W. Kipp of Pennsylvania, John J. Whitacre of Ohio, Charles A. Talcott of New York, and Thomas L. Rubey of Missouri, Democrats; and Gilbert N. Haugen of Iowa, James C. McLaughlin of Michigan, Willis C. Hawley of Oregon, Joseph Howell of Utah, Louis B. Hanna of North Dakota, Frank Plumley of Vermont, James S. Simmons of New York, and William H. Andrews of New Mexico, Republicans.

The first car of new Texas wheat to reach Fort Worth arrived on June 3 from Sanger Mill and Elevator Co. to Dazel Moore Grain Co. It graded 3 red and tested 58 lbs. It was not sold on arrival.

[For the "American Elevator and Grain Trade."]

BOSTON AND NEW ENGLAND AS MARKETS FOR WESTERN GRAIN AND FEED.

BY L. C. BREED.

In reporting the volume of business done by the wholesale grain dealers and brokers of Boston, it is proper to state that the grain receipts of the city represent only the grain sold to the local trade and exported. By far the larger part of their business is in sales to the country trade for shipment from the West, since nearly all New England points take the Boston rate of freight.

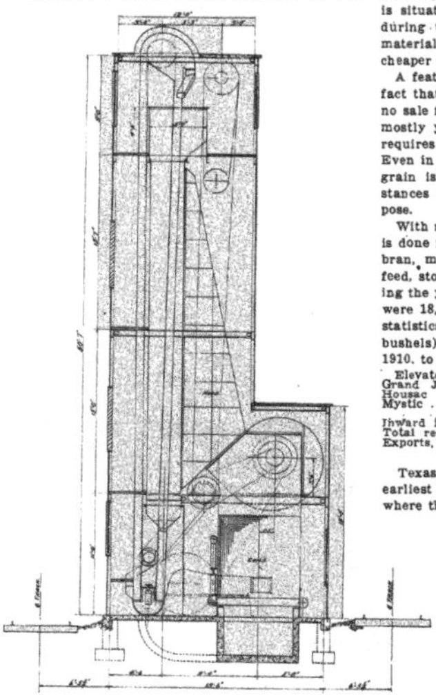

CROSS SECTION

INDIANAPOLIS ELEVATOR CO.'S ELLIS DRIER.

New England is an extensive importer of grain and feed, owing to the large number of great cities within its borders, whose people consume milk and dairy products, etc., and whose horses must be fed. The West produces grain on a cheaper basis and the mills also are situated in that region, from which supplies of feed are procured.

In supplying this trade, Boston wholesalers are obliged to share the business with New England jobbers and Western shippers and millers. Complaint is made that a steady encroachment is going on, through which the West is increasing its business with country retailers direct, and the growing development of the automobile industry is cutting down the sale of oats and other feeding stuffs to the local trade.

Compared with, say ten years ago, one observes that the attendance on the floor of the exchange of parties identified with the grain trade is much smaller than it used to be. This is explained by the fact that of late years the practice of doing business by telephone has become quite general. Leading men in the trade express regret for this change, in that it prevents getting and keeping in touch personally with their old and new customers, thus curtailing their ability to size up those parties and to judge of the business conditions pertaining to them from time to time. With the country dealer the time and expense of frequent trips to Boston is quite an item, consequently the convenience of the telephone naturally appeals to him.

The steady increase in the development of manufactures and mercantile pursuits, and the decline in the production of grain because of Western competition, renders New England an important and growing market for corn, oats and feedstuffs. With Western shippers, the sections which can supply this demand are governed mainly by freight rates. During the winter, when all-rail rates apply exclusively, it makes less difference where the shipper is situated; but the practice of laying in supplies during the prevalence of lake-and-rail rates very materially curtails the volume of business while the cheaper freights are not available.

A feature of the grain trade of this section is the fact that it calls for prime stuff. There is little or no sale for low grade oats; and in case of corn it is mostly yellow or high mixed. The long haul also requires that corn should be dry when shipped. Even in case of off grain for poultry feeding, burnt grain is a hard seller and consumers in some instances even purchase milling wheat for this purpose.

With regard to feeding stuffs an immense business is done in this line. The kinds mostly dealt in are bran, mixed feed, middlings, gluten feed, hominy feed, stock feeds, cotton and linseed oil meals. During the year 1910 the receipts at Boston of mill feed were 18,874 tons, but for New England at large no statistics are available. The receipts of grain (in bushels) at the regular elevators from January 1, 1910, to January 1, 1911, were as follows:

Elevator.	Cars.	Corn.	Wheat.	Oats.
Grand Junction......	1,699	142,206	1,989,732	....
Housac	4,166	1,580,312	3,444,371	37,661
Mystic	2,234	1,263,368	1,057,105	59,525
Inward inspection...	8,099	2,908,693	6,081,239	97,185
Total receipts........	.....	3,424,452	5,707,404	4,306,794
Exports, Boston.....	.....	2,749,967	6,337,243	136,914

Texas began cutting wheat on May 17—one of the earliest harvest dates on record for Denton County, where the wheat was cut.

INDIANAPOLIS ELEVATOR COMPANY'S NEW DRYING PLANT.

Within the past month the Ellis Drier Company of Chicago has completed the erection of a drying plant for the Indianapolis Elevator Company of Indianapolis, Indiana. The erectors have attached unusual interest to this plant, for it embodies process patents recently obtained by them, covering a system of air returns, the use of which provides for exceptional ecenomy and increased rapidity in the operation of the drier.

The building is a steel frame structure sided with ferrolithic steel plates and plastered with concrete, both inside and out. There is not a piece of wood in the entire plant, making it absolutely fire-proof. Considerable difficulty was encountered in the design of the building owing to the very limited space available, as a glance at the photographs will show. In addition to the erection of the drying plant, a twin steel leg was installed within the elevator. Power for the operation of this leg is furnished by the drier engine, and inasmuch as this leg connects with sufficient storage capacity to supply the drier for a 24-hours' run, it is possible to operate the plant entirely independent of the main house.

Power is furnished for the operation of the complete plant by an Ames Automatic Engine, the exhaust from the engine passing directly to the coils. The coils, which are of a special design for the utilization of exhaust steam, are placed on the ground floor, and should any break or leak develop the broken coil can be slipped out and repaired without the necessity of tearing down walls, floors, or partitions. A Dean Automatic Receiver Pump returns all condensation from the coils directly to the boiler.

Particular care has been taken in the designing of the plant to keep all machinery and moving parts as free as possible from dust. The engine is housed entirely separate from the drying room. As an aid to the lighting effect of the plant, the drier, cooler,

STEEL FRAME OF ELLIS DRIER FOR THE INDIANAPOLIS ELEVATOR CO.

fans, etc., are painted a light gray, which in combination with the color of the concrete, makes a pleasing combination.

The drier is composed of one unit 30 ft. high, 10 ft. 2 ins. long and 3 ft. wide; the cooler unit is 30 ft. high, 5 ft. 4 ins. long, and 3 ft. wide. Air is supplied to each of the units by a Special Multivane Steel Plate Fan. The plant has a drying capacity of 850 to 1,000 bushels per hour.

A special feature of the drier, which is of con-

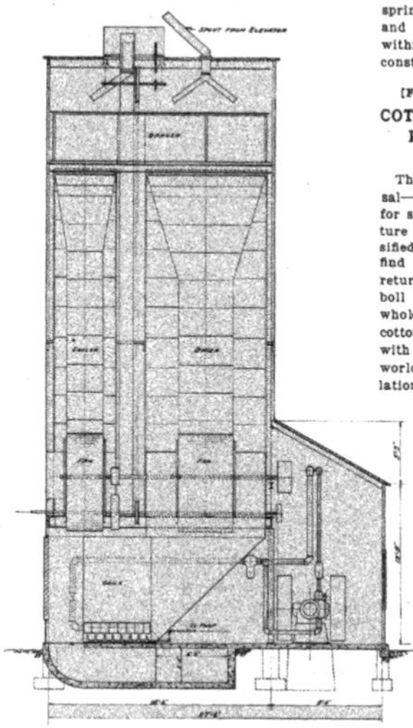

LONGITUDINAL SECTION

INDIANAPOLIS ELEVATOR CO.'S ELLIS DRIER.

siderable importance, is the ability of the operator to test the grain flowing from the drier with one hand and at the same time, without so much as moving a step, he can reach out and touch the finished product as it flows from the cooler. An accurate and constant knowledge of the drying process is very essential, as an over-reduction of the moisture content means a waste of time and money. Both the drier and cooler are operated as continuous feed machines; the merits of this system are now well established.

Owing to the application of the patented system of air returns, live steam is not required to make up any heat deficiency, and so perfect are the adjustments in this particular that it is possible to obtain a drying temperature of 165° Fahr. with exhaust steam only. Not only is it possible to greatly economize in heat by means of the new system, but it is practicable, owing to the slight vacuum created at the exhaust chambers, to greatly facilitate the removal of moisture and hence increase the rapidity of the drying process.

To further the general utility of the drier means have been provided to transform the entire plant into a cold-air drier. For the purpose of raising grades, when a shrinkage of one-half to three per cent is sufficient, or in the conditioning of hot corn, cold air only is applied. The conveyors, legs, etc., are designed to meet the added load when running in this capacity. To the writer's knowledge the cold-air process has been used almost exclusively up to the present time. The economic value of the new system of air returns in combination with the ability to convert the entire plant into a cold-air drier is of greater importance than appears at first sight. It means that the modern drying plant need no longer lie idle until the advent of an off-year, but under good management can be profitably operated every day in the year.

Owing to the anxiety of the Indianapolis Elevator Company to get the plant in operation for the spring work, extra effort was made in the erection, and the complete plant was placed in operation within seven weeks from the day of starting its construction.

[For the "American Elevator and Grain Trade."]

COTTON LINT AND COTTON SEED AND THE POSSIBLE PARTING OF THE WAYS.

BY N. L. WILLET.

There is a strong and general—I may say universal—feeling that cotton lint has moved up, at least for some years to come, to a higher level. Agriculture in the South is becoming each year more diversified; even with higher prices for cotton, planters find that other crops beside cotton bring in equal return in dollars and cents. The ever-advancing boll weevil, too, which in time must ravage the whole South, is seemingly saying to the Southern cotton industry, "So far and no farther." Along with decreased crops comes, on the other hand, a world's greater want in the cotton lint line. Population is steadily increasing; and savages are being transformed into semi-savages, and semi-savages into civilized people; and this makes a greater demand and use for cotton cloth.

No matter, too, how high lint in price may obtain, there is to date no fit substitute for cotton. It is the world's standard clothing; and outside of clothing a vast number of new uses for cotton and outlets for it have been found in the past few years. Farmers in the South who can grow cotton successfully seem, therefore, to be assured, at least for a few years ahead, of high prices for their lint.

The future, however, for cotton seed, if we look conditions squarely in the face, does not seem so bright. Cotton seeds for all of these years have been moving up in price along with cotton lint—indeed, comparatively, attaining a much higher ratio. The high price of $33 or more per ton for cotton seed, however, has found for cotton seed a rival, or, indeed, many rivals. These rivals have grown in amount, each one so enormously, that they are, in fact, threatening the cotton seed business. Your nearest oil mill will confirm what I say in very truth. Cotton lint and cotton seed seem, therefore, to have come to the parting of the ways. Conditions are so depressed today that it really does seem as if the outlook is for a lower level for cotton seed than has obtained for several years past.

For the reasonableness of this view I cite the following data: Northern Europe is a butter and cheese country. At one time vast exports from America were made of cotton meal for the various cattle countries in northern Europe. But cotton meal at last became prohibitory in price; the dairy men of northern Europe could not offer to buy it; and they moved heaven and earth to find a substitute. And they have found a substitute. And they have found a substitute which they like better. That substitute principally is soya bean meal. There is probably no better or stronger feed on earth than bean meal.

ELLIS DRIER OF INDIANAPOLIS ELEVATOR COMPANY AS COMPLETED.

The growth of the soya bean industry in Manchuria, China, reads like a fairy story. The importation of beans for pressing purposes into northern Europe has almost stopped the importing of cotton seed meal into those countries. Indeed, if it were not for the import duty of 25c per bushel, beans could be profitably brought to America for pressing purposes in competition with home grown cotton meal for feed purposes. There has been, too, in America, in one line, I feel sure, a considerable disuse in the matter of cotton seed meal. I refer to the feeding of droves of cattle for fattening purposes. For several years this has been unprofitable. In this immediate territory, where largely this custom obtained, it is practically carried on today in only the most limited way.

Turning from northern to southern Europe, we find countries in which the human largely subsists on oil. Time was when vast amounts of cotton seed oil went to southern Europe for human use. But as it came in direct competition with the olive oil industry of Italy, Spain, Greece, Austria and France, these countries at once made discriminations against the importation of cotton oil. Austria practically excluded it. Before it can go into Spain it must be denatured. Even when shipped to Europe, the oil mills had in 1910 many cargoes rejected technically on the smallest grounds. It is getting to be a dangerous proposition, indeed, to ship cotton seed oil into southern Europe. While cotton seed oil has been largely barred out, southern Europe has welcomed other products for grinding and pressing into oil.

Marseilles, France, is the center of the oil pressing business in southern Europe. In 1910 Marseilles imported nearly 700,000 tons of oil seed for its mills. Three-fourths of this was peanuts from Africa and China, the rest being cocoanut cake and benne seed. Strange as it may seem, Marseilles exported to America last year nearly 50,000 barrels of peanut oil. Peanut oil, we might say here, ranks higher as an oil than cotton seed oil. The pressing of nearly 400,000 tons per year of peanuts into oil in the one city of Marseilles shows a tremendous industry that is directly opposed to the cotton seed industry of America. Opposed to cotton oil, too, is lard. Lard has fallen nearly 50 per cent in the past twelve months; and when we take note of the immense and recent hog industry in south Georgia and Florida and elsewhere in the South, it might seem indeed as if lard and kindred stuffs may remain on lower levels.

The fall in these kindred stuffs is seen by the following: Pure lard at Chicago, this time a year ago, sold at approximately 13¾c per pound, against less than 8½c per pound at present. Pork is more than $10.50 a barrel cheaper and ribs 5c a pound cheaper. Compound lard, at this time last year, sold at about 10¼c, whereas it is difficult to obtain 7½c at this moment. Tallow, last year at this time, was 7¼c, against 6c at present; lard stearine, 15c, against 9½; oleo-stearine, 17c, against 7½c at present; oleo-oil, a year ago, sold at about 14c and is now quoted at 8½c to 8¾c.

There is a question as to whether the peanut cannot and will not be grown in America, possibly in the immediate future, in competition with cotton seed. It is declared, indeed, that peanuts, if they could be bought at 40c per bushel, would become here a strong and important rival of cotton seed. It requires different machinery for pressing peanuts than cotton seed, but the correct machinery could be quickly had of course. The Southwest Oil Mills are preparing to crush peanuts.

Now, it is easy to grow, even on poor, sandy land, from 40 to 50 bushels of peanuts per acre; furthermore, when the vineless variety is grown, these tops make a ton to a ton and a half per acre of valuable hay, worth at least $12 per ton. We have here a product of at least $30 per acre from peanuts, even at 40c per bushel. These peanuts—Bunch-Spanish varieties—are quick maturing, and can be planted after grain and truck in the late spring. Therefore, these peanuts afford a second crop on the same ground within twelve months. Furthermore, they are a leguminous crop and fertilize the soil for future crops.

The literature of agriculture is always interesting. While there seems to be no doubt as regards a high price for cotton lint in the next few years, yet I repeat that there is not the same optimistic feeling as regards this same high price for cotton seed for pressing commercially into oil and meal. Cotton seed oil that under contracts sold for 60c per gallon in summer of 1910 is today 40c or less; and meal that sold for $30 per ton can be bought, of the Sea Island variety, at something like $18.

THE TEXAS ASSOCIATION.

The annual meeting of the Texas Grain Dealers' Association was held at Dallas on May 25 and 26, with about 125 members present. In his annual address President James C. Hunt of Wichita Falls attacked the reciprocity agreement as "signifying lower prices on wheat and flour;" but a resolution to give expression to Mr. Hunt's views, introduced later in the session, was tabled.

Following an address of welcome by Rev. W. M. Anderson, C. W. Lonsdale of the Kansas City Board of Trade was called on, and spoke chiefly on the work of the Crop Improvement Committee. He asked the Association to appoint a committee of three to co-operate with the general Committee.

PRESIDENT'S ANNUAL ADDRESS.

President Hunt in his annual report in part said:

With Chicago wheat ranging in July as high as $1.15 and as low as $1.02 the same month; in September as high as $1.10 and as low as $1.02; in January it went to $1.03 only to drop in February to 89c; and then on down in March to less than 86c, it would take men of more than ordinary intelligence to know what course to pursue. As one dealer expressed to me: "It made no difference the past season whether you bought or sold, the market would show you a loss before you got through with it." Wheat promised to go to $1.25 per bushel in Texas and did sell to the mills in this state at $1.15 in January, declining to a little more than $1 in March. We must give the grain dealers and millers credit for having several grains of wheat sense if they have been successful the past season. Still we are not pessimists and, as a whole, we are content to simply "hold our own" in a year like the past one.

One thing that has tended probably more than any other to unsettle the grain market has been reciprocity. Mr. Taft has touched a responsive chord in his appeal to the people for lower prices, especially for the necessaries of life, and from present indications reciprocity with Canada will soon be accomplished. Canadian wheat will doubtless affect the grain trade more than any other cereal.

Canada raises about 150,000,000 bushels of wheat, a large part of which usually moves for export. The duty on this wheat, if brought across the border, is 25 cents, so that when wheat is worth 80c per bushel on the Canadian border, it would cost $1.05 to get it across the line. In this way we have been protected against cheap Canadian wheat. Should reciprocity be accomplished, this wheat could be moved into Indianapolis and other border cities on as cheap or cheaper freight than at present obtains from a number of nearby states in the Union. I can therefore see no reason why the price of wheat will not decline, not, however, in the ratio of the duty taken off, since that is always an equalization process under conditions of this kind, but there will be a decline in the value of wheat in the United States in my humble estimation of about 10c per bushel.

On the basis of this argument Mr. Hunt predicted a decline in wheat land values of no less than $3 per acre for the entire Nation if the agreement is consummated.

Commending the very high-class work done by the Association's arbitration committee, Mr. Hunt turned to the telegraph and telephone companies, business with whom, he said, was full of "trials and tribulations," and which he thought should be brought under state government control.

SECRETARY'S REPORT.

Sec'y G. J. Gibbs in his annual report said, among other things, that the Association had had some trouble with the Oklahoma Association because the latter had hitherto had no provision for arbitration except with its own members, while the Texas Association requires its members to arbitrate with the world; but on May 24, 1911, the Oklahoma Association had unanimously adopted a resolution patterning after the Texas Association's by-law in this particular.

Twenty-one new members were admitted during the past year, making a present net enrollment of 107. Receipts $3,573.76, total disbursements $3,362.72, on hand $211.04.

The secretary reported that he did not attend the last session of the legislature because "there was so much pro-Bailey and anti-Bailey he had been advised there was little opportunity to secure business legislation."

One member of the Association was expelled from membership because he had refused to abide by the arbitration committee's finding in a case decided against him, which he carried to the courts.

L. G. Belew of Pilot Point in his report of the "tri-state appeals committee," said there had been but nine cases coming before this body. He suggested to members the wisdom of toleration in viewing disputes from the other fellow's standpoint, and the advisability of permitting appeals from the state board to the tri-state board. He also said that much trouble can be avoided by exercising care in making contracts.

SHRINKAGE IN TRANSIT.

W. M. Priddy of Wichita Falls opened a discussion on shrinkage in transit by saying that his mill does not make a claim for loss unless there is a shrinkage of more than 200 pounds to a carload;

OFFICERS OF THE TEXAS GRAIN DEALERS' ASSOCIATION.
Read left to right: Standing—C. L. Moss, Dallas; H. B. Dorsey, Ft. Worth; E. R. Kolp, Ft. Worth; sitting—T. G. Moore, Ft. Worth; J. C. Hunt, Wichita Falls; G. J. Gibbs, Ft. Worth; E. W. Crouch, McGregor.

then a claim is made for the loss and it is insisted upon. He said the practice of roads to charge for the transportation of the original weight regardless of the weight upon arrival at destination was wrong. He suggested that the Association should co-operate with the railroads in inspecting railroad scales. He complained of the railroads' dilatory tactics in settling claims and called attention to imperfect cars furnished shippers as a reason for much loss. But he added: "I suggest that a spirit of fairness be cultivated and fostered throughout the Association and that men deal with each other and with corporations and carriers more as individuals."

D. W. McLeod, in charge of the claim department of the Santa Fe System, said the railroads are as willing to come up and toe the mark as are the grain dealers. The railroads have made exhaustive investigations into this matter of losses, and it has been found that there have been imperfections in scales and in weighing. The solution of this vexed question may be found in an outside agency of some kind to supervise scales and assure the railroads that they are getting all that is coming to them. The speaker admitted his road knows some of its equipment is imperfect for the handling of grain, but this the roads are trying to overcome. He complained that the courts are against the roads, as a rule, but he said that, "If the railroads will get acquainted with the grain people, and vice versa, we ought to be able to get together as do other business men and get on a common ground for settling claims."

He insisted there should be a uniform system of scale weights and scale inspection, which will guarantee to the railroads as well as members of the Association that the weights are correct. "And when you find our cars in defective condition, I really think you should call this to the attention of some of our representatives. This will assist us in correcting this source of loss. It is an actual fact that in some cases of losses we get sworn statements of scale weights when it has developed that there were no scales within five miles of the shipper, but the weights were estimated from a measurement." He said also that trouble comes when cars are delivered to industry tracks and are out of the surveillance and ought to be out of the custody of the railroads. Then often seals are broken during the night and contents removed, and then claims are presented. In one case it was developed that an elevator sold several thousand bushels more grain than it had bought, although it should, on the contrary, have been considerably short, as the railroads had paid claims for many thousands of bushels claimed to be short.

C. D. Kemp of Electra and J. Z. Keel of Gainesville made short talks supporting the argument that had been made by Mr. McLeod, the point made being carelessness in scale weights. "I believe," said Mr. Keel in closing, "that the Santa Fe is correct in its contentions."

A. A. Martin, chief clerk in the claim department of the Texas and Pacific Railroad, spoke upon the relationship existing between the claim agent and the claimant, saying that he handled some of the letters from the grain dealers almost with tongs for fear they would explode. He insisted that there should exist a broad spirit of comity between these two interests.

H. B. Dorsey of Fort Worth said he did not think there is any natural shrinkage in Texas, but there may be variation in scales.

STATE CONTROL OF TELEPHONES.

On the second day the matter of telephone service was taken up; and on motion a committee was appointed to ask Gov. Colquitt to lay before the next called session of the Legislature the question of placing telephone and telegraph corporations under the supervision of the Railroad Commission or to create a corporation commission for that purpose. The following compose the committee: H. B. Dorsey, Fort Worth; S. E. Moss, Dallas; J. A. Hughes, Howe.

EXCHANGE ON DRAFTS.

The question, "Who should pay the exchange on drafts?" disclosed on discussion a marked difference of opinion. Allen Early of Amarillo, who read a paper on the subject, thought that if the grain is sold f. o. b. the buyer should pay; if delivered, the seller. T. G. Moore of Fort Worth thought that plan would enable him to escape paying any exchange—he could sell f. o. b. and buy delivered.

"The country banks," he suggested, 'are largely responsible for some of our ills, by requiring the exchange in some cases to be attached to the invoices. I think the shippers ought to pay their own exchange without regard to whether sales are made f. o. b. or on a delivered basis. That is a system that is in vogue in every other state, and it is only in Texas that the receiver is required to pay exchange." J. Z. Keel of Gainesville argued that the net amount of money due the shipper should be paid to him at the place where the grain is sold f. o. b.; if sold delivered, then he should be paid the amount due him at that place.

A point of order being made that the debate had no motion behind it, it was moved that a rule be made that the shipper in all instances should pay the exchange; to which amendment was made, that all drafts payable on presentation shall be drawn without exchange and all drafts payable on arrival shall be drawn with exchange.

The debate was then resumed; and Sec'y Gibbs urged that the question should be disposed of, as 40 per cent of the time of previous conventions had been consumed in the discussion of this matter. He argued that the shipper should in each case pay the exchange, but if a different modus operandi is desired in individual cases let it be so stipulated. Mr. Keel agreed with Mr. Lasker of Galveston that a change of rules would merely lead to confusion until a new basis should become established. If a change were made and the seller required to pay the exchange, the seller would have to ask a little more for his grain. He argued that the present rule of the association is tracking the law and said it is to the interest of the miller, little shipper and the buyer to leave the rules as at present. Accordingly, O. F. Witherspoon of Denton moved to lay the whole matter on the table, which was done by an almost unanimous vote.

DISPOSITION OF OFF-GRADE STUFF.

In a paper by T. P. Duncan of Waco on the disposition by unloading of shipments not up to agreed grade, the writer took the position that when the contract is made under the usual conditions, the buyer assuming the duty of inspection and weighing, the buyer has the right to unload grain not up to the contract grade.

F. J. Becker said that at Galveston grain is occasionally handled with the understanding that if it doesn't come up to the grade contracted for, that fact is taken up by wire with the shipper. In response to a question he said that if the grain is merchantable but off-grade wheat would be taken out and docked at the regular scale.

President Hunt said this subject was being discussed to determine whether, when there is not more than 1c difference between the shipper and buyer, the wheat should be unloaded without going to the expense of notifying the shipper. J. T. Stark of Plano contended that the millers had no right to confiscate the wheat of the shipper without notifying him. Mr. Chambers of Sanger said that in Oklahoma the custom prevails of unloading the wheat and charging the shipper the difference.

H. B. Dorsey, former secretary, read the trade rule which he said means that the miller has the right to unload the grain and apply to it the market difference. Secretary Gibbs said that in twenty-five years' experience as a shipper he had never had any trouble; that he always sold what he had agreed to, but he had always had a specific understanding in his contracts as to mis-grade stuff.

ON STATE CROP STATISTICS.

The perennial demand for better crop statistics for the state was voiced in a paper by J. T. Stark of Plano, who thought that for the present they might be confined to wheat and oats; and that in the absence of state action the Association could appoint members of the Association in each county and justice precinct to gather statistics and report them to the Secretary for tabulation. The data could be gathered from the men who own thrashers (1) upon the number of bushels of wheat thrashed this year; (2) the number of acres of ground this represents, and (3) what proportion of this will be used at home.

F. M. Duncan of Killeen, in discussing the same subject, suggested that the essential features needed are acreage, condition and progress of crop. He recommended the system used by most of the large cotton houses in collecting data upon the progress of the cotton crop, by means of return postal cards. To this Mr. Stark added the suggestion that weekly reports from March to July be furnished by the dealers to the Secretary for tabulation, the reports to embrace oats, wheat and corn crops only; but, Secretary Gibbs said he had already tried this plan several times, and perhaps it would surprise members to know that out of 100 inquiries sent out he would receive only fifty-two replies, and that in some instances the dealers would furnish misinformation.

H. B. Dorsey of Fort Worth said the only solution of this question is to have the Legislature pass a law requiring the farmer to swear to the acreage he has planted and then have reporters all over the state and pay the tax collectors for gathering this information.

MISCELLANEOUS BUSINESS.

A motion to change the Association headquarters from Fort Worth to Dallas was laid on the table.

A resolution offered by W. E. Werkheiser of Temple that, "It is the sense of this association that a ½ of 1 per cent deduction for variations in weight by the carriers in settlement of claims is not unreasonable," was tabled.

The following committee of three to work for seed improvement was appointed: G. J. Gibbs and Jules Smith of Fort Worth and A. B. Crouch of Temple.

Rule 7 of the Trade Rules, relative to unfinished shipments, was amended.

ANNUAL ELECTION.

A motion by President Hunt, that hereafter the presidential term be limited to one year, having been tabled, the Association proceeded to the election of officers, with the following result:

President, James C. Hunt, Wichita Falls (re-elected).

First vice-president, W. W. Manning, Fort Worth.

Second vice-president, E. W. Crouch, McGregor.

Secretary, G. J. Gibbs, Fort Worth (re-elected).

Executive committee—C. F. Witherspoon, Denton; G. T. Stark, Plano; C. L. Moss, Dallas.

Committee on arbitration—A. B. Crouch, Temple; J. Hughes, Howe; Kent Barber, Fort Worth.

Members to represent Texas on tri-state appeals committee—Levi G. Below, Pilot Point (re-elected).

After the election the motion limiting the presidential term to one year was taken from the table and adopted.

The meeting then adjourned.

The members in attendance were royally entertained by Dallas, at a popular resort on the 25th and at a banquet at the Oriental Hotel on the 26th.

SOUTH DAKOTA CROPS.

The leading crops of South Dakota in order of value are wheat, corn, oats, hay, etc., barley, flaxseed and emmer and spelt. The acreage in 1909 and 1899 with yield in bushels for 1909 are as follows:

	Acreage		Yield,
Crop—	1909.	1899.	1909.
Wheat	3,104,622	3,984,659	45,289,818
Corn	1,975,558	1,196,381	53,612,093
Oats	1,480,075	691,167	41,255,569
Hay and forage (tons)	3,429,527	2,287,875	3,649,577
Barley	1,057,533	299,510	20,325,498
Flaxseed	507,286	302,010	4,649,237
Emmer and spelt..	259,674	......	6,095,683

A Canadian judge, in the case of the Ogilvie Milling Co. who protested against their elevator at Brandon, Man., which is on C. P. R. property, being assessed, held that so long as the property was used for strictly railway purposes it was not liable to taxes, but once it was used for other purposes it must pay taxes to the municipality.

A NEW FARMERS' ELEVATOR.

The elevator, of which the plan drawings are reproduced herewith, and which is now under construction at Minonk, Ill., by McAllister & O'Connor of Chicago, will be on its completion one of the best farmers' elevators ever built in Illinois. With a wisdom not common to the management of farmers' companies, the owners of this fine property, the Farmers' Elevator and Supply Co., gave the designers and builders the order to make the plant a good one; and they have embodied in its construction their theory of compactness and other features which make the houses of McAllister & O'Connor more or less distinctive.

The ground area covered is 36x38 feet; the height is 60 ft. to top of bins, above which is a cupola 16x24 ft. in area and 18 ft. high, making the total height of the building to the square of the cupola 78 ft. The frame will be covered with Genuine Galvanized Corrugated Iron for the sides and Genuine Galvanized Iron Standing Seam Roofing.

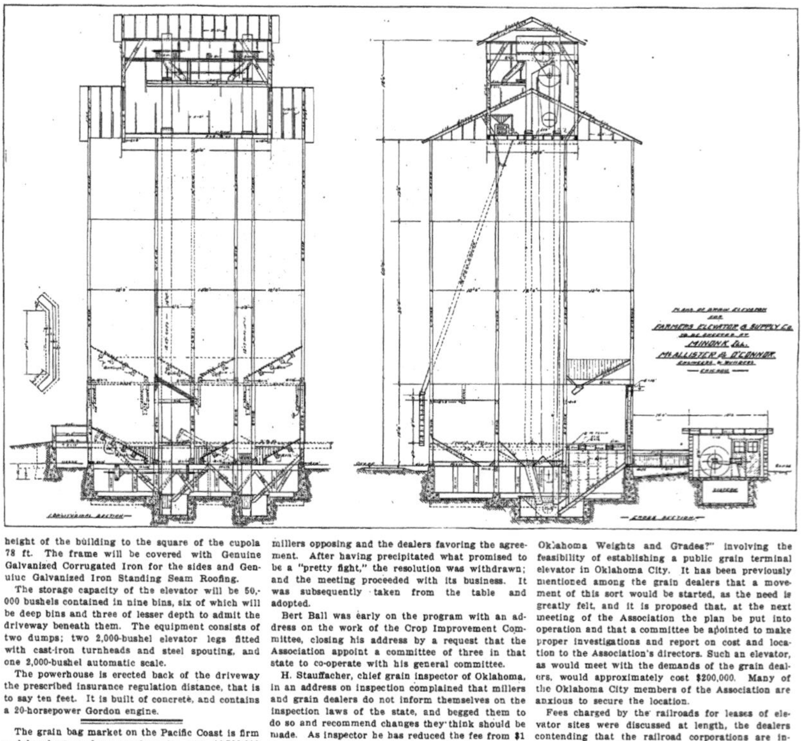

The storage capacity of the elevator will be 50,000 bushels contained in nine bins, six of which will be deep bins and three of lesser depth to admit the driveway beneath them. The equipment consists of two dumps; two 2,000-bushel elevator legs fitted with cast-iron turnheads and steel spouting, and one 2,000-bushel automatic scale.

The powerhouse is erected back of the driveway the prescribed insurance regulation distance, that is to say ten feet. It is built of concrete, and contains a 20-horsepower Gordon engine.

The grain bag market on the Pacific Coast is firm and has been so for several weeks, with 44,500,000 sacks in sight. Of these 32,000,000 have been imported; 7,500,000 have been made at the prison factory of San Quentin, Calif., and Walla Walla, Wash., and 5,000,000 were carried over from 1910. A Portland dealer places the requirements for the season at 60,000,000 against 58,000,000 actually used last season. On the other hand, this pessimistic outlook is somewhat discounted by the fact that there has never yet been an actual deficiency of bags on the Coast, though in some years, particularly in 1905, there were grave fears that the farmers would not be able to sack all of their wheat. The crop that year was a great one, and a shortage of bags was figured out before harvest; yet the entire crop was marketed without loss.

THE OKLAHOMA MEETING.

The "live wire" of the meeting of Oklahoma millers and grain dealers at Oklahoma City on May 23 was a resolution by J. S. Hutchins of Ponca City asking the senators from Oklahoma at Washington to vote no on the reciprocity agreement, the millers opposing and the dealers favoring the agreement. After having precipitated what promised to be a "pretty fight," the resolution was withdrawn; and the meeting proceeded with its business. It was subsequently taken from the table and adopted.

Bert Ball was early on the program with an address on the work of the Crop Improvement Committee, closing his address by a request that the Association appoint a committee of three in that state to co-operate with his general committee.

H. Stauffacher, chief grain inspector of Oklahoma, in an address on inspection complained that millers and grain dealers do not inform themselves on the inspection laws of the state, and begged them to do so and recommend changes they think should be made. As inspector he has reduced the fee from $1 to 50c per car; has appointed Mr. Topping and Mr. Prouty (who selected a third) as appeals committee; has compiled new grading rules; and appointed as deputies only men approved by the trade (millers and dealers).

The officers for the ensuing year were elected on May 24, as follows: W. M. Randalls, Enid, president; R. H. Dramman, Oklahoma City, vice-president; C. M. Prouty, Oklahoma City, secretary-treasurer (re-elected); directors, D. J. Donahue, Ponca City; J. E. Farrington, Chickasha; D. C. Kolp, Jr., Oklahoma City; George Harbaugh, Altus; W. L. Lyons, Enid; committee on arbitration (appointed by the president)—U. F. Clements, Marshall; P. J. Mullin, Oklahoma City; M. E. Humphrey, Chickasha; delegate to represent the Oklahoma Association on the tri-state arbitration appeals committee, J. H. Shaw; committee on reciprocity (by president)—U. F. Clemons, Marshall; D J. Donahue, Ponca City; J. S. Hutchins, Ponca City; committee on weights and grades (by president)—Milbourn, Drennan, Donahue and Vandenburgh.

There was a paper by Jesse Vandenburgh of Blackwell on the question: "Can We Establish Oklahoma Weights and Grades?" involving the feasibility of establishing a public grain terminal elevator in Oklahoma City. It has been previously mentioned among the grain dealers that a movement of this sort would be started, as the need is greatly felt, and it is proposed that, at the next meeting of the Association the plan be put into operation and that a committee be appointed to make proper investigations and report on cost and location to the Association's directors. Such an elevator, as would meet with the demands of the grain dealers, would approximately cost $200,000. Many of the Oklahoma City members of the Association are anxious to secure the location.

Fees charged by the railroads for leases of elevator sites were discussed at length, the dealers contending that the railroad corporations are injecting clauses into the leases which are unjust and detrimental to the interest of the millers.

In his report Sec'y C. M. Prouty said the net result of the year's campaign for members was an "even break" and congraulated the new grain inspector on his good work. As to Trade Rules he said:

Our Trade Rules, as we understand them, cover our present needs. The agitation pertaining to their revision is wise only as it tends to broaden their scope and add to their general usefulness, as, for instance, it is my earnest opinion that some rule should be formulated which could be adopted by this organization and put into effect, regulating the time limit in making returns. This feature alone is causing more dissatisfaction among our shippers than any other, and is causing a breach in the friendly feeling heretofore existing between receiver and shipper. It has been the custom ever since I have known anything of the grain business to leave ample margin on all shipments; and while this custom is still in existence, it is not practiced to the extent it should be, nor has been in former years. The reason is simply that when our shippers leave a margin the receivers take their own sweet will in making returns. When the shipper is compelled to wait for two, three, six months and in many instances much longer for their returns, simply for the reason that a margin is in the shipment and something is due the shipper, can you blame them for quitting the long established custom and drawing up in full? Our shippers are doing this in the way of self-protection, more especially on grain going to Texas and Southern markets. The same rule governing this feature should apply to Kansas, Texas and Oklahoma, and if uniform laws in regard to this matter could be adopted by all three associations, it would be of great benefit to us all.

The financial report showed receipts of $4,012.64 and expenditures of $3,736.85.

The following resolutions were adopted:

ST. LOUIS AS A MARKET.

"Whereas, The state of Oklahoma is one of the great grain producing states; and

"Whereas, In order that the producers of grain may receive the greatest benefit through competition of markets and derive a direct benefit from such competition it is necessary to reach the great grain markets where grain is accumulated for future sale; and

"Whereas, St. Louis is one of the most important primary markets where grain may be sold upon consignment upon any business day in the year; and

"Whereas, The great grain producing section of this state is tributary to St. Louis, and buyers and shippers of grain in this territory should receive the benefit of St. Louis competition; therefore, be it

"Resolved, It is to the interest of the producer, shipper and carrier that rates to St. Louis be harmonized with prevailing rates to other points and be made not to exceed rates to Memphis, Tenn. It is also

"Resolved, That our membership employ all reasonable and legitimate means in securing the benefit of this competition. Also

"Resolved, That a copy of this resolution be furnished to the chief traffic officers of the lines serving St. Louis, and to the Oklahoma corporation commission.

MARKET QUOTATIONS.

"Whereas, The price of grain cannot be established by any one market unless compared with the same grade in Oklahoma newspapers; and

"Whereas, The prices of grain at St. Louis are not printed daily in the Oklahoma newspapers; be it

"Resolved, That the Oklahoma Millers' and Grain Dealers' Associations, through their secretaries, shall request the leading newspapers of Oklahoma to print a comparative market report of the principal grain markets tributary to Oklahoma, giving each market equal prominence. It is also

"Resolved, That members of these associations, individually, request the editors of the newspapers of Oklahoma to ask the Associated Press and other press associations for this information. It is further

"Resolved, That a copy of this resolution be furnished to each of said newspapers, to the Associated Press, and to other press associations serving Oklahoma papers.

AGAINST FEDERAL INSPECTION.

"Whereas, The grain trade of the United States has struggled along under about as much technical regulation from the Agricultural Department as it can stand;

"Resolved, That the Oklahoma Grain Dealers' Association in annual convention at Oklahoma City this 24th day of May, 1911, do hereby protest most vigorously against the enactment into law of Senator McCumber's bill, known as S. F. 223, which is designed to place the grading of all grain in this country in the hands of the employes of the Agricultural Department; be it further

"Resolved, That our secretary be instructed to send a copy of this protest to each of our representatives in the United States Senate and to request each member of the Association to protest to our senators against the proposed legislation."

The members after adjournment were the guests of the Yukon Mill & Grain Co. (Krontil Bros.) for luncheon.

THE KANSAS INSPECTION ROW.

The Kansas state inspection department is not earning money enough to pay expenses, and as any surplus of the past has been paid into the treasury, the department was on Uneasy Street for some time, when the state auditor refused to permit the use of the governor's contingent fund to help out. This situation has developed since the new law increasing the fees went into effect, several of the elevator companies operating in Kansas City having refused to pay their inspection fees or to have their grain inspected or weighed. At length the attorney-general of the state held in a written opinion that the governor could use the fund named to cover a temporary deficiency in any department; and so back salaries were paid and the department goes on with its work. At May 15 the department was behind with its pay roll nearly $5,000 and fee collections are expected to become steadily less until after harvest. By that time the department is likely to be $10,000 behind and the governor's contingent fund is only $10,000 a year.

The Kansas Association, on behalf of 4,500 grain dealers and farmers, filed its answer to the state's bill of complaint in the case, in which it is charged that the fees under the law are unreasonable, exorbitant and arbitrary and not in proper proportion to the service performed; that the manner of inspecting grain is such as to put a premium upon dishonest and incompetent inspection and that the grain grades given by the department are unreliable and untrustworthy; that either through the antiquated or unscientific methods of inspection or the incompetence of the employes, the grain grades and weights are not dependable; that as much of the grain shipped by Kansas dealers goes to mills and elevators outside the state, the collection of the fees works as an export tax on the grain, which is prohibited by the constitution of the United States.

It was originally intended that during the progress of the suit, the contested fees accruing in the course of business would be paid and turned over to trustees appointed to hold them in escrow until the litigation should be terminated; but this idea has been abandoned; and if the state finally wins out, it will have to make collections from the individual farmers and producers who shipped the grain.

If the state does not "win out," it is understood Gov. Stubbs will recall the legislature in special session to enact an inspection law that will meet the views of the Supreme Court of the state. A final adjudication of the matter is not expected before next fall.

The first new barley on exhibition in California this season was at Willows, Glenn County, on June 1.

The "provisional government" at Juarez ordered the restoration of flour and grain duties in May 29. Did they "need the money?"

The Agricultural College at St. Anthony's Park, Minn., has established a division of chemistry, in which experiments will be made to grade grain according to its actual value as food and especially to estimate the value of wheat as a bread producer. By investigations and chemical tests the effect of fertilizers, soils and climate upon the quality of the grain will be ascertained. Clyde Bailey, a Minnesota graduate of '05, will be the head of the new department. It is hinted that upon the results of these tests modification may be urged in the future rules for the grading of grain in Minnesota.

EAR CORN CRUSHER.

In response to the growing demand for a machine that will rapidly crush corn and cobs for coarse feed or prepare them for further reduction on buhr-stone or other grinding mills, the Barnard & Leas Manufacturing Company of Moline, Ill., has designed and put on the market the crusher shown in the engraving. The designer has taken into consideration convenience of operation and economy of power, as well as strength, simplicity and uniformity and efficiency of work.

The material to be crushed is fed into the hopper, where it is broken up and crushed by a revolving cone which is provided with sharp projections, or teeth. After being broken up by the cone, the material is forced between the grinding disks and further reduced. These disks are made larger than usual and thus give large capacity with comparatively little power. In this matter of capacity and economy of power, this crusher, it is believed, has no superior and consequently has become a favorite wherever used. The disks are also made adjustable and can be set for fine coarse grinding. Both the cone and disks are made of very hard, white iron, and will stand long and hard usage.

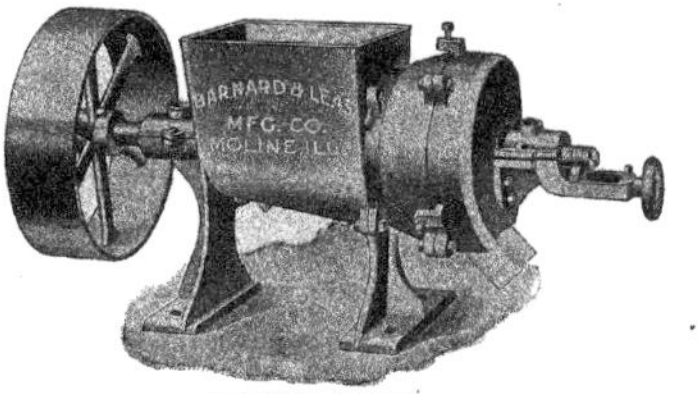

EAR CORN CRUSHER.

While this machine is not intended to crush fine enough for fine feed, still with proper adjustment, the material can be reduced as fine as necessary for coarse feed; it is mainly used, however, for preparing corn and cobs for after reduction on buhr-stone or other grinding mills.

Only the best of material and workmanship are put into its construction, and purchasers can rest assured they will get a thoroughly practical and efficient machine. The manufacturers will be glad to send further details and prices on application.

NORTH DAKOTA CROPS.

In North Dakota in 1909 the leading crops in order of valuation were wheat, oats, flaxseed, barley, hay and forage, corn, emmer and spelt. The acreage to each in 1909 and 1899 with field in 1909 were as follows:

	—Acreage—		Yield,
Crop—	1909.	1899.	1909.
Wheat	8,178,304	4,451,251	116,349,677
Oats	2,143,546	780,517	65,787,236
Flaxseed	1,065,239	773,999	10,319,062
Barley	1,213,239	287,092	26,336,755
Hay, etc., tons.....	2,537,181	1,410,534	2,723,741
Corn	186,787	62,373	4,999,703
Emmer and spelt .	95,474	......	2,421,434

A country shipper who forwarded a car of No. 2 red wheat to Chicago on May 25 succeeded in getting it in store and it sold on May 31 at $1.04½. The same man shipped a car May 27 which reached the elevator yards same morning, but failed to get in store, and was sold at the same time at 91c, there being a difference of 13½c in price between the wheat in the elevator bin and that in cars a few feet from the elevator.—Inter Ocean.

ILLINOIS GRAIN DEALERS.

The Illinois grain dealers, at the opening of the eighteenth annual meeting of their state Association, at Bloomington on June 13, were shocked to learn that their president, Geo. D. Montelius, of Piper City, was confined to his bed by serious illness. This information was conveyed to the Association by Vice-President H. A. Hilmer, who presided, and who read a letter from Mr. Montelius in which the latter expressed régret at his inability to be present and sent his good wishes and kindly regards to all present. Mr. Montelius has been ill for several months, but he himself said he was feeling better and hoped soon to be well again; and such is the wish of all who know him. In this connection Mr. Strong announced that Mr. Montelius had sent for distribution to the Secretary a souvenir to the members in the form of a neat leather bill folder, which were later distributed with Mr. Montelius' compliments. The members were touched by the sentiment of the giver thus expressed, and the souvenir was accepted with more than common feeling.

There being no formal address of welcome, Chairman Hilmer proceeded at once to the regular program, asking, however, that the members give their attention to the work in hand and visit after the sessions are ended.

On motion of Mr. Tyng the minutes were adopted as printed in the trade journals.

SECRETARY'S REPORT.

Secretary Strong then made his annual report, as follows:

Secretary's Financial Report, May 31st, 1911:

Balance on hand June 1st, 1910.....		$1,036.83
RECEIPTS.		
Received from dues of members...	$5,070.00	
Received from fees of new members	310.00	
Received from fees of arbitrations.	154.00	
Received from advertising in Eighteenth Annual Directory....	1,305.25	
		$6,839.25
Total		$7,876.08
EXPENDITURES.		
Supplies for the office for the year.	$ 117.51	
Expenses of officers for the year..	260.15	
Postage	322.24	
Stenographers	388.40	
Expense 17th Annual Convention..	365.92	
Office rent	152.50	
Refunded arbitration fees...........	126.00	
Telephone, telegraph and express.	116.41	
Assistant secretary	392.53	
Printing	121.88	
Salary of secretary..................	2,500.00	
Traveling expenses of secretary...	849.15	
Publishing directory................	763.21	
Dues to National Association.......	352.50	
		$6,828.41
Balance in treasurer's hands, May 31st, 1911		$1,047.67

The foregoing financial report of the Association shows a good, healthy standing; and the organization is to be congratulated upon increased membership, a better understanding of the business, and the fact that all the state, where there are elevators, is now covered by the organization.

There are some things which the organization in my judgment, at this time should undertake, looking to future action and to the better working of the society for the protection of the interests of the members.

The present Constitution and By-Laws were adopted many years ago. Committees which were then needed, having fulfilled their work, are now useless; but in accordance with the law of the organization they are still appointed year after year, with nothing for them to do. It would seem to me to be good judgment for the Association to revise during the coming year its Constitution and By-Laws; and the secretary would recommend such a consideration to the convention.

The Association is now the largest and strongest grain association in the country; and if its activities were properly exerted, its wants and wishes would be respected and its members thereby benefited.

The voting power of the members should be more fully protected; the floor, or the privilege of the convention platform, should be more confined to those who are entitled to it by right of membership.

There are quite a number of grain shippers in the state who have all the benefits of the Association, who use its committees, who take advantage of its arbitration court, who are benefited by its claim department, and who are always at the conventions, and yet who still do not apply for membership. Some action should be taken by the Association to secure the union of those grain dealers with the organization,—a little effort by the Association members, or by a committee to procure new members of the Association; and their added payments would allow of much greater accomplishment by the organization.

Instead of the committees which are now provided for by the by-laws, as the work for which they were appointed at the first as has been said, is practically done, there should be committees whose duty it should be to supervise or investigate on complaint the actions of inspection and weighing departments at the various terminal markets. There should be a committee on legal matters, whose duty it should be to see that the Association is rightly directed under the law, and its rights secured.

There is a question, just at the present, affecting shippers as to the action of inspection departments at some of the terminal markets, which obligates the shipper to guarantee the grade of grain until it reaches the elevator where it is to be unloaded, no matter how many days may elapse from the time the car is delivered in the terminal until it is unloaded.

Another practice at Chicago, by the inspection department, is to stamp "subject to future inspection—too full" indiscriminately. Complaint has been made to the Chief Grain Inspector at Chicago of this practice with the full expectation that it will be corrected and stopped.

But all such subjects should be safeguarded by committees ready at any time to act; and if the members of the Association would take the necessary action to add to its membership those dealers who secure its benefits without supporting the organization, these committees could be paid their expenses, at least, when they are attending to the duties of their various lines.

Committees should not exceed three members; and these ought to be selected from those who are, by reason of their experience, best able to handle the subject matter referred to that committee; and provision should be made for the payment of the expenses of all committees when in the service of the Association, to the extent of their expenses.

The loyalty of the membership of the Illinois Grain Dealers' Association, I venture to say, is not surpassed by any organization in the country. The liberal voluntary payment of dues, the readiness of members to serve on committees at any time and pay their own expenses, and without any remuneration, cannot be exceeded by any other body of men; and the very liberality of these grain men makes them support many who do not from one cause or another assist the organization.

I want to now express as best I may my sincere thanks to the members of the Association for their very liberal support, for their never-ending friendliness, for the hearty welcome which is ever extended to me whenever and wherever I meet them; and I assure each one of you that the organization is well equipped and provided to care for your wants and will do so at any time, if you will only call for what you want or may need.

The report was adopted and ordered filed.

On motion of Mr. Tyng, the recommendations of the secretary's report were referred to the committee on resolutions to report at this meeting.

On motion of Mr. Shellabarger a committee was ordered and directed to send a telegram of sympathy and good will to President Montelius.

The chair appointed Messrs. Shellabarger, Collins and Tyng.

The report of H. I. Baldwin, treasurer, was read and adopted. It agreed with the financial statement of the secretary.

The report of the finance committee, acting as auditors, was read and adopted as follows:

BLOOMINGTON, ILL., June 10, 1911.

We, the finance committee acting as auditors, have this day examined the books and accounts of S. W. Strong, Urbana, secretary, and H. I. Baldwin, Decatur, treasurer, respectively of the Illinois Grain Dealers' Association; and beg leave to report:

We find the books and accounts of both officers are correctly and lucidly kept; that all moneys paid to the secretary have been remitted by him to the treasurer; and the secretary has on file in his office receipts from the treasurer which were exhibited and duly examined by the committee.

We find that all moneys remitted by the secretary to the treasurer are duly receipted for by him and entered in his books of account.

We find that no payments have been made by the secretary out of the funds of the Association whatsoever.

We find that all payments made by the treasurer were made on orders signed by the president and by the secretary; said orders were exhibited to the committee and duly examined by them.

We find that the balance June 1st, 1910, in the hands of the treasurer was $1,036.83, and that after all receipts were credited, and all orders paid charged, there remains the sum of $1,047.57 in the treasurer's hands to the credit of the Association at this date.

We commend the manner in which the books and accounts are kept; and we recommend also a continuance of the system.

The committee have examined the copies of monthly reports of the business of the Association made to the president each month and recommend a continuance of the method.

F. L. WARNER, Chenoa, Chairman.
L. E. SLICK, Bloomington.
VICTOR DEWEIN, Warrensburg,
Committee.

CONVENTION COMMITTEES.

The chair appointed the following committees to serve through the convention:

Resolutions.—Lee Metcalf, J. W. Probasco, William Shellabarger, A. W. Ford, H. C. Roberts.

Nominations.—B. P. Hill, E. M. Wayne, P. K. Wilson, H. O. Benson, Jas. Inkster.

CROP IMPROVEMENT.

Bert Ball, Chicago, secretary and manager of the Crop Improvement Committee, made an address on the work of this more or less famous committee. The work is based on the selfish query, How can you grain men get more grain to handle to add to your incomes? Coming here through Illinois, I saw the beautiful fields of waving grain; but, I thought, if the boys in South Carolina can get 200 bushels of corn per acre, then something better than has been done by the men of Illinois will have to be done if the state is to maintain her reputation as an agricultural state.

The above question was raised at a meeting of the Council of Exchanges; and as pure seed is a prime essential to larger crops, an examination into the situation disclosed the fact that it was practically impossible to get pure seed in any market in quantity. This led to the organization of the committee; but as many lines of business other than grain dealers are interested in larger crops, these other lines have been approached and brought into this work. The activities of the many have been brought under one general direction and energy is conserved thereby. The I. H. C. is now taking a census of the working forces engaged in the propaganda of crop improvement, and when this is completed the weak spots will be laid bare and there the campaign can be concentrated by the organization on locality work. This will be done with the united support of all business men interested. The farmers are in a receptive mood and it will be easy to get the work in motion when there are men to take it up.

Mr. Ball then went on to show what will be done in the way of locality work: the substitution of specialty railroad laborers in the place of trains of many professors talking to many separate groups of auditors at one time and place; the circulation of literature; the making of a seed census in order that supplies may be located and so on. He closed by suggesting that this Association appoint a seed improvement committee to act in conjunction with the committee represented by him.

Ralph Pickell, editor of the Hay and Grain Reporter, Chicago, delivered an address on the "Ethics of the Grain Trade," the theme of which was that "The best service is that which earns a reasonable profit"—it doesn't pay, in good men's opinion, to be a hog, so to say.

On motion of Mr. Wayne all resolutions were ordered sent to the committee on resolutions directly.

The following telegram was reported sent to President Geo. D. Montelius:

The Illinois Grain Dealers' Association in convention assembled extend their warmest sympathy and regret your inability to be with us. Your many acts in behalf of the Association are daily forced upon our attention, and we sincerely hope and pray for your early recovery.

The convention then adjourned until 1:30 p. m.

AFTERNOON SESSION—FIRST DAY.

The afternoon session was opened by an address by J. S. Tustin, F. C. A. Mo. Pac. Ry. Co. and president of the Freight Claim Agents' National Association. He made some clever hits in opening, aimed at claimants, the editorial "we" used by some editors and the man with a tape worm, and then plunged *in medias res* with the following paper on "Pharoah and His Corn Crop," which he enlivened with some happy interpolations that might entitle the gentleman to "distinguished consideration" as an entertainer if his success on this occasion be a criterion:

It is my aim on this occasion to preach a little sermon; and I assume that in Illinois no state license is required to perform this function. We will consider, along with the main narrative, some of the moral off-shoots of what was likely the first successful grain corner in the world's history. The recorded incidents may be read by those who care to do it in fifteen minutes, and the whereabouts of my text is within the knowledge of some of you who constitute today's congregation.

'Way back in the long ago, when, viewed from the present, fact and fiction form a soft blend, a lad was sold by his brothers to a band of commercial travelers who were moving along with their camels and goods, and was carried off into slavery. Eventually he reached Egypt, about one hundred and twenty-five miles away, and through a chain of events came to the notice of the ruler of the "ribbon kingdom," which then as now extended hundreds of miles along the Nile. A woman got mixed up in the story, as she has been other times before and since, and Joseph, the slave boy, discovered even in that early day that "hell hath no fury like a woman scorned." He was proof against her advances, not having absorbed the sophistication that men may sometimes properly lie out of a bad situation and that anyway, to some minds, two lies are admissible generally—one in the protection of vested interests and the other in the obscuration of those feminine circumstances for which a man will perjure himself like an English gentleman.

A dream also was an important incident, the important incident I should say, in the development of the commercial coup. As a general thing people look askance at the dreamer and place emphasis on the "stuff" and the "main chance." Reflection and meditation have become outlaws in our common view and the blue ribbon belongs to immediate decision. That a man's life consisteth not in the abundance of things which he possesseth may have been good ethical preachment long ago, but few men now-adays, especially young ones, subscribe to it. And yet I have a fondness for dreams, not that sort, to be sure, which declares that to dream of a rat forebodes misfortune and to dream of a robin betokens good luck; there is a stern practical mind that discovers no truth in Alice In Wonderland and would take from our literature the charm of Santa Claus. Perhaps it is my liking for dreams that fits me for the job of a railroad claim agent—if I am fit.

A facetious critic of the vocation which I follow has said in post prandial good humor that if Lazarus who was raised from the dead had been a freight claim agent, when the Voice cried, "Come forth," Lazarus would have come fifth. I am of the disposition today to concur in this opinion, at any rate to urge that we lower the speed limit to conform to midsummer weather in the prairie lands of our Middle West. You will recall the apocryphal story of the French scientists who undertook to define crab: Having concluded that "it is a small red fish, which walks backwards," they decided to defer to Cuvier, who exclaimed: "Wonderful! that is, with three petit exceptions: a crab is not a fish, it is not red, and it does not walk backwards. Otherwise the definition is superb."

I am urging you to walk backwards on this occasion, taking a warrant from our wise legislators who at times turn back the hands of the clock to lengthen the official day. With us, however, we need to recall the calendar, pass in our retreat the enactment of the inter-state commerce law, the Declaration of Independence, Hannibal crossing the Alps, the invasion of Gaul which Caesar recorded, until we reach the shadow land of history.

Joseph, the manager of Pharoah's grain corner, had been raised in the country and was an early example of the army of people who have come off the farm and have succeeded in the professions, in mercantile life, and in general industry. But few in any capacity can travel backwards any considerable distance without coming to a hardy sire who followed the plow; indeed, the most fascinating study of life is the history of ancestry. Taking our cue from the man who agreed to pay the blacksmith a cent for the first nail, two for the second, four for the third and doubling in progression until the horse was shod, each of us, have no doubt, has thought of his two parents, four grandparents, eight great grandparents, and the continuing process until if we dared think back to Pharoah's day a sense of bewilderment would absorb the reflecting processes and we would stand uncovered at the problem of life. Somewhere back the lives of our ancestry converge; but notwithstanding this mixture we have not become uniform, and happily so, either in face or thinking; and great is the mystery thereof.

A story is told, I believe of Madam DeStael and Talleyrand. The former, somewhat cross-eyed, is said to have met the latter, somewhat bowlegged. "Good morning, Talleyrand," said she, "how are your legs?" "Crooked, as you see, Madam," he replied.

Along with our blood mixture, with its kaliedoscopic aspect, an ideal morality survives which must ultimately prevail. There is no ugliness without an ideal beauty, nor wrong without an ideal right, nor vice without an ideal virtue.

Vehicles of transportation in Pharoah's day were boats, camels, donkeys and the slave's back. Evidence that the carriage of people and property was a business of magnitude, and that the forehanded were on the work, may be reasonably inferred from the controversial epic called the book of Job. Before trouble came to this argumentative Oriental he owned three thousand camels; and notwithstanding the deluge of disaster around which his career centers, he ended up with six thousand ships of the desert and a restoration, with compound interest, of his losses, save in the destruction of his family. Job as well as Pharoah had the rare power of acquisition, and could engineer in our day of steel, tobacco or oil combination, and, judging from the exposure of their mental processes, would perhaps keep within the rule of reason. Job was a dealer in transportation supplies.

The camel today ambles across the desert stretches of Persia, Arabia and other Eastern lands, carrying figs, rugs, salt, grain and spices. But occidental ideals are invading the land of mystery, and railroad building goes on apace. Less poetry may be involved in an Oriental rug carried from Moshed to Constantinople in a freight car than on a camel; the slow jog of velvet feet and the sleepy indolence of the man who drives her are whips to fancy, when we study the matchless weaves of the peripatetic people who gather from the deeps of contemplation colors and combinations that the sands fain would produce. The human mind is the master weaver, and from its repositories, vivified by controlled passions and impulses, comes the satisfaction which things alone fail to give. Imagination suitably educated extends the span of life backwards to that degree that the bombardment of Sumpter is no more real than the passage of Napoleon to Egypt. We may think to that degree of realism that the memory of the ark and Ararat are as well within our knowledge and experience as the Lusitania and London.

In due time when Western culture does its perfect work, a Camel Owners' Protective League may spring full-grown into the arena, and then may crystallize Oriental opinion on hours of labor, maximum and minimum tariffs, the rate on figs from Babylon to Bloomington and on gum arabic from Sarouk to Sioux City. There are some social phenomena for which language is ready made, among them the laborer's demand for his wage, a mother's plea for her child, the management of the opposition newspaper, and the regulation of transportation minutiae.

But we must not permit the attractions of philosophy or fancy to entirely sidetrack the story we are considering this summer day in Bloomington. In this fragment of history, we should reckon with the tendencies of the human mind, which have not fundamentally changed since Adam except in their application to altered commercial and social conditions. Jealousy, the bias of self-interest, and the strife for gain, are discoverable despite our evolved ethical standards. In our retreat into dreamland days we fail to find in the cuneiform writings on earthen tablets evidence of trade journals, grain dealers' associations, the scientific operation of law (?), democratic legislation or other modern instrumentalities, which, while they usually instruct and educate, at times also confuse. Pharoah, in engineering his corner, was not bothered by the problem whether the standard of measurement was the same in Memphis, his capital, as in Heliopolis, a distance away. He seized all he could get against the day when people would come to his granaries and turn in all they had to satisfy hunger.

In our day, of course, all measurements are uniform and all scales weigh alike. Some wise people with a bump of curiosity are bold enough to declare that in a big run of grain one modern market will show an average difference of a thousand pounds while another an average of a hundred. We are not going to spend valuable time today with those inquisitive fellows, although I have seen claims against railroads for ten pounds short from a carload of twelve hundred bushels; and this is enough to provoke discussion. The ancient grain growers and dealers in Egypt had no railroads to bother with, nor were camel owners responsible if sands buried, Philistines stole or animals died.

Was eight cents a ton per mile, as one of our early American railroad tariffs provided, too high, or the present average of three-quarters of a cent per ton per mile too low, or not low enough?

Was grain a highly perishable commodity when the curing season was unfavorable, to be rated with peaches and strawberries; or non-perishable, to be rated with coal and pig iron?

What cared Pharoah or Joseph, or the slow driver—"Come and get it, pay for it and haul it away or go hungry."

The spokesman of the Camel Transportation Company had no convenient penny piece of chewing gum to illustrate by comparison the cost of carriage as against the cost of other service. No one could break off a fourth of it and holding the stump in his fingers exclaim that "this represents the average gross pay—not the average profit—of hauling a ton of freight a mile." Such an achievement is distinctly, and, I believe, exclusively American.

In handling grain in his subterranean storage bins Manager Joseph had no pure food inspectors to deal with, nor board of trade weighmasters to check against him. Likely in the hot, dry climate of Egypt he was not compelled to run his grain from one pit to another to keep it from the dreaded "no grade;" nor did it concern him in any manner if the people who bought or others who transported occupied a week or month getting the grain to the consuming market. There were no red-ball caravans to hurry things along; there was no Egyptian Commerce Commission to announce that two hundred and eighteen thousand million tons of freight had been hauled one mile, as was done in the United States a year or two ago; nor was there a multitude of experts ready to declare the rate that should be charged on ostrich feathers, brick bats and balloons. Ah! we are a long ways from Pharoah. Does grain get hot in elevators? Cure it and charge the owners. Does it get hot in cars? Charge the railroads. Does it get off-grade at destination? Charge Providence. Does it cost twenty or twenty-five cents a ton a mile to haul to the shipping station? Charge incidentals. Does it cost a fraction of a cent for the same service by rail? Charge, charge the "Octupus."

A while ago I read a book that contained a chapter headed, "Subjective Synthesis." Maybe you know what that means, but I am not sure that I do. The argument, as far as I was able to understand it, understook to sustain the proposition that any truth is part of a general universal truth; that the fact of a star, the fact of a wheat field, and the fact of ultimate morality all have union somewhere, either in ideal human thinking or in the ultimate end of things. Maybe we have not dwelt as we profitably may on the word "co-ordination," a better word sometimes than co-operation. Let me venture a simple illustration. A shadowy impression reaches the human brain—vague, illusive and unformed. The period of mental gestation is fulfilled, a psychic relation is established with the muscles of the throat, and lo! a spoken word is born. Sometimes in certain nervous ailments the connective is broken and, as in perverted morals, we have a malformation that shatters the ideal, provokes ignoble passion, raises self-interest to the throne, and ignores the truth that the principle which works for the general good works by reflex for the maximum individual reward. Unconscious bias, from which few are immune, leads too often to the organized expression of disagreement, eclipsing the fact that there must be, unless the creation and order of things is chaos, a fundamental social and commercial morality, the attainment of which is the supreme personal and collective prize.

Meanwhile, where have we left Pharoah and his grain pits? Let me read from the ancient narrative:

"There was no bread in all the land; for the famine was very sore. And Joseph gathered up all the money that was found in all the land of Egypt, and in the land of Canaan for the corn which they bought; and Joseph brought the money unto Pharaoh's home."

The early morality of this young man stood by him and was proof against the temptation of cash. The story proceeds to relate that in time he secured all the cattle, horses and miscellaneous flocks; afterwards he got the farms and ultimately the people themselves—the clergy alone being exempt.

And there you have government ownership to a fare-ye-well. Talk about commissions to regulate one thing or another, Henry George's land tax and Washington crossing the Delaware—here is the whole business of transportation, agriculture and commerce in its ramifications, centered in one great head, who bossed the entire job. Forsooth, what's the use of thinking, if we can get some colossal chief to do it for us?

I shall not undertake to attach a moral to this remarkable denouncement, as we are all pretty apt at this business (as it affects the other men), but I will revert for a concluding moment to our friend of the Subjective Synthesis, with his unification of truth. In the Congressional Library at Washington, among the mural mottoes, is this striking and suggestive one, which I fear a fallible memory may forbid me to quote exactly, but its essence is: "One God, one law, one far-off Divine event to which all creation moves!"

[Incidentally it might be repeated that he said the railroads in a single year had paid $30,000,000 to claimants for loss and damages.]

CLAIMS DEPARTMENT.

Wm. R. Bach, manager of the Association's claim department, did not quite stick to his text, "Progress of the Claims Department," for he opened by saying that while the railroads may have paid 30 millions in claims there were some still unpaid, probably for the reason that the president of the F. C. A. Nat. Ass'n had used so much time searching the Congressional Library for material for the paper just read—a "Roland for some of Mr. Tustin's clever Olivers, that the latter seemed to enjoy as much as did the audience. Mr. Bach did not fail to give Mr. Tustin credit for meeting the claims problem fairly and squarely and for having suggested material parts of the agreement mentioned below by him, which has been of so much benefit to Illinois shippers. The substance of Mr. Bach's address was as follows:

Practical Suggestions in Connection with the Preparation and Handling of Grain Claims and Incidentally of the Progress of the Claims' Department of the Illinois Grain Dealers' Association:

1st. It is the first duty of every consignor to do all in his power to prevent, if possible, having a claim against the railroad company which carries his grain.

This duty requires that the consignor shall maintain accurate scales and shall keep the same properly adjusted and shall have the same carefully tested and examined at reasonable intervals.

The person entrusted with the weighing of the grain should be capable and honest. He should carefully weigh the grain and record the weight at the time of weighing. All figures made by such person at the time of the weighing of grain into the car should be preserved, as these figures, and not the record in the office made therefrom, will be of any service in case suit is brought against the carrier.

No doubt every shipper is already carefully observing all of these suggestions, yet I deem it of sufficient importance to call your attention thereto.

In this connection let me suggest that in case a shortage amounting to more than $3.00 is reported on any car, you should at once, while the matter is fresh in the minds of the persons weighing and loading the car, cause them to swear to and sign an affidavit, such as we have caused to be prepared in blank, after the same has been properly and accurately filled out according to the facts in the particular case.

The utmost care should also be exercised by the person loading cars to see that the same are properly coopered and the grain doors properly set. If it were generally known by the persons handling grain claims for the various railroads in the state of Illinois that these suggestions were being rigidly followed by the members of the Illinois Grain Dealers' Association, I venture to say that our claims would be paid more promptly than they now are and that rejection on account of discrepancies in weight when the record of handling shows no exception to condition of car and where original seals are intact would be the exception.

So much for matters at point of shipment. Let us now consider some matters of vital importance at point of destination. And first in regard to out

A PORTION OF THE DEALERS PRESENT AT BLOOMINGTON—SEE OPPOSITE PAGE.

turn weights. It is absolutely essential both to the shipper and carrier that out turn weights of grain should be authentic. Both are interested therein. Some recent observations on this point in connection with the handling of grain in shipment incline me to believe that when the market is off to any extent there is usually considerable variation between the loading weights and out-turn weights. Whether this is intentional on the part of the weighers at destination or not I do not say. It is significant to say the least.

Circulars have been mailed to every member of the association suggesting that consignor should request of consignee sworn certificates of out turn weights whenever the loss in weight amounts to more than $3.00 in value. I notice that only a few shippers are observing this suggestion. Not being in the bsuiness myself there may be some good reason why this is impracticable and if there is I should like to hear from some of the members present in regard to the same. It occurs to me that it is one of the more important matters in connection with the filing and collection of claims for shortage.

We have in Illinois a statute already referred to by me in my former address to you which is of vast importance to the grain dealers.

It provides among other things that where the railroad company neglects or refuses to weigh the grain at point of destination the sworn statement of the person to whom the grain is delivered or his agent, having personal knowledge thereof, shall be taken as true as to the amount of grain delivered.

You can see at a glance that this statute is of great benefit to a shipper in case suit is brought on a claim for shortage. The sworn statement of the weigher who weighed the grain for the consignee is thereby made evidence of the amount of grain in the car, obviating the cost and delay of taking depositions. Then too if the affidavit of the weigher is not taken immediately by the time the case is reached for trial the weigher has forgotten the matter or is so hazy in his recollection that his evidence counts for but little.

Personal experience in this particular matter causes me to urge upon you the importance of the same.

I am inserting herein a blank form of affidavit with the suggestion that if it meets with approval at your hands a sufficient number may be placed in the hands of the trade so that when occasion requires an affidavit may be furnished without any inconvenience to any one.

I would suggest the following form:

State of.........., ...County, ss.

................, being duly sworn on his oath deposes and says that on the......day of........,A. D. 191.., he carefully and accurately weighed for.... ....of.........., State of..........., to whom the grain, hereinafter specified, was delivered, the contents of...... Car No..... That the correct weight of the contents of said car was......pounds. That at the time of weighing said grain the scales by which the said grain was weighed were in good repair and properly adjusted.

Dated......day of........, A. D. 191..

Subscribed and sworn to before me this....day of ......, A. D. 1911.

....
Notary Public.

The important question in connection with this affidavit is, How can we get the purchaser of grain to furnish these affidavits?

It may be difficult and require some correspondence to get these affidavits, but if every member of the Illinois Grain Dealers' Association will insist on the same, there will very little objection raised to furnishing same.

We would suggest that the following be attached to the papers at the time of forwarding bill of lading:

Notice.—If there is a shortage of more than $3.00 between the out turn weights and the weight specified in Bill of Lading attached, a sworn statement of the person weighing the grain in the form presented by the Illinois Grain Dealers' Association must be furnished consignor, for which we will allow you 25 cents to cover cost of its execution.

It will not take trade long to adapt itself to the mode of furnishing consignors with the necessary evidence of out turn weights.

We are confident that much time will be saved thereby both in attending upon court or before persons authorized to take depositions and in correspondence in regard to the matter.

The shipper would have the satisfaction of knowing that if deductions were made on account of loss in transit he would have furnished to him the evidence by which he could recover his loss.

I come now to the practical results that have been attained through the organization of the claims department of your association.

We recognize that the department has not reached perfection by any means. The fact is that it has only started. Many benefits have already been obtained through it, not only to our members who use the department, but also to every grain dealer in Illinois.

When the claim department was first organized, some few claims were being paid by the railroads, principally to the larger shipper with several elevators, and located at junction points where grain might be shipped over two or more railroads. Most of the claims for shortage were being rejected, where the evidence furnished showed that the original seals were intact and no exceptions were noted to condition of car.

As a result of several important conferences with various members of the F. C. A. Association of Illinois, a working agreement was reached between our association and nearly all of the important railroads in Illinois, as follows:

Agreement or Understanding entered into this date by a Committee of the Illinois Grain Dealers' Association and a Committee of the Freight Claim Association in relation to the adjustment of claims for loss of grain.

(1) No claim will be filed for shortage where the amount of loss does not exceed $3.00 per car.

(2) Where there is no exception against the condition of the car, no leakage shown, the seals intact, an allowance will be made for so-called scale variation or natural shrinkage, of one-quarter of one per cent on corn and one-eighth of one per cent on other grain, but no claim will be made for $3.00 or less, as provided in No. 1.

(3) Where there is an exception to the condition of the car that is that it is shown to be leaking, seals tampered with, or having been repaired by the railroad company in transit, no allowance whatever will be made for so-called scale variation or natural shrinkage, but no claim will be made for $3.00 or less, as provided in No. 1.

(4) It is understood that a report will be made by the Railroad Company on each claim within ninety days of the date of presentation.

(5) Each claim when presented will be accompanied with proper papers, including affidavit of shipper as to condition of scales, weight, etc. (as per form now in use by the Illinois Grain Dealers' Association). The claim will also be accompanied by the Bill of Lading and Freight Bill or their absence explained.

The above agreement was not intended in any way to interfere with the investigation of any particular claim where there is reason to believe that the claim is not correct, further that it does not bind any of the companied to pay any claim which they think should not be paid. These rules are simply to be applied to cases where the claims are to be paid, and it is simply an understanding or working basis so that there may be no unnecessary correspondence in regard to allowance that should be made or the minimum that should apply. The agreement is more a matter of convenience than anything else, and it was so intended by all parties present.

It was further understood that this agreement should not prejudice the rights of shippers to contest a claim which has been rejected by the Railroad Company.

Some grain shippers in Illinois are not members of the Illinois Grain Dealers' Association and therefore would not be bound by the agreement, and there are some members of the Illinois Grain Dealers' Association who may refuse to abide by it, but the Association will, as far as may be in their power, endeavor to have it lived up to in all cases.

The following were present:

Illinois Grain Dealers' Association.—G. D. Montelius, President; S. W. Strong, Secretary.

Railroad Companies.—H. C. Howe, F. C. A., Chicago & Northwestern; C. H. Newton, F. C. A., Wabash; J. S. Tustin, F. C. A., Missouri Pacific; J. W. Newell, A. F. A., Chicago, Burlington & Quincy; H. P. Elliott, F. C. A., Chicago, Milwaukee & St. Paul; J. H. Howard, F. C. A., Chicago Great Western; H. B. Belt, F. C. A., Chicago & Alton & Clover Leaf; C. M. Kittle, F. C. A., Illinois Central; J. M. Denyven, G. F. A., Mobile & Ohio; F. W. Main, A. F. G. A., Chicago, Rock Island & Pacific; B. H. Stanage, A. G. F. A., Frisco Lines; J. F. Seger, F. C. A., Louisville & Nashville.

September 21, 1910.

Since the adoption of this agreement but few of our claims have been rejected and it is our further desire to so convince the Freight Claim Agent of every railroad in Illinois by our fairness and accuracy in the preparation and filing of claims that our claims department and our members are entitled to the money represented by their claims when the same are filed. I am convinced that this claims department can be so perfected that every legitimate claim will be paid upon presentation within ninety days or less.

Some arrangement should be devised whereby a member who is compelled to sue a railroad company for a legitimate claim that has been approved by the proper committee will be furnished with counsel by the association.

As it is now we know of several instances where it is necessary to sue on claims and where service cannot be had on the railroad in this county. In each case the fee of foreign counsel is prohibitive owing to the fact that they are not regularly employed by the association. As a result the claimant, though having a meritorious case is denied justice, simply because the railroad company knows that it will cost him as much more to fight the case as he will realize from the same.

If it were known that the Illinois Grain Dealers' Association would furnish counsel in every contested claim, which had been approved by a committee of the association appointed especially for that purpose very few claims would ever be compelled to be sued. This could easily be done by setting apart certain of the annual dues of those members of the association who desired to avail themselves of the benefits thereof. The matter would be purely optional with the members. On the whole I desire to here state that there is very good feeling existing between the freight claim agents of the Illinois railroads and the claims department and we trust that such condition will continue to exist.

We are just as anxious to defeat and deny a dishonest claim as any freight claim agent in Illinois or anywhere else. And any member who would knowingly present a dishonest claim should be expelled from membership in the association.

It is true that quite a few claims have been rejected by us before being sent in to the railroads. Some have been voluntarily withdrawn when it was found that some mistake had been made.

During our connection with the claims department there have been filed 603 claims of all kinds by one hundred and two different members of our association.

Of these, claims amounting to over $6,000, as near as we can figure it, have been paid. And in this connection let me suggest that each member who has sent in claims through our claims department, carefully check up his claims and remit our fees that have not already been paid. Also send us list of unpaid claims in order that our records may be made as accurate as possible.

I am convinced that some claims have been paid direct to claimant which have not been reported to us. You can realize at once that report should be made at once when railroad company pays a claim direct to claimant. Since the organization of this department two years ago there has been collected

A PORTION OF THE DEALERS PRESENT AT BLOOMINGTON—SEE OPPOSITE PAGE.

by us as fees from all claims collected the sum of $730.33.

We believe that every member of the association should send its claims through the department. Many of you will say, I can collect my claims myself without any attorney fee. Suppose every member felt the same way. How long would it be until conditions would be as they were prior to the organization of this department? You owe it to your association to patronize this department that has done so much for the entire membership. The small shipper gets his claims paid under the present arrangement just as quickly as the larger one. Do you think that without such an arrangement we could make such a statement.

Some member may say: "What's the use of having an attorney to handle these claims? Why can't we handle them ourselves?"

Every railroad with which you deal has counsel in every county seat and besides has general counsel upon which the F. C. A. calls for advice. Some attorney must advise your organization and he must receive compensation. If he will specialize sufficiently to know and understand the intricate matters and points of law involved, he must be paid.

In closing I desire to state that several members of the association, particularly our esteemed secretary and local members of the executive committee, have materially assisted me in the organization and operation of the claims department and I wish to here publicly thank them for their good work.

It is our desire to make this department efficient, practical, helpful and valuable to the members. To qualify ourselves in the law applicable to every phase of the business.

I feel that my connection with your organization and association with the members has been indeed pleasant and valuable to me.

I had not intended to make this an address and perhaps it should not be so considered.

What was desired was to make a few practical suggestions and discuss them with you to the end that the same may be generally understood and put in use by our members.

It would please me to answer any questions that any member might see fit to ask concerning the operation of the claims department and matters arising in the preparation and handling of your claims.

I am at your service and want you to feel free to make suggestions and inquiries relative to the business.

ILLINOIS CROP STATISTICS.

Hon. J. K. Dickirson, secretary of the State Board of Agriculture, took up the matter of the regrettable condition of the machinery for collecting the crop statistics of the state. He said, in substance:

We have a good law in this state (see Hurd's Rev. Statutes, 1908, Chap. V. Sections 24, 25, 26 and 27) requiring the assessors to secure the facts as to the acreage of the principal crops and other agricultural statistics and to give these facts to their respective county clerks and providing for the tabulation of the same and the return to the office of the State Board of Agriculture of the statistical data so obtained. But there seems to be a prejudice in the minds of some farmers against giving this information, and there being no penalty for non-compliance with the law, it has become almost a dead letter.

Every year, in compiling the agricultural statistics of the state it is necessary to estimate acreages by surrounding counties, to average and make comparisons until, endeavoring always to be conservative, the figures for acreage and yield have fallen far below what they should be to fairly and truthfully show the agricultural importance of Illinois. These statistical reports are, to put it mildly, no credit to the state, and this condition should not be allowed to continue. The facts as to the great importance of Illinois as an agricultural state should be available, so that this information, which is asked for almost every day, may be given out by the proper authority. The State Board of Agriculture should not be obliged to apologize for the inaccuracy and incompleteness of its statistical publications.

Persons seeking investments, others wishing to establish business along progressive methods of farming and stock breeding, railroad companies and promoters of interurban lines are constantly asking for information which it is impossible to give them, concerning the productions and agricultural conditions in Illinois.

This data is not wanted, as is supposed by some, for the benefit of the boards of trade in the various states. Stock brokers send their agents out over the country and pay them good salaries to get just such information for their own benefit, and they get it without the consent or even the knowledge of the farmers who oppose giving it to the proper authorities who would use it for their (the farmers') benefit. These facts, carefully gathered and tabulated and given out by the authority of state officials, would afford to investors and to every one interested in our progress and prosperity the confidence in the substantial value of the state that rightfully belongs to Illinois as one of the greatest agricultural states in the Union. This would increase the value of property and be helpful and not detrimental to our interests.

This year a special effort is being made to secure this information, through an appeal to county officers to use their influence to have the law enforced, and encouraging response has been received from a number of counties.

There being no way of arriving at an accurate statement of acreage, the rest of the work is difficult, but, he said:

"The Board has crop reporters to the number of 300, acting without compensation, who report on the condition of growing crops, the acreage compared with the previous year (in percentages), the yield per acre and ruling price of crops. If we could secure the acreage of crops, then the yield per acre and price per bushel given by the crop reporters would be of value, and the total yield and value of the crops could be estimated. Correct agricultural statistics cannot be compiled until the acreage of the crops for each year is secured. The acreage of the present year is secured by multiplying the acreage of last year by the percentage given by the reporter under the head of 'Area 1911 compared with 1910.' Now, if the area had been but half the usual acreage, say 5,000 acres in 1910, and in 1911 the usual acreage, or 10,000 acres, had been sown, the crop reporter would report 100 per cent for 'Acreage compared with 1910,' as 100 per cent is the basis in representing acreage in comparison with that of last year yield or condition in comparison with a fair average, or in any other comparison made for tabulation, and an increase of one-tenth, or 10 per cent, is recorded 110; a decrease of 5 per cent will be marked 95, etc. The area, then, for that county will be recorded as 5,000 acres, or 100 per cent, as compared with 1910, whereas the conditions at time of seeding the crop were most favorable and the full 10,000 acres seeded. This of course reduces not only the acreage, but the yield, and, therefore, the value of the crop in an alarming manner."

But as there is no way but a guess to arrive at a basic acreage, the comparisons are manifestly worthless (comparatively, at least) so Mr. Dickirson made it a point a year ago to secure the co-operation of the county clerks to enforce the law above referred to; subsequently he repeated the request to county clerks and treasurers and this is the substance of the reports he received in reply:

Pulaski County Clerk: If your office is in a position to pay for the information, we could possibly get it ready in 30 days. If there are no funds available for this work, then, of course, your office would not expect us to put in overtime getting the information for you.

DeWitt County Clerk: The farmers refused to give the information, and the assessors lost considerable time to procure the same and received no compensation therefor. It has turned out that, as far as this county is concerned, all attempts to secure these statistics have amounted to nothing but botheration and expense.

Winnebago County Clerk: Unless the law is so amended as to make it compulsory for the farmers to give the assessors this information, the whole thing will continue to be a failure and a farce.

Bond County Clerk: Unless there is some way to compel the farmer to give the information, it is of no use. Last year I furnished all the supplies to the assessors and got no returns; so you can readily see a county clerk is at sea, without oar or rudder.

Pike County Clerk: I believe if the various supervisors of assessments in the state will take the matter up with the local assessors and insist that they get the agricultural statistics, you will receive a good report from the state. The local assessors look upon the supervisor of assessments as their boss and do not pay much attention to county clerks.

Tazewell County Clerk: Unless there is a penalty connected with a failure to have same filled out it is a useless expense to the counties to furnish the books and blanks.

There were 29 of the 102 counties that complied with the law in 1910 and sent in agricultural statistics, as follows: DuPage, JoDaviess, Carroll, Bureau, Boone, Iroquois, Williamson, Whiteside, Wabash, St. Clair, Saline, Randolph, Moultrie, Ford, Kankakee, Massac, Winnebago, Edgar, Kendall, Lee, Hamilton, Clinton, Effingham, Sangamon, Piatt, Coles, Macoupin and Putnam.

Of course such a showing amounts to but little. Then Mr. Dickirson went to the legislature, with no result, for, he says, a bill was introduced in both the house and senate to compel assessors to secure this information relating to acreage and to fine them for the non-performance of such duty. Senate Bill 171, "An Act to amend an Act entitled an Act to secure the collection and publication of agricultural and other statistics," passed the senate on March 15, was tabled in the house April 7. House bill 246 (same bill as Senate Bill 171) was tabled April 7. House Bill 244, "An Act making an appropriation for the State Board of Agriculture and county and other agricultural fairs," asked for $1,000 for collection of agricultural statistics, an increase of $400. This was not allowed by the appropriation committee, the sum of $600 only being allowed, which barely covers the printing of reports and postage for the issuance of same.

Mr. Dickirson thinks a good law might be enacted if the Association will take an interest in it and help it along. As it is all reports now published are mere guesses, pretty fair guesses, but still guesses based on 17,000,000 acres, about half the improved area of the state having been well reported on this year.

After some announcements, the convention adjourned for the day.

SECOND DAY—MORNING SESSION

The second day was one of more than ordinary interest. The attendance was large—in the neighborhood of 400, and it was evident that the main topic of the morning involved vast possibilities. Dr. J. W. T. Duvel, crop technologist B. P. I., Dept. of Agr., Washington, opened the session with an address on "The Use and Advantages of the Moisture Test in Handling Grain." His attention was devoted exclusively to corn because that grain is most in evidence in Illinois and because most of the work of his Bureau has been devoted to the study of corn. Moisture, he began, is the most important factor in the keeping quality of corn. A knowledge of the moisture content is therefore indispensable in its commercial movement. The moisture test therefore has come to stay, although it may have been abused in its use; for the time has come when the American consumer will buy only on the basis of the actual dry-matter value, and Europeans will soon do the same.

The tester has been abused and its results rendered unauthoritative by (1) carelessness in weighing the sample to be tested; (2) by inaccuracy in the proportion of oil used; (3) by use of a higher temperature than 190°, for if a higher temperature is used more moisture than necessary is eliminated and the character of the dry matter is changed by the burning of the grain and the breaking up of the stand cells; (4) by inaccurate handling of the tester thermometer; (5) by error in reading the result of the test, the percentage being indicated below the oil carried over with the eliminated moisture; (6) by neglect to insure continued accuracy of the thermometer; and (7) neglect to secure an absolutely clean graduate by removing all moisture of former tests.

There is a natural shrinkage in the curing of corn—from 22 per cent of moisture as it goes into the crib in the fall to 12 per cent when it comes out in the spring dry. The actual weight loss is greater than the indicated loss of moisture; and a study of this shrinkage is valuable commercially to both the farmer and the shipper. The discount in value, all things being normal in the market, with corn at about present prices, is say ⅝c per bushel for each 1% excess of moisture down to 12%; but the discount must vary in proportion to the price. There are also the conditions under which the grain must be handled by the receiver. When 21% corn arrives, it must be dried to 16 to 17% to carry, and the receiver must pay the cost and stand the shrinkage—all of which conditions affect the cash discounts from the basic price. There is a variation in the moisture content with the season and from year to year. The crop of 1909 was better than that of 1910. In October, 1909, the corn of Illinois examined by Dr. Duvel's laboratories, averaged 20.3% moisture; in March, 1910, it was 18.9% against 18.7 in February; in June 14.1 and in August 12.7, the tests being made from corn taken in many points in Illinois. The crop of 1910 was indeed much worse than he had thought. Of 1,906 cars tested at New Orleans from 125 stations and 24 counties in the very heart of the corn belt of central Illinois, covering all Illinois shipments to New Orleans, the average moisture (all grades, 2, 3 and 4) was 20.4%. This was the best corn Illinois had; so that when we consider that it had more than 20% of moisture, it need hardly be said that there is something radically wrong. You know that 20% corn is not a safe commercial article.

Now look at what this means. Last year (1910) the corn crop measured three billion bushels, of which Illinois grew 414 millions. Of the entire crop 22.2% went out of the county where it was grown, of which amount Illinois ships 48%, or 199,104,000 bushels or 28% of the entire movable corn of the Union. Illinois, therefore, has the call ou—rules the moisture problem. Now on account of its poor quality Europeans have stopped buying American corn when they can get corn elsewhere; and when that substitution becomes permanent, our surplus corn must stay at home. I think that today if Europe would buy freely in this country our price would be 3c a bushel higher than it is. So you are interested in these conditions and you can improve them if you want to. The corn of 1910 sold for early shipment all had at least 5% excess of moisture, equal to 9,955,000 bushels, 9,955 cars; and if this moisture went to New Orleans the freight alone would equal $750,000.

Dr. Duvel referred to the appreciation of the moisture tester in Illinois and also to the criticisms made upon it; but he thought some line houses are deceived by managers who when they got stuck on corn badly bought by them did not always send to headquarters strictly accurate samples, and the company was disappointed at outturn at the terminal market.

Dr. Duvel answered numerous questions relating to the tester, particularly as to test temperatures which must not be above 190° and must be arrived at slowly; thermometers must be handled carefully and frequently compared with the standard.

Mr. Shellabarger said he knew of thermometers that had been in use in a certain terminal market for more than two years without any correction or examination; to which Dr. Duvel replied by citing cases coming to his knowledge where the abuses were even worse than that—where one thermometer had been turned upside down and had 16° of mercury lodged in the top; but it was in use just the same!

MR. HUBBARD ON THE TESTER.

Geo. H. Hubbard of Mt. Pulaski, former president of the Association, gave the country dealer's side of the tester. His company has three testers in use—two for three years and one for two years; and our experience has been satisfactory. We think very much of these machines. By their use we have learned much about corn and its carrying quality at different degrees of moisture content. On the crop of 1908, our machines saved us about $10,000. About two years ago we went out in July and bought about 200,000 bushels of the corn then growing—"mine run." Of course, none of you do that—you are too clever! [Laughter]. What was the result? We sold it out all over the country, and when it began to come in we had to take it just as it was. The deal netted a loss of $6,000 to $10,000! We have since stopped that kind of business. If any of you here contemplate such a program, I'd advise you to stop now. Then there was a sale of oats bought at 30c in the same way and sold at 38c—oh, it was easy money until the deal was closed. But, why linger!

In February, 1909, a farmer called us up and said he had about 6,000 bushels of No. 3 yellow corn. We offered 38c, subject to discount if it missed grade. And he started shelling, and we took it. We didn't test it all—only when it seemed on the line. When about half was hauled the moisture seemed to increase and we began testing, finding that it ran 19.5 to 20½%. When he came in to settle he was told that it was about half and half three and four. But he could not understand why; nor could we, as all the corn was grown on the same land, harvested and cribbed and shelled alike. As it had been housed in separate bins it was understood that each part should be marketed separately, and that if we were wrong I agreed to buy him the "best hat in town." It was so shipped, and it graded on sale exactly as we anticipated.

Then I began asking more questions and found that he had cribbed it in a shingle roof crib, standing north and south; and the damper corn had come from the bin on the east side of the driveway which had been protected from the prevailing west and northwest winds. And it was so—that was the secret, and the tester had demonstrated the fact. Had we not used the tester how would we have come out on that deal? Would we not have cussed the inspection?

There is one man responsible for uncured corn—the farmer, the grower. I think, added Mr. Hubbard, that it is your duty as grain dealers to urge upon him the necessity of planting a seed corn that he knows will mature in this latitude. Now what is the best way to teach him this important lesson? Touch his pocket book. Discriminate against his damp corn in buying. Put it up to the farmer to raise commercial corn and to cure it, or suffer the pecuniary consequences. (Applause). Show him the condition of the corn and make him take only the price that it is worth. Summarizing up the whole matter, Mr. Hubbard concluded by saying:

During the pioneer days, when the growing of corn to feed the live stock upon the farm was the only purpose for which it was used, the use of a moisture tester was not dreamed of. The amount of moisture in the corn was not to be considered of vital interest or importance, either to the producer or to the consumer; it concerned either but little, whether it contained 17 per cent or 20 per cent of moisture. Some of the older members present, perhaps, can remember the time when some farmers of central Illinois burned one crop of corn in order to plant and grow another on the same land, to the one doing so it mattered but little how much moisture it contained, provided it would burn.

It is only of very recent years that there has developed the merchandising of corn, especially merchandising the larger part of the crop during the winter months. In the earlier period of merchandising corn in the winter months it was delivered to the local dealer by the farmer on the cob and placed in cribs and there allowed to dry out and get into a merchantable condition before merchandising. Merchandising corn in this manner, the question of amount of moisture was not so very important; but, gentlemen, allow me to say that conditions have changed, and under the new manner of merchandising corn the question of the amount of moisture in said corn is one of the most vital ones that enter into the merchandising of corn at present.

The manner of determining the amount of moisture in corn, up to a very recent date, was by guessing at it, and some of the older and apparently more intelligent dealers seem to desire to continue the guessing, in preference to adopting a mechanical and scientific analysis made by a moisture tester that is not only exact but rapid and easily operated. Any person of ordinary intelligence can in twenty minutes determine to a certainty the amount of moisture in a sample of corn.

It seems to me that to be able to determine the amount of moisture in corn is of inestimable value to the country grain dealer. It not only enables him to arrive at the value of it, but, in addition, it is there to tell you unmistakably of its carrying qualities; it also acts as a guide in determining the proper market to ship to.

I am constrained to say that I believe that the strongest objection to the moisture tester emanates from those buyers that do not own or use one in their business.

Permit me to say that in my judgment the better thing to do is to cease complaining of the moisture tester, and go immediately and buy one, and use it; and you will rejoice at your good fortune in having a moisture tester, and you will wonder how you got along without one or how it was possible that you had been so foolish as to have ever opposed progression.

After you have used a moisture tester for one year, you will see your losses on account of discounts on off-grades disappear; the instances of having No. 4 and sample grades of corn at destination, which you paid No. 3 prices for, will be but few.

We are sometimes met with the argument that you can get samples out of the same car that will show difference in the test. We are ready to admit such a thing is possible; but it is just as true that there is a difference in the corn. That being true, it proves the accuracy of the machine.

The selection of the sample for the test is of very great importance; this being carefully done, the rest is easy.

Believing, as I do, what I have said about the moisture tester to be true, it seems to me rather preposterous to assume or to think of eliminating the moisture tester. It is here to stay; its uses may be improved upon, but to be discarded—never.

The address was repeatedly interrupted by applause or by laughter at the clever hits.

THE RESOLUTIONS.

The committee on resolutions, by Lee Metcalf of Illiopolis, reported the following which were adopted singly and as a whole:

IN MEMORIAM.

Whereas, it has pleased Divine Providence, in His infinite wisdom, to remove by death from among our valued members:

E. S. Greenleaf, Jacksonville, January 10, 1911.
A. R. Sawers, Chicago, June 23, 1910.
S. A. Hendee, Bushnell, June 20, 1910.
J. P. Faris, Niantic, July 28, 1910.
N. A. Mansfield, Niantic, July 30, 1910.
T. E. Wells, Chicago, August 3, 1910.
P. B. Webster, Lodge, October 21, 1910.

Therefore, be it

Resolved, That we extend to the families of the departed our deepest and most heartfelt sympathy in their sad bereavement and commend them to the care of Him who doeth all things well. Be it further

Resolved, That this resolution be spread upon the minutes of our meeting and a copy mailed by the secretary to each of the families of the deceased.

REVISION OF CONSTITUTION.

Whereas, The Secretary has recommended in his report that the By-Laws of the Association, which have been in effect for the past eighteen years, should in his judgment be revised and,

Whereas, The said report has been by motion accepted by the convention; therefore be it

Resolved, That the President, the Secretary, and one member of the Board of Directors, to be selected by the President, are hereby declared a committee to revise the Constitution and By-Laws of the Association, and that said committee shall, within ninety days from this date, make such revision; and the Secretary shall mail a copy of such revision to the President, the Vice-President and each member of the Board of Directors; and the President is hereby directed in fifteen days of receipt of a copy of the revision of said By-Laws to call a meeting of the Board of Directors of the Association. And it is further

Resolved, That the Board of Directors to be elected at the present eighteenth annual convention of the Association be and are hereby empowered to approve, amend and adopt or reject, as it may be deemed in their judgment wise to do, said revision of the Constitution and By-Laws as may be made by the committee hereinbefore provided. And be it further

Resolved, That such revision of the By-Laws, when made by the committee and if approved by the Board of Directors, shall be referred to the convention at its nineteenth annual meeting for ratification or rejection.

INSPECTION "SUBJECT."

Whereas, It has become a practice of the track samplers connected with the State Grain Inspection Department to mark many cars of grain "subject to approval," supposedly on account of the cars being too full for thorough inspection or sampling; be it hereby

Resolved, That the Chief Grain Inspector at Chicago be requested to look carefully into this matter and see that cars are not inspected "subject" except when absolutely necessary, believing that the marking of cars "subject" when they are not too full for thorough inspection or sampling is detrimental to the interests of the shippers to the Chicago market and likely to lead to severe losses.

SCALE TESTING.

Resolved, That the President is hereby requested to appoint a committee of three members of this Association to investigate and if found practical to inaugurate a department for scale testing for the benefit of the members of this Association.

DISCOUNTS AND PREMIUMS.

Whereas, The majority of bids for corn are made on basis of number three grade and,

Whereas, A discount is made on number four or lower grade corn applied on contract, and no premium is allowed when number two or better grade corn is applied on contract, therefore, be it

Resolved, That this convention, as a body and as individuals, protest against this practice as not equitable to the country dealers as well as the producers; and that we hereby request the call board committee of the Chicago Board of Trade and all firms and commission merchants of other markets to hereafter put out all bids on basis of number 3 white, yellow and mixed corn and to amend their rules so that the market premium can be paid ou better grades when applied on number three corn contracts. Be it further

Resolved, That a copy of these Resolutions be sent to the Secretary of all exchanges and Boards of Trade tributary to this state.

ILLINOIS AGRICULTURAL STATISTICS.

Deploring with the State Board of Agriculture the lack of accurate statistics of farm production, this Association directs its Legislative Committee to cooperate with the State Board of Agriculture to secure such legislation as is needed to obtain the same. The Association extends to Secretary J. K. Dickirson its thanks for his personal efforts to improve the character of Illinois state crop reports.

MOISTURE TEST RULE.

Whereas, The present Moisture Test Rule with reference to the inspection of corn put in effect about two years ago by the Railroad and Warehouse Commission and rigidly enforced (and properly so) by the Chief Inspector of Grain at Chicago, has, after a thorough trial, proven impracticable, and has resulted in a serious loss to the producer and country shipper of grain; be it

Resolved, By the Illinois Grain Dealers' Association, in convention assembled, at Bloomington, Illinois, June 14th, 1911, that the Railroad and Warehouse Commission be requested at the earliest possible moment to eliminate from the inspection rules of this state the moisture test as THE determining factor in the inspection of corn, believing the present rule, if in effect after October first, of this year, will result in further serious loss to the producer and country shipper of corn. And the Secretary of this Association is hereby instructed to send a copy of this resolution to the Railroad and Warehouse Commission and to the Governor of the state.

CIVIL SERVICE ACT.

Whereas, The 47th General Assembly has passed and the Governor has signed a comprehensive state wide Civil Service Law covering practically all the state employes; and,

Whereas, The application of this law will undoubtedly prove a great benefit to both the producer and shipper of grain, as well as the many state institutions whose employes will be brought under the operation of the merit system of employment and promotion; therefore, be it

Resolved, That we, the Illinois Grain Dealers' Association, in convention assembled, commend the members of the 47th Assembly for the enactment of this law and the Governor for signing same, and we, as citizens, pledge ourselves to co-operate with the executive in the enforcement of the act.

FAST FREIGHT MAIL.

Whereas, The Post Office Department is preparing to forward trade journals between large centers by freight, thus delaying the delivery of trade information to us three to six days; be it

Resolved, By the Illinois Grain Dealers' Association, in convention assembled, at Bloomington this 14th day of June, 1911, that we protest against such delay, and petition the Illinois representatives in the U. S. Senate and House of Representatives to use their best efforts to scure the prompt forwarding of our trade publications to us in the mail cars. Be it further

Resolved, That our Secretary be instructed to send a copy of this resolution to the President of the United States, the Postmaster General and each of our Representatives in Congress at his earliest convenience.

THANKS TO OFFICERS.

Resolved, That a vote of thanks be extended to the officers and directors for their faithful services during the past year.

THANKS TO CITIZENS OF BLOOMINGTON.

Resolved, That a vote of thanks of this Association be extended to the Bloomington grain men and their ladies and all others associated with them in the entertainment of this, the 18th annual convention of this Association.

MOISTURE TEST DEBATE.

The resolution on the moisture test precipitated a sharp debate, of course, opened by Mr. Wayne, who moved to table.

Mr. Newell suggested that all should vote understandingly, realizing what would be the import of such action.

The motion was lost.

The motion being one to adopt Mr. Wayne, who in time past had on more than one occasion expressed his disbelief in the entire fairness of the inspection rule in regard to moisture in No. 3 corn, said he had become convinced that the trouble is not so much with the moisture test as with the discounts. He agreed with Mr. Hubbard's view of the tester and felt that if dealers used it more they would find less fault with it. As for himself, he had not used it, but he intends now to do so. He felt, however, that the discounts exacted in some markets were disproportionate to the intrinsic value as established by Dr. Duvel. He would then like to continue the use of the tester; he had made money when he had insisted on buying grain on its merit and lost when he had not, and he thought the Association would make a mistake in adopting the resolution.

Mr. Shellabarger voiced the opposition to the tester. He dwelt upon its deficiencies, real and artificial, charging the last to the machine and emphasizing the former. He did not charge deliberate intent on the part of anyone to misuse the tester, but in practice the inspection rule did act to the disadvantage of many shippers by robbing corn otherwise sound and in every way desirable of the benefit of its good qualities because it has a technical excess of moisture which might or might not be real.

Mr. Cole favored the use of the moisture tester—he had found it useful; but he did not agree with the grade rule that excess of moisture as the sole defect of grain should be the factor determining absolutely the grade—the good qualities should be allowed to count.

Mr. Tyng said the elimination of the moisture test is a return to the old system of inspection by guess—to anarchy in the inspection system. If we do not retain this test, we shall all be at the mercy of the inspector.

Mr. Metcalf said there seemed to be a misunderstanding—the recommendation does not contemplate elimination of the test but does change the rule that makes it the [sole] determining factor of the grading.

Mr. Hubbard insisted that moisture is the determining factor. Most of you are young men and you don't remember the old conditions—

[At which point he was interrupted by Mr. Shellabarger who raised the point of order that the speaker was not talking to the question before the house. Mr. Shellabarger was over-ruled by the chair and Mr. Hubbard continued:]

Moisture is a determining factor; you can't get away from it—you never have been away from it. It has always affected the grading.

The resolution was then adopted by a vote of 42 to 17 [with 200 or more people in the house, most of whom as will be seen voted neither to adopt or reject the motion.]

ELECTION OF OFFICERS.

Mr. Hill then made the report of the nominating committee recommending the election of the following officers:

President—Lee Metcalf of Illiopolis.

Vice-President—S. C. Taylor of Kankakee.

Treasurer—H. I. Baldwin of Decatur.

Directors—Messrs. Tyng of Peoria, Truby of Joliet, Hilmer of Freeport and Sinclair of Ashland.

On motion the report was adopted, and the chair declared that thereby all the officers had been duly elected.

Adjourned to 2 p. m.

WEDNESDAY—FINAL SESSION.

Mr. Lee Metcalf occupied the chair during the final session. He said in opening that he appreciated the honor conferred on him by the Association of which he had been a more or less active member ever since its organization. As such he had endeavored to do what he could through it for Illinois and the grain trade and the farmers of this state. Of the Association he could say that in all questions affecting the farmer and the members it has stood for fairness and honesty with them and with each other. As to the future, he asked that those who had any word or suggestion to benefit the Association and broaden its purposes or its influence would come to him with it.

WHAT THE ASSOCIATION HAS DONE.

Very appropriately, at this point Secretary Strong, on urgence of the directors, read the following paper on the work of the Association:

The first meeting of grain dealers, of which I have been able to get any account, was held in this city, Bloomington, about twenty-five years ago this summer, in a building which stood on the east side of the square, but which has since been removed. At that time the first grain dumps for unloading wagons at an elevator were coming into vogue. Many dealers had installed dumps, and some parties had sent out notices of infringement of patent, with threats of suit. A meeting of grain dealers of central Illinois was called to consider what was best to do in the matter. After that subject had been disposed of, a number remained and talked of the conditions of the trade, trying to determine if anything could be done which would in any way relieve the trade of the many evils and disadvantages with which it was beset.

And, indeed, to look at the then condition of the grain trade was well likely to discourage if not dishearten even a grain dealer. The business was infested throughout the whole country with unscrupulous dealers, brokers, track-buyers, scoop-shovelers and commission merchants. There were few regular boards of trade or exchanges for the buying and selling of grain. There were rebates at every station, on every railroad, and particularly at junction points. Telegraph franks were common; special rates were often given on a large shipment of grain. The country grain dealer was the banker for the farmer; and it was the general custom to advance any amount of money asked, without interest and for almost any length of time. Free storage without limit was the rule; and the elevator operator in the country looked to the commission house in the terminal for a supply of money to carry his customers. The usual practice was to bid on every wagon load of grain which came to town; and the bright progressive dealer would often have a man employed who would be at the cross roads a mile or more from the town to bid on grain as the farmers were driving to the elevators. The man at the cross roads would make a bid, but the farmer well knew that there would be a better bid at the elevator than from street bidders. The market price was not bid; it was a kind of haggling between bidders and the farmer; and to get the top of the market required much delicate finesse on the part of the seller. Each dealer received market reports by telegraph at his own expense, and the farmer depended on the weekly paper, or an occasional trip to town, or on hearing it from his neighbors.

There were dockages in every market or terminal, sometimes acknowledged, but often tolerated, practiced and denied.

There were few weighing departments with supervision of a board of trade or state weigher; but much of the grain was weighed by the employes of the commission houses.

After that first meeting an occasional conference was held by some of the principal dealers who really desired to see a betterment of trade conditions, usually in Chicago, Decatur or Peoria. Several attempts were made to organize an association, and to some extent they succeeded; but in a short time, for one reason or another, the effort failed, till eighteen years ago, this month, in the city of Decatur, the present organization was effected.

The present Constitution and By-Laws were adopted, and the organization was named the Illinois Grain Dealers' Association, and all reputable grain merchants, track-buyers, brokers and commission men were invited to become members. The objects of the Association were to promote uniformity in the customs and usages of grain dealers; to inculcate principles of justice and equity in the trade; and to correct and eliminate abuses arising in the buying, selling, handling, inspecting, weighing and transportation of grain.

The activities of the organization are exerted through committees, of which there are nine; and every phase of the business of a grain dealer is covered by a committee, whose duty it is to attend to all complaints made by members through the organization. If you have trouble of any kind, no matter what, whether it relates to railroad matters, or to receivers, or car service, or if you desire information of any kind, you should write to the office of the organization, where all the means are provided to furnish information or give assistance in any line of work. Nine committees are appointed annually by the president, who are ready at all times to look after the interests of the organization and its members. One committee is growing rather rusty, the appeal committee, which has five members, who have been appointed yearly by the President and who have never had a case before them.

Since that time the Association has followed a well defined purpose: to eliminate from the trade every unnecessary charge of expense; every dishonorable dealer, be he commission merchant, track-buyer, receiver, or country elevator operator; to secure fair and honest methods throughout the various branches of the business; to see to it that grain should be handled from the producer to the consumer with only necessary reasonable charges and an honest and legitimate profit to the dealer, and that the full weight of the product should at all times be accounted for to the seller.

For many years there was a general understanding in the trade that there was great risk to the seller in shipping grain south of the Ohio River, for the reason that there were no organized markets in that section of the country. Today, through the efforts of associated shippers of grain, in organizations known as associations, throughout the country, from the east to the west, from the north to the gulf, there are boards of trade or grain exchanges in every terminal, which are charted by the states in which they are situated; where grain is handled under well-known rules, duly adopted by those organizations, with fees and charges regulated by the exchanges under the laws of such states and which give to every shipper equal rights, protected and secured to him by adequate regulations.

All rebates have been abolished; dockages, which were a pernicious form of robbery, have been discontinued in every market; telegraph franks are a thing of the past; freight rates have been equalized; and the inspection, and weighing of grain has been reduced to a matter of almost scientific certainty, or as nearly so as the judgment of man makes possible.

Today "arbitration" is the slogan of the grain dealer; and the man or firm who does not willingly submit to arbitration a difference with another grain dealer is a marked man, and he received discipline by loss of business and confidence from the trade, which very few firms care to incur.

The present condition of the grain trade is characterized by the highest standard of dealing; and no more honorable men are found in the world of commerce than those engaged in handling grain, who pride themselves on the good name of their firm, their company, exchange or Association. The very highest test of organization is required—the efficiency of association work among its members to insure every transaction to be one which cannot be questioned in any way.

No charge of unfairness or dishonest dealing has ever been proved against the Illinois Grain Dealers' Association. The organization does not buy or sell grain, but endeavors to instruct its members that equity, fairness, honorable dealing redound to the credit of dealers and conduce to profit making.

Elevators in Illinois have been developed from the "blind-horse" power stage to the electric power, automatic scale, gravity loaders, manlift, sheller and cleaner standard.

The Association through its committees has supervised the rules and workings of every terminal market in the country; and has assisted in organizing a number of the exchanges. Now a shipper may send his grain to the East and to the South with perfect confidence that the transactions regarding the inspection, weighing, selling will be done in an honorable manner and due return made immediately thereon to him, with full and explicit account and official certificates showing every step in the handling.

The Association secures for its members reliable statistics from time to time of the amount of grain in the country; the condition of growing crops; and such other information as may assist the dealer in determining the market value of grain.

All claims for losses which arise from shipping grain on railroads are collected for the members by the organization. The Illinois Association has an agreement with the Western Freight Claims Association, covering twenty railroads in this state, for the payment of losses in transit, with an adequate department under the management of a competent attorney, where every member can secure prompt adjustment of any losses which may occur in the shipping of products to any market in the country.

The Association maintains also a department of arbitration, through which in the past six years more than 2,800 claims between shippers and receiver have been adjusted. One moment of thought will suffice to assure you that this feature alone makes for a vast saving to the members, as the fee required would not be a retainer for an attorney, and it is the entire and only charge made by the organization for arbitration. Of the 2,800 and more cases adjusted through the arbitration department, let it be known to the great and lasting credit of the grain dealers, members of this organization, that not one case has ever been left unadjusted and never has a member refused to abide by the award of the committee of arbiters.

This committee is appointed by the president annually. Is composed of three men, who must be members of the Association, and no compensation is paid the committee other than is sufficient for their expenses. No greater tribute could be paid to the integrity of purpose of the grain dealers of the Illinois Association than the record of the arbitration department; and it is a pleasure for me to testify that invariably—in every case—are awards complied with promptly and fully.

Through the committees of the Association, legislation, both National and state, is scrutinized for the purpose of safe-guarding the interests of the members. The legislative committee, whose duty it is to attend to this work, are unselfish and untiring in their attention at every meeting of the General Assembly in Illinois and through the National organization supervise all measures introduced in the Congress at Washington.

Insurance, railroad rates, trade rules and many other features which affect the daily profits of the shipper are given careful consideration by the Association through its committees.

Now, all this has been accomplished by the Association; and the query naturally arises who make up that body? The country grain dealers of Illinois—a set of men, than whom there are none of greater probity of character or of higher standards of honesty, who value their good name and the good name of their Association as above price; who back it with their time, attention and money and who are ever ready at the call of its president to attend meetings, work on committees and give freely and without stint to the assistance of an organization which stands for righteousness and truth, which stands for fair dealing among men, who believe that honesty of purpose inspire all transactions.

Commercial firms, no matter where established, never hesitate to buy or sell to a dealer in Illinois whose name in the Directory is preceded by an asterisk; and why? Because that sign indicates that he is a member of the Illinois Grain Dealers' Association; and all men are thereby assured that all transactions with that firm will be conducted under the rules of the Association, which require honesty as a fundamental principle in all business.

Too much credit canont be given to the members of the Association for their splendid support of the organization and for the care with which through the finance committee they husband the funds of the organization. Every dollar received by the secretary must go to the treasurer; and no payments are made from the Association funds except by a warrant signed by the president and countersigned by the secretary. Every member who has ever sent a check to the office of the secretary will find the endorsement of the treasurer on that check when it is returned.

Every grain dealer in the state is benefited by the work of the Association; and it is more and more getting to be esteemed a privilege to belong to an organization whose certificates of membership are an asset of true value. The fact of being a member gives a commercial standing to a dealer everywhere, and to the Illinois Association men in the grain trade look for instruction and guidance in the business. The splendid attendance upon the annual meetings of the organizaiton testify to its worth in the estimation of the trade; and a grain dealer now feels that he misses one of his established rights if he is prevented from attending.

The members of the Illinois Grain Dealers' Association can look upon their achievements of the past eighteen years, with a pride which none will question who are at all conversant with conditions of the trade when this society was first organized; and I bespeak a future for the Association, which will be fraught with other and greater accomplishments, for there are many things to be done in the trade which will be profitable to every one who has to do with the handling of grain; and the work of the organization should continue until the grain business shall become a great public service organization, with established regulations at every station on every railroad in the state, by which any one and every one who has grain to sell may receive that just and prompt service at the market price which is the true intent of the Illinois Grain Dealers' Association to enforce.

GRADING FROZEN CORN.

Mr. W. L. Richeson of New Orleans, who had been asked, with Mr. S. H. Smith of Chicago, to speak on "Grading corn that has been frozen, on warm, damp days," sent word that unexpected engagements prevented his attendance.

Mr. Smith, while expressing his pleasure to be present for the assignment, said that after all there was not much necessity therefor. You all know that corn in that condition is in a bad way. Always in the spring the moment warm, damp air strikes cold corn it begins to sweat just as a cold water pitcher sweats. If you put it into a car it heats very quickly. You can have that kind of corn hot in 24 hours. In car lots of 1,000 bushels it is not so dangerous as in bulk. This is all simple enough, and if you have corn to market that has been frozen, get rid of it as quickly as possible.

In answer to a question he said that it is safe to put cold old corn into bins now. All corn should be aired, but old corn is much the easier to handle. During the germinating season old corn should be handled frequently,—once a month at least in the germinating season.

Frozen corn, soft new corn, should be handled through the winter and spring from time to time in the atmosphere to withdraw the frost gradually and to warm it up as the temperature outside rises. But if you take out cold corn now in the warm, damp air, it will sour immediately.

THE CALL.

The "call" on the Chicago Board of Trade was a topic for discussion. Mr. Wayne thought he saw in the "call" a piece of Board of Trade machinery for benefiting the commission houses at the expense of the country shipper.

Both Mr. Radford and Mr. Stevers controverted this idea, maintaining that on the contrary it was one of the most successful devices ever invented by the Board of Trade to guarantee to the country shipper opportunities he never had had before the call was invented to sell his grain at the highest price and to conduct his business as safely in all respects as the elevator men can who use all the devices of the Board of Trade rules. Before the call was established all the benefits of the premiums went to the elevator men; now the country shippers get them.

Mr. Paddock of Toledo was called on. There the call has been in operation for a year and a half and I believe it is the best thing that ever happened to insure to the country shippers stability of prices and greatest opportunity.

STORING GRAIN.

Geo. W. Cole of Bushnell spoke on the question: Does it pay to store grain? He said he would answer by asking, Why not make it pay? It was in brief his idea that grain men could earn money on sometimes empty space by storing grain wherever the farmer wanted to use it. He would charge 1c a bushel per month and then his space was filled and he needed it for his own business he would send it elsewhere to be stored and use the space. There is no reason why one dealer should take to "cutting up" because his neighbor should store when he did not want to do likewise. We should get together on this point, adopt a uniform policy and work our empty space to earn us income.

A testimonial fund of about $150 having been paid in to purchase a testimonial to Geo. D. Montelius, Messrs. Frank Supple and Oscar White were appointed a committee to purchase the gift and present it in the name of the Association.

ON BREEDING CORN.

Just before adjournment, Eugene Funk of Bloomington was called upon. Mr. Funk as is well known is one of the most celebrated seed corn breeders of this country. He has been at it for many years. Corn improvement is a leading question. He said he had kept a bushel of seed corn of every crop he had raised for each of the past ten years and the improvement shown by them is remarkable—you would not believe it unless you saw it. And the effect on the country is shown by reports from our customers. Out of 1,000 reports coming from all parts of the United States, we get a general average of the increase and we find it to be about 15 bushels per acre, and the quality of the corn compares with the increase in yield.

Mr. Funk said he knew Dr. Duvel when he first engaged in this work of testing corn. We use one of Dr. Duvel's first testers in the seed house and in our elevator and we find that it has helped us in our work in all departments.

Mr. Wayne: Is not the new corn too large?

Mr. Funk: Yes, it is. But the seed men have to supply what is demanded—cater to their customers. We thought years ago that big ears would be demanded and we bred them. The result is that we now are compelled by the demand for the seed to grow a corn that will not mature in this climate, and the moisture tester men help to rectify that condition.

On motion adjourned *sine die*.

ENTERTAINMENT AT MILLER PARK.

The general entertainment of the meeting was the luncheon at 7 o'clock, p. m., at Miller Park Pavilion. Miller Park is a large tract of land on one side of the city, beautifully laid out with drives and broad spaces for public use for picnics and outdoor life. There is also a considerable pond with swimming and boating. The Pavilion is a beautiful two-story building with balconies and basement. The floors are used for refectory, assemblies, dancing and banquet. It is a real public convenience like the pavilions of the new parks of all up-to-date cities that tempt their people into the out-of-doors. Here the luncheon was prepared by the ladies of Bloomington who served an attractive menu. Before entering the dining room in the basement story, the H. J. Hasenwinkle Co. of Memphis, Tenn., issued rattles, which sometimes permitted an excellent brass and reed band to be heard during the evening. The luncheon was excellent and the service good, and at its conclusion the company adjourned to the second story assembly room, where a short speaking program was carried out. Mr. Bach of Bloomington, attorney of the Claims Department, made an excellent toastmaster, and characteristically sent off his speakers with the facility of all good "starters."

Mr. Wayne was the first speaker, taking as his subject the work of the National Association, of which he is president.

Then Chester A. Legg, counsel to the executive committee of the Chicago Board of Trade, made an interesting and lucid argument in defense of the functions and purposes of the Chicago Board of Trade.

Hon. S. S. Tanner, a former president of the association, made one of his telling speeches, short but crisp and full of fun as usual.

Then there was a violin solo by Mrs. Della Phillips Swode, 'The Gypsy's Dream,' that was the performance of an artist, and the evening was concluded by a moving picture show.

On the same afternoon the ladies present, of whom there were quite a number, were given an automobile ride and a dinner at the Country Club.

NOTES OF THE CONVENTION.

Fred W. Kennedy, Shelbyville, Ind, exhibited his paper car-liners.

The W. U. Telegraph Co. placed an operator on the convention floor.

The Adder Machine Co., Wilkes-Barre, Pa, had a machine on exhibition.

C. A. Burks & Co., Decatur, gave out rubber 'phone receiver ear-guards.

The National Scale Co., Bloomington, gave out souvenir celluloid six-inch rule scales.

B. S. Constant Co.'s "Uncle Sam" (see extreme right of group picture), gave out street maps of the business center of Bloomington.

The Union Iron Works, Decatur, represented by Chas. Ward, had as its souvenir a vest pocket memorandum book, with renewable pads.

The Bloomington dealers entertained about thirty-five receivers at dinner at the Country Club on Thursday evening. It was an unusually pleasant function.

M. L. Vehon, who on June 13 began business on his own account, was formally initiated into the curb circle, the ceremonies being regardless of expense or the quiet of the neighborhood. The candidate next day got even by showering the ladies with bouquets.

THOSE PRESENT.

Memphis was represented by: E. E. Burton and J. H. Hasenwinkle, of the Hasenwinkle Gr. Co.

Nashville, Tenn., was represented by: R. W. Hale, with J. R. Hale & Sons, and S. W. Polk, with J. H. Wicks & Co.

Buffalo, N. Y., was represented by: C. W. Bartlett, with Churchill Grain & Seed Co.; H. T. Burns, with Eastern Grain Co., and F. G. Heinmiller, with Alder Grain Co.

Government officials present were: Dr. J. W. Duvel, Dept. of Agr., Washington; L. M. Jeffers, Dept. of Agr., New Orleans; C. A. Russell, I. E. Roberts and R. C. Mill, Dept. of Agr., Decatur.

Louisville, Ky., was represented by: A. Drohn, with Zorn Grain Co.; Fred W. Scholl, with Bingham-Hewett Gr. Co.; A. C. Schuff, of A. C. Schuff & Co.; L. T. Williams, with Zorn Grain Co.

Insurance men were represented by: B. J. Alley, Peoria; C. A. Garver, Champaign, Ill.; E. P. Jones, Millers' National Ins. Co., St. Louis; T. H. VanHorn, Ill. Millers' Mutual, Chicago.

Cleveland, Ohio, was represented by: J. H. Bray, with The Union Elev. Co.; F. C. Cain, with E. I. Bailey; J. M. Foglesong, with Cleveland Gr. Co., and F. W. Blazy, with Star Elev. Co.

Peoria was represented by: R. A. Lynch, with H. W. Lynch; G. H. McHugh, Peoria Board of Trade; Louis Mueller, T. A. Grier & Co.; C. R. Miles, P. B. & C. C. Miles; N. R. Moore, of Rumsey, Moore & Co.; J. H. Ridge, with S. C. Bartlett Co.; F. B. Tompkins, chief inspector of Peoria; A. G. Tyng, of Tyng, Hall Co.; F. L. Wood, with C. H. Feltman.

Toledo, Ohio, was represented by: J. F. Courcier, Sec'y Grain Dealers' Nat. Assn.; E. H. Culver, chief inspector Toledo Produce Exchange; Henry L. Goemann, of Goemann Grain Co.; W. H. Haskell, of W. H. Haskell & Co.

Machinery men present included: F. H. Morley, Jr., Invincible Grain Cleaner Co., Chicago; J. F. Bassett, Durable Wire Rope Co.; E. B. Bargery, Avery Scale Co., Chicago; Max H. Hurd, Union Iron Works, Decatur; A. N. Dawson, Root & Van Dervoort Engine Co., East Moline, Ill.; Fred W. Kennedy, Shelbyville, Ind.; H. P. McKee, Simmons Hardware Co., St. Louis, Mo.; H. E. McLeod, National Automatic Scale Co., Peoria; H. C. Michels, B. S. Constant & Co., Bloomington; Willard B. Smith, Richardson Scale Co., Chicago; C. N. Ward, Union Iron Works, Decatur; F. J. Temple, Union Iron Works, Decatur.

A. E. Schuyler and J. A. Schmitz represented Weighing Dept., Chicago Board; Samuel H. Smith was from the State Grain Inspection Dept., Chicago; W. S. Powell was from the Cairo Board of Trade, Cairo; Wm. R. Bach was present as attorney of the Claim Dept., Bloomington; J. Ralph Pickell and W. W. Reed represented the National Hay & Grain Reporter, Chicago, and Charles S. Clark the Grain Dealers Journal, Chicago. S. S. Tanner was there from Minier, Ill., because he wanted to be there; Bert Ball represented the Crop Improvement Committee and E. G. Osman the "American Elevator and Grain Trade."

Railroad men present were: C. W. Austin, Erie Railroad, Chicago; C. C. Backus, I. C. Railroad, Bloomington; Frank Baker, Erie Dispatch, Peoria; W. T. Bowlus, Wabash Railroad, Springfield; J. H. Chandler, L. & N. Railroad, Evansville, Ind.; C. L. Daly, Continental Line, Peoria; Wm. Dare, Erie Railroad, Chicago; M. G. Flannigan, I. C. Railroad, Freeport; W. H. Goff, I. C. Railroad, Bloomington; Rudd H. Hemmel, Big Four Railroad, Peoria; Jas. R. Love, New York Central Line, Peoria; J. S. Tuston, St. Louis Pacific, St. Louis; W. S. Bunder, Big Four, Peoria; R. A. Webster, Traders' Dispatch, Peoria; Jos. W. Webb, C. & A., Bloomington; Jas. Mann, C. & A., Springfield; Jos. E. Sunderland, Wabash Railroad, Springfield, Ill.

Chicago Commission Houses were represented as follows: M. M. Adrian, Hulburd, Warren & Chandler; James M. Adams, Rosenbaum Brothers; John H. Ashum, Walter Fitch & Co.; D. W. Burry, F. E. Winans & Co.; Merle Dent, Lamson Bros. & Co.; J. F. Duvall, J. Rosenbaum Gr. Co.; L. C. Emerson, Jas. E. Bennett & Co.; H. R. Emerson, Norris & Co.; P. S. Goodman, Clement Curtis Co.; Gordon Hannah, Pope & Eckhardt Co.; W. M. Herschy, J. C. Shaffer & Co.; Louis S. Hill, B. S. Wilson; L. S. Hoyt, Carhart Code Harwood Co.; W. G. Kelly, Lamson Bros. & Co.; Fred B. Lewis, J. P. Griffin & Co.; H. L. Miller, ReQua Brothers; Dean L. Moberly, Sawers Grain Co.; T. E. Moran, Walter Fitch & Co.; H. H. Newell, Rogers Gr. Co.; Wm. P. Quinlevan, Walter Fitch & Co.; J. W. Radford, Pope & Eckhardt Co.; H. A. Rumsey, Remsey & Co.; H. R. Sawyer, J. H Dole & Co.; F. D. Stevers, Geo. H. Sidwell Co.; H. Clay Shaw, Rosenbaum Bros.; Harry G. Smith, Lamson Bros. & Co.; Henry Stanbert, Rogers Grain Co.; J. J. Stream, J. C. Shaffer & Co.; R. J. Sullivan, Geo. H. Sidwell; C. H. Thayer, E. W. Bailey & Co.; W. M. Timberlake, B. S. Wilson Co.; E. F. Thompson, Lamson, Bros. & Co.; T. C. Taylor, C. H. Thayer & Co.; B. F. Traxler, Nash Wright Grain Co.; L. I. Van Ness, Van Ness & Co.; L. O. Vincent, Lipsey & Co.; M. L. Vehon, M. L. Vehon & Co.; J. A. Waring, Hulburd, Warren & Chandler; Oscar C. White, Philip H. Schiffin & Co.; A. E. Wood, E. W. Bailey & Co.; E. H. Young, W. A. Fraser Co.; G. S. Hutchinson, The Albert Dickinson Co.; W. A. Worth, Beach W. Grain Co.; C. H. Thayer, C. H. Thayer & Co.

Commission merchants and brokers from various markets present were: H. I. Baldwin, H. I. Baldwin & Co., Decatur; W. C. Brubaker, Farber Bros. Co., Bloomington; G. A. Burks, C. A. Burks & Co., Decatur; F. G. Crowell, Hall Baker Grain Co., Kansas City, Mo.; F. J. Currus, McQuilland Co., Cincinnati, O.; A. J. Cope, Lamson Bros. & Co., Urbana; James A. Connor, Connor Bros. & Co., St. Louis, Mo.; Bert A. Boyd, Indianapolis, R. C. Baldwin, Baldwin Grain Co., Bloomington; W. F. Bishopp, Bishopp Hominy Co., Sheldon; D. M. Cash, McLane, Swift & Co., Battle Creek, Mich.; C. A. Dryer, Dryer & Burt, Champaign; F. H. Funk, Eugene D. Funk and L. H. Leaton, Funk Bros. Seed Co., Bloomington; W. B. Foresman, Crabbs-Reynolds Taylor Co., LaFayette, Ind.; W. P. Foote, H. I. Baldwin & Co., Champaign; F. E. Fleming, Ellis & Fleming, Cincinnati, O.; A. C. Gale, Gale Bros. Co., Cincinnati, O.; J. T. Gehring, Cleveland Gr. Co., Indianapolis; R. W. Hale, J. R. Hale & Sons, Nashville, Tenn.; T. J. Hanley, Hanley & Cormaker, Bloomington; H. J. Hasenwinkle, H. J. Hasenwinkle & Co., Memphis, Tenn.; Ralph Hasenwinkle, Hasenwinkle Gr. Co., Bloomington; J. E. Hawthorne, Hawthorne Grain Co., Bloomington; B. F. Harber, J. W. Harber and Jos. S. Joplin, Harber Bros. Co., Bloomington; J. C. Hight and Geo. L. Hight, Hight Grain Co., Decatur; Henry Hunter, Taylor-Hunter Gr. Co., St. Louis, Mo.; F. R. Ludwig, Ludwig & Grady, Champaign; A. V. S. Lloyd, Hasenwinkle Gr. Co., Bloomington; H. E. Kenney, H. E. Kenney Co., Indianapolis, Ind.; W. K. Klosterman, Morton & Co., St. Louis, Mo.; Harry Livingston, The Livingston Gr. Co., Bloomington; H. G. Marshall, Cleveland Gr. Co., Champaign; B. B. Minor, Indianapolis, Ind.; J. W. McNoldy, Hasenwinkle Gr. Co., Bloomington; Geo. C. Martin, Jr., Goffe & Carkauer Co., St. Louis, Mo.; J. C. McCord, Bloomington; John P. Miller and C. W. Miller, Stockbridge Elev. Co., Jackson, Mich.; J. Nichols, Ware & LeLand, Decatur; R. S. Nelson, Nansom Com. Co., St. Louis, Mo.; S. W. Polk, J. H. Wicks & Co., Nashville, Tenn.; J. A. Parks, Finley, Barrell Co., Bloomington; Jas. D. Parrott, Parrott Day Co., St. Louis, Mo.; W. H. Reedy, Bloomington; J. H. Ridge, S. C. Bartlett Co., Peoria; W. J. Riley, Cary Jackson Grain Co., Indianapolis, Ind. Albert Rothschild, S. S. Carlisle Com. Co., St. Louis, Mo.; Ed. K. Shepperd, Cleveland Gr. Co., Indianapolis, Ind.; Edw. C. Seele, Seele Bros. Gr. Co., St. Louis, Mo.; Willis E. Shelden, Jackson, Mich.; E. E. Snow, Harber Bros., Bloomington; Frank Supple, Bloomington; Marcus L. R. Tankersley, Tankersley & Co., Champaign; W. B. Triege, Hasenwinkle Grain Co., Bloomington; B. L. Williams, Henderson Elevator Co., Henderson, Ky.; Frank H. Witt, Stebbins-Witt Con. Co., Indianapolis, Ind.; Fred E. Walkens, Cleveland Gr. Co., Indianapolis, Ind.; Wm. Zierfuss, Livingston Grain Co., Bloomington; J. H. Ridge, S. C. Bartlett Co., Peoria; Champaign; A. V. S. Lloyd, Hasenwinkle Gr. Co., L. R. Tankersley, Tankersley & Co., Champaign.

Illinois county shippers present and the firms they represented were, as follows: A. B. Applegate, Applegate & King, Atlanta; A. R. Aden, Carlinville; E. P. Armstrong, E. P. Armstrong & Son, Parnell; Frank W. Aldrich, Aldrich Grain Co., McLean; J. R. Aston, Emden; H. Bachenhimer, Livingston Gr. Co., Bloomington; Paul A. Babcock, Pontiac; O. C. Benson, Fairmount; John Benson, F. R. Ludwig, Watkins; Ben B. Bishopp, Eastern Grain Co., Sheldon; C. U. Bower, Covel; Walker Boulware, Walker Boulware & Co., Foosland; J. W. Brown, Jenkins Gr. Co., Jenkins; M. K. Busey, Wm. Wykle, Mahomet; R. K. Byerly, Catlin; G. Brauer, San Jose; C. G. Brotherton, McClure & Brotherton, Guthrie; Geo. D. Cash, F. P. Smith & Co., Clinton; D. H. Claudon, Claudon Brothers, Ludlow; A. B. Cleland, F. C. Harney, Decatur; C. P. Cline, Evans Elev. Co., Decatur; N. B. Claudon, N. B. Claudon & Son, Fairbury; A. S. Carter, P. S. Carter & Co., Girard; J. Winifield Close, Mansfield Ford Gr. Co., Illiopolis; D. H. Claudon, Claudon Bros., Meadows; H. H. Corman, American Hominy Co., Decatur; H. B. Coyle, Coyle Gr. & Coal Co., Gridley; A. L. Culbertson and W. J. Culbertson, Delavan; J. E. Collins, Atwood Gr. Co., Garrett; B. F. Colehower, Long Point; G. A. DeLong, Foosland; S. G. Crawford, Bondville; Geo. W. Cole, Bushnell; Victor Dewein, Warrensburg; G. M. Duzenberry, G. M. Duzenberry & Co., Henning; Mathew M. Dee, Wm. Dee Clay Mfg. Co., Springfield; L. L. Harrison, Harrison Bros., Dwight; J. E. O'Hara, O'Hara & Gaddis, Carlock; E. E. Hamman, Hamman Bros., Milmine; C. E. Hitch, Hitch Bros., West Ridge; Charles C. Davis, Davis Grain Co., Galesburg; Alex. C. Durdy, Ohlman; W. C. Darnall, Darnall & Spence, McLean; J. L. Douglass, Shirley; Geo. Dunaway, Ill. Valley Gr. Co., Utica; E. Donovan, Fisher; H. S. Eckart, Central Mill & Elev. Co., Bloomington; M. K. Elliott, Merritt & Elliott, Henning; A. P. Eaton, S. W. Allerton, Allerton; A. H. Edwards, Champaign; W. N. Ewing, Aldrich Grain Co., McLean; John Fryer, San Jose; A. W. Ford, Scottsburg; A. F. Files, W. H. Small & Co., Evansville; T. H. Greenfield, Arrowsmith; Chas. Graff, Sutter Siding, Hopedale; Frank Gordon, Bartlett Frazier, Lincoln; W. T. Hardin, DeLand; G. T. Hanson and T. D. Hanson, T. D. Hanson & Co., Villa Grove; A. Harris, P. K. Wilson, Clinton; T. E. Hamman, Hamman Brothers, Milmine; Wm. Hasenwinkle, Hasenwinkle Gr. Co., Hudson; B. P. Hill, The B. P. Hill Gr. Co., Freeport; J. Q. Hitch, Hitch & Kirk, Champaign; A. N. Hilton, Symerton; H. A. Hillmer, H. A. Hillmer Co., Freeport; Henry Holmes, Spellman & Co., Lincoln; Ben Hoffman, Puterbaugh Walker & Co., Mackinaw; V. L. Horton, Horton Bros. & Co., Tolono; M. C. Hobart, Rumsey & Co., Momence; E. C. Hollis, Hasenwinkle Gr. Co., Heyworth; F. E. Horner, Horner Elev. & M. Co., Lawrenceville; G. H. Hubbard, Mt. Pulaski Gr. Co., Mt. Pulaski; James Inkster, Inkster Brothers, Herscher; L. J. Jeter, Jeter & Boston, Yorkville; Al Jackson, Ellsworth; C. E. Johnson, Tankersley & Co., Champaign; R. C. Jordan, Supt. Central Elev. & Whse. Co., New Orleans, La.; J. M. Jones, Dewey; F. W. Kee, L. T. Hutchins, Sheldon; Horace J. Kapp, O. H. Cannon & Co., Decatur; J. J. Camp, Lexington; J. M. Kautz, Kautz & Maus, Mt. Pulaski; J. M. Kearby, Kearby & Holmes, Stanford; James Karr, Seymour; M. A. Kirk, Hitch & Kirk, Bondville; J. A. King, Applegate & King, Atlanta; Wm. Kleiss, Kleiss & Gilles, Pesotum; L. Lamoreaux, Lamoreaux & Inkster Bros., Melvin; J. O. O. Lambert, The H. Lambert Co., Beaverville; H. B. Lacharite, Lacharite Gr. Co., Assumption; F. S. Larrison, El Paso; Samuel Mangas, Elkhart; J. Mahan, Mansfield; H. F. Maus, Kautz & Maus, Latham; E. E. McConnell, Eastern Grain Co., Lima, O.; M. L. Merritt, Dwight Grain Co., Dwight; Geo. L. Merritt, G. L. Merritt & Co., Rossville; Lee Metcalf, Metcalf & Kinnahan, Lanesville; W. C. McGuire, Maroa; M. L. Miller, El Paso; C. R. Mitchell, Ashmore; R. T. Miles, Fisher; Wm. Murray, Champaign; Bert Muthersbaugh, F. P. Smith & Co., Decatur; S. S. Neeman, Warrensburg; J. H. Nafziger, Anchor Grain Co., Anchor; Wm. Noble, Noble Bros., Foosland; Thos. Ogden, Dewey; P. Powers, Rees & Powers, Bradford; R. C. Parks, Kirksville; C. H. Fratt, Cropsey Elevator Co., Cropsey; F. M. Powell, Decatur; Scott Price, Herrick; Howard H. Piper, J. W. Probasco, Bloomington; Chas. D. Parrett, The Farmer City Grain Co., Farmer City; J. W. Probasco, Bloomington; John W. Prather, Prather & Groves, Williamsville; Leslie Reel, Congerville; E. G. Rees, Rees & Powers, Bradford; Harry Riddle, Paul Kuhn & Co., Terre Haute, Ind.; R. J. Riley, Forrest; H. J. Railsback, B. T. Railsback & Sons, Hopedale; Wm. Richardson, Elsworth; S. G. Ross, Ross, Ross & Barr, Chalmers, Ind.; J. C. Roe, J. C. Roe & Co., Hayes; Frank Rybun, Heyworth; F. N. Rood, La Rose Grain Co., La Rose; H. E. Roberts, Blandinsville; C. O. Swift, C. O. Swift & Co., Normal; A. C. Strong, Urbana; U. J. Sinclair, Central Ill. Grain Co., Ashland; Frank G. Shearburn, Lowder; John K. Seagrave, C. B. Munday & Co., Litchfield; L. E. Slick, L. E. Slick & Co., Bloomington; J. P. Sledge, Champaign; L. Shulhafer, I. H. French & Co., Champaign; W. L. Schmitz, Moschel Dodds Co., Tremont; Robt. W. Leetch, Cooksville Grain Co., Cooksville; W. D. Schad, Yuton Grain Co., Yuton; Harry Scott, Thorpe, Scott & Co., Wapella; Chas. Shelby, Paxton; A. P. Schantz, Lexington Grain Co., Lexington; C. L. Smith, Hopedale; Frank Simpson and Jesse Simpson, Danvers Farmers El. Co., Danvers; F. E. Schwartz, Carlock Farmers El. Co., Carlock; J. A. Simpson, J. A. Simpson & Sons, Minonk; W. L. Shellabarger, Shellabarger El. Co., Decatur; C. B. Spang, Georgetown; H. A. Stotler, Taggart-Stotler, Wenona; Frank J. Somers, Strawn Farmers El. Co., Risk; M. J. Stotler and O. H. Stotler, Stotler Bros., Strawn; E. S. Summers, Summers Bros., Kappa; C. N. Sutter, Hopedale; S. C. Taylor, Taylor Bros., Kankakee; E. R. Talbott, Springfield; J. C. Tobey, J. C. Tobey Co., Odell; L. A. Tripp, Assumption Grain Co., Assumption; Geo. C. Tucker, Freburg & Tucker, Walnut Grove; H. T. Truby, M. Truby & Son, Joliet; S. B. VanNess, Dumall & Spence, McLean; H. C. Vollmer, Illinois Granaries Co., Lostant; O. T. Unland, Smith-Hippen Co., Pekin; Fred Verry, Verry & Son, Armstrong; C. H. Wade, Paris; Wm. Wholler, Melvin; L. J. West, Glenavon; Bruce Waller, M. R. Allsup, Marva; T. M. Walsh, M. R. Walsh, Campus; Ames Woodman, Woodman & Parrot, Fullerton; J. R. Wagner, Metamora; E. M. Wayne, Wayne Bros. Grain Co., Delevan; W. A. Webb, S. F. Webb Grain Co., Weldon; P. K. Willson, Birbeck; Geo. L. Weirather, Bushnell; Wm. Wykle, Mahomet; John Wiemer, San Jose; J. P. Woolpold, Galton; Wm. Wrightsman, J. A. Mouch & Co., East Lynn; F. E. Webber, A. H. Webber & Son, Padna; W. L. Wilson, Bloomington; H. C. Clark, Springfield; E. W. Crow, E. W. Crow, Blue Mound; Thos. Shepland, Spires Elev. Co., Spires; P. M. Faucett, Champaign; E. L. Coyle, Coyle G. & C. Co., Gridley; Edw. D. Evans, Evans Milling Co., Indianapolis; Wm. Close, Mansfield Ford, Illiopolis; F. H. Hunting, E. W. Wagner & Co., Champaign; F. C. Martens, Martens Bros., Randolph; W. T. Hardin, DeLand; A. L. Nicol, J. W. Probasco, Bloomington; W. M. Skinner, A. W. Skinner & Co., Hudson; C. F. Quinn, Farmers Elev. Co., Shirley; W. H. Adams, Ila N. Adams and O. R. Adams, W. H. Adams & Sons, Atlanta; D. M. Burner, New Holland; I. F. Groves, Prather & Groves, Williamsville; Edward Barry, Samuel Mangus, Elkhart; W. M. Myers, Kenney; P. H. Hayes, Hayes Bros., Galesville; Trave Elmore, V. C. & Trave Elmore, Ashland; F. M. Hubbard, Mason City.

Cincinnati grain dealers have imported hay from Canada and rye from Germany and did so at a profit. The rye sold as high as $1.15 a bushel, while first grade hay went up to $24 a ton.

NINTH ANNUAL MEETING OF INDIANA GRAIN DEALERS' ASSOCIATION.

The Indiana Grain Dealers' Association met in their ninth annual meeting at the Board of Trade, Indianapolis, on Thursday morning, June 15.

THURSDAY MORNING.

The meeting was called to order by President William B. Foresman of Lafayette, with about one hundred and fifty members and visitors present. The welcome from the grain trade of Indianapolis was delivered by Mr. H. E. Kinney and in the absence of Vice-President A. W. Taylor of Stillwell, the response was given by Mr. J. D. McCardell of Indianapolis. President Foresman next read his address to the Association.

Members of the Indiana Grain Dealers' Association and Friends: Having once more closed another year of work in the interest of the Indiana Grain Dealers' Association, we have this morning gathered together in commemoration of our ninth annual meeting.

This Association is, I believe, one of the oldest grain associations in the country, and it should indeed be a power for good in the grain trade in our state. Its influence should be felt in every market where its members do business and it should wield a powerful influence for the adoption of better business methods by the grain dealers of Indiana.

Far too many Indiana dealers take little or no interest in their state organization, and few appreciate the wide scope of its usefulness, or the work it is doing in the interests of the entire grain trade of the state. What a powerful organization this would be for good in the grain trade if all the dealers in Indiana could be made to realize the possibilities of what could be done through thorough cooperation in this organization. But many of them do not realize its strength or what it can do if they give it a chance.

An old adage of trade was "Competition is the life of trade," but modern methods of trade are so vastly different that this old adage should be re-written to read "Co-operation, not competition, is the life of trade." There are many legitimate ways in which our state organization is proving itself invaluable to its members; it is not necessary to consider controlling prices or attempt any illegal process in our organization, but through the exchange of ideas, becoming more familiar with our trade troubles and their solution, widening our acquaintance one with another, and cementing our friendships as we become better acquainted, we learn at our meetings to adopt the best ideas for the conducting of our business and to adopt the more modern methods of business. We realize our competitors are not nearly the mean fellows we considered them; in fact, we find that we had prejudiced ourselves against them and are apt to be too easily offended at their acts, we learn to see more of their good points, and find that if we but give them a chance or meet them half way that they are inclined to be fair with us.

We learn from this exchange of ideas from associating together that it costs more to do business now than it did in days gone by, and we find it is more profitable to let our competitors have their fair share of business. We make a better return to handle half as much at a reasonable margin than all at no margin at all. In fact, in promoting good fellowship among dealers, I believe that our local, state and national associations are doing their greatest work.

The work of the local associations throughout the state, when properly supported, is of great importance. No grain dealer with sufficient investment to justify the title should withhold his connection with and support of the local organization.

The work of the state association is a necessity and it is doubtful if the locals would long exist were it not for the influence of the state association and the constant efforts of its officers. However, the good that results from co-operation is greatly augmented by the interest maintained in local organization and its work.

It is the opinion of the present administration that many of the locals, as now organized, cover too much territory, and the Secretary advises that it is his purpose to try and increase the number and reduce their size.

Men who are closely situated geographically, can better understand each other, especially where conditions are similar and the interests are identical, so I urge you to co-operate with the Secretary in the development of more locals and in securing better attendance upon their meetings.

The Association has at different times during the past five years declared in favor of maintaining a freight claims department, whereby members could receive proper assistance in the preparation and collection of their claims. At the meeting of the board of managers in March this year, a committee was appointed to inaugurate the department, and it seemed to be an auspicious time to begin, as Mr. Riley, the present Secretary, with the experience of his five years' connection with the Railroad Commission, was so familiar with transportation mattrs that the department was soon established, and many claims have already been filed and in process of adjustment.

The purpose in establishing this department is three fold: First, it is believed it will prove highly beneficial to the average dealer who may have occasion to patronize it. Second, it is believed the carriers will treat with the department on more satisfactory terms, in the main, than with the many individual dealers. Third, the careful scrutiny of each claim received by the department is valuable to shipper and carrier alike, as claims without merit are excluded and those that have merit, but usually are discriminated against, because of technical defenses are pushed for settlement.

In view of this new department being wholly dependent upon the patronage of the grain dealers, we recommend and urge you to support it by sending your claims in for preparation and settlement.

The Secretary advises that his department is at all times ready to advise and confer with members about transportation matters generally, and you are urged to avail yourselves of this opportunity.

By the assistance of representatives of this Association, some legislation was secured at the recent session of the General Assembly, which materially aids in the adjustment of intrastate claims, a provision being made for filing same with the Railroad Commission under certain conditions.

You have been advised by circular from the secretary's office the result of the legislative effort and in addition to the beneficial legislation procured, some vicious propositions were defeated. One in particular we wish to refer to; that was a bill providing for a board of examiners to prescribe qualifications for stationary engineers, and prohibiting engineers not thus qualified and licensed from operating engines. The movement seemed to have been inspired by certain interests that would have been profited thereby and would have compelled the employment of expert engineers by many men whose business could not have stood the additional burden. The grain men of Indiana are not wholly mercenary, and took the stand that this great burden could possibly have been assumed, if the conservation of life and property would have been augmented thereby, but we think statistics do not justify the condemnation of the present system, nor demonstrate the success of the proposed system, which has worked disastrously in some of our sister states.

Much has been said in this Association about the storage of the producer's grain by the country grain dealers, and the consensus of opinion is that the practice is detrimental from a financial point of view. Not only is it believed to be unprofitable, but in many cases the dealer is compelled to violate the laws of the state by shipping out and otherwise appropriating the grain before he can secure title thereto. The secretary mailed to each dealer in the state Circular No. 1 which contained a copy of the law concerning storage, and it is to be hoped that you have read it and will be governed by its provisions. Very few of you can justify the practice and certainly you should not persist in a practice that is neither legal nor profitable. Should there be those who cannot yet abandon the practice of storing the farmer's grain, you should scrutinize carefully your tickets or receipts issued on account thereof; and for your benefit, I suggest, the secretary has prepared a form of receipt that will protect you against the legal difficulties, but no one can protect you against the financial loss that follows the unrestricted practice.

With each recurrent year in the grain trade, the value of correct information concerning conditions of crops and stocks of grain on hand, becomes more important; not infrequently do we find some of our members have been influenced in their investments in grain by reports that are wholly unreliable, if not inspired for the benefit of certain interests.

The government has accomplished much in the matter of reliable information, but much yet remains to be accomplished and it is believed the gathering, compiling and circulating information as to crop and other elements that enter into and affect the grain business, is legitimate and proper Association work.

The secretary sent out on June 8th over 100 blanks with which to obtain correct information as to crop conditions, and I understand he will be able to give you the result of this first effort. This with a view to having you determine whether or not such a bureau shall be established.

I am fully satisfied the effort will prove highly important and will merit your approval and support.

It shall be my purpose and pleasure to appoint a committee to whom this subject may be referred for its consideration and report at this meeting, so that the work may be speedily inaugurated.

The success of this Association, as other similar organizations, is dependent largely upon the financial support of its members. When this Association was organized nine years ago, a membership fee of $10 was required from an applicant, together with their dues; at the present time, and for some years past, no membership fee has been collected, so the revenues are wholly dependent upon the dues, payable semi-annually in advance. Much of the secretary's time and the money of the Association is expended in the effort to collect the dues and to add new members to take the place of those that default or drop out on account of change of business, etc. Without going into detail further as to the value of and the necessity for the existence of the Association, for that is admitted by all, I feel it is my duty to say that no member should delay the payment of his dues and you should each resolve yourself into a committee of one to bring in a new member within the next thirty days. Your dues to the Association are not a liability, but the most valuable asset of like magnitude you have.

There are loyal and consistent Association men before me now, who have contributed of their time and money to make this Association one of the best of all the state associations, and they have not only paid membership fees and dues to the full limit, but they have advanced money to tide it over when some extraordinary demand developed. Let us make the coming year a "red letter" year in our membership and in the accomplishments of this Association. I am advised that practically all other similar organizations are growing rapidly in membership and it is doubtful if any of their members need the protection that is needed by the average grain dealer.

During my term I have attended meetings in states other than our own, but I do not think any of them have accomplished more than have we, and not one of them has members who are more loyal than some of our good old war horses, organizers, and never-quitting members of this Association. To them I wish to extend my most sincere thanks for their loyalty toward me, I trust they may be able supporters of my successor and that they may have the pleasure of meeting with us many more times on these annual occasions. I wish also to thank our secretary and assistant for courtesies and efficient attention to the office and work, and trust that the coming year will be the banner one for the Association.

SECRETARY'S REPORT.

Following President Foresman, Secretary Chas. B. Riley of Indianapolis presented his report:

As your secretary at the present time, it is my duty and pleasure to submit in this report an outline of the business and accomplishments of the Association, covering the current period.

Since March 1 I have been giving the business of the Association my entire time as Secretary and have attended twenty local meetings in different parts of the state and at Sheldon, Ill.

Mr. M. T. Dillen, who has since March 1 acted as assistant to the Secretary, attended fifteen local meetings, making in all thirty-five meetings attended since that time.

The attendance at the local meetings has not been what we desired, but good interest was generally manifested, and the Association spirit fostered.

At the January meeting of the Association, the Secretary reported 324 members, which embraced twenty who had been delinquent and not in good standing since July, 1910; that number should have been eliminated from the number above mentioned, leaving only 304 in good standing at that time, of which latter number twenty-seven have since become delinquent and are not in good standing, or have retired from business, thus leaving 277 as the actual membership from the list of 324 reported.

Since the January meeting there have been added twenty-seven new members, thus bringing the membership back to 304, all in good standing; and we trust so imbued with the spirit that they will each perform such effective missionary service that the next report will show a 50 per cent increase in our membership.

Since our January meeting there have been no new arbitration cases presented, and the two that were pending upon appeal to the National Association, have been settled and discharged.

Since our freight claims department was inaugurated April 22 last, we have received, audited and filed twenty-six claims with the proper department of four separate railroads. One claim has been settled and paid, all the others are in process of adjustment, with the promise of speedy consideration by the departments in charge of same.

We are pained, though compelled, to report the death of one of our members, Mr. John Chambers, of the firm of Walker & Chambers, Wheatland, Ind., whose death occurred in May, 1911, after a brief illness.

Thanking the members one and all for their support and co-operation and trusting the future has in store many good things for each, I respectfully submit the financial report, which is as follows:

Financial Report of Secretary C. B. Riley up to June 15, 1911:

RECEIPTS.

Cash on hand Jan. 1, 1911	$ 324.10
Account Delinquent Dues	60.00
Account Current Dues	858.75
Account Current Dues, Additional Stations	172.50
Account Advanced acct. Dues, etc	1,202.50
Account Arbitration	1.50
Account Directories Sold	2.00
Account Advertising in Dir. & Consti. & By-Laws—Pamphlets	78.85
Account Traveling Expense refunded	15.05
Total	$2,715.25

DISBURSEMENTS.

Chas. B. Riley, Secretary, Salary	$ 523.00
Chas. B. Riley, Traveling Exp. Acct	90.60
M. T. Dillen, Salary	600.00
M. T. Dillen, Traveling Exp. Acct	248.64
N. D. Ross, Salary, Stenographer	236.00
Board of Managers, Trav. Exp	3.90
Gr. Dealers Nat. Assn. Dues, Bal. due for yr. 1910	28.00
Printing & Postage	192.77
Office Expense & Rent	187.30
Arbitration Refund	25.16
Pd. to Treasurer, account Advances	150.00
Total	$2,285.37
Cash on hand June 14, 1911	429.88
	$2,715.25

Treasurer Bert A. Boyd of Indianapolis next presented his report which tallied with the Secretary's financial statement.

Auditing committee appointed consisting of Messrs. Witt, Schoemaker and Hutchinson.

SECRETARY'S INDIANA CROP REPORT.

Next in order, Secretary Riley distributed among the members his Indiana crop report for June 15, as follows:

The following report was compiled from answers

to questions submitted to 108 grain dealers and answered by 54 dealers located in various parts of the state:

Explanation:—Figures for answers following the words "largest," "same," "less," "normal," "early," "late," "light," "moderate," "free," represent the relative condition, based on the whole number of answers made to such questions.

SOIL CONDITION: (1) "Too wet" 2, "too dry" 25, or "normal" 23.

TEMPERATURE: (2) Thus far this season the temperature has averaged "above" 42, "below" —, or at "normal" 9.

GROWTH CONDITION: (3) Basing the Government "Normal" at 100 the percentage comparison of growth condition of winter wheat is. (Ans.) 86.6%. (5) Of oats. (Ans.) 81.12%. (6) Of corn. (Ans.) 93.15%. (7) Of clover. (Ans.) 77.1%. (8) Of timothy. (Ans.) 71.2%.

PROSPECTIVE PRODUCTION: (9) The present conditions give promise of the final crop conditions compared with last year. Wheat "larger" 23.2%, "same" 30.3% or "less" 46.5%. (10) Of oats, "larger" 30.2%, "same" 40.8%, or "less" 40.8%. (11) Of hay, "larger" —%, "same" 14% or "less" 86%.

STAND OF CORN: (12) Basing a perfect stand of corn at 100, the percentage comparison of stand as shown by the crop at this time is. (Ans.) 93.3%.

GROWING SEASON: (13) The growing season is "normal" 33%, "early" 66%, or "late" —%. Number of days. "Normal" —, "early" 9.3, "late"—.

MOVEMENT: (14) Anticipated "free," "light" or "moderate" movement at present values during the last half of June oats. (Ans.) "free" 3%, "light" 63%, "moderate" 34%. (15) Of corn. (Ans.) "free" 6%, "light" 67%, "moderate" 27%.

FARM SURPLUS: (16) Percentage of farm surplus of wheat estimated has been sold by the farmers. (Ans.) 91%. (17) Of oats. (Ans.) 91%. (18) Of corn. (Ans.) 81%.

PRICES: (19) The price being paid to the farmers for wheat. (Ans.) 83.3. (20) For oats. (Ans.) 32.7. (21) For corn. (Ans.) 49.8.

Five counties report fly in wheat.

MISCELLANEOUS BUSINESS.

President Foresman then called upon Secretary John F. Courcier of the Grain Dealers' National Association. Secretary Courcier responded with an informal talk, taking up first the question of the action of the Illinois Grain Dealers' Association at Bloomington in condemning the moisture tester. Mr. Courcier also touched on the question of Federal Inspection, the Trade Rules of the Grain Dealers' National Association, appealing for a better general knowledge and observance of them, and mentioned the coming publication of a volume of the decisions of the arbitration committee of the Grain Dealers' National Association.

A membership committee, comprising Messrs. D. C. Moore, Waynetown; Walter Castle, Dayton; P. E. Goodrich, Winchester, and Thos. Morrison, Kokomo, was next appointed.

"Big Chief" Culver of Toledo was called upon, and talked on the moisture test problem, characterizing the opposition to it as "a mule that kicks backward," and strongly advocating its adoption. Mr. Culver told of analyzing corn selected from crib for a group of Ohio farmers who were skeptical on the moisture test, and finding a percentage of from 29 to 32 in the samples brought in, and stated that the average of over 50,000 tests performed in his office on No. 3 corn was 18 per cent. He mentioned the possibility of legislation compelling a maximum of only 17 per cent in No. 3 corn.

Various representatives from the different terminal markets next were called upon for short talks.

A resolution committee, consisting of E. E. Elliott, Edward Shepard, and Fred Fox, was appointed and recess was taken for luncheon.

THURSDAY AFTERNOON.

The first order of business in the afternoon was the appointment of a nominating committee as follows: H. H. Deam, chairman, John Hazelrigg, J. R. Barr, William Nading and James Wellman.

Next in order was a paper by Mr. P. S. Goodman of Chicago on "Reciprocity with Canada and how it will affect the grain, farming and other interests of the United States."

At the close of his paper, Mr. Goodman gave, by request, a brief summary of French crop and market conditions, indicating the relation of the French duty on wheat to the crop in that country, and imports from outside.

Discussion of the Reciprocity question, as affecting the grain, milling and farming interests was next held, led by Mr. A. E. Reynolds of Crawfordsville. Mr. Reynolds argued strongly against Reciprocity, stating his belief that while the measure might not affect adversely the purely merchandizing grain business, it would lower the price of farm products and farm land, and would drag the American farmer, for whom so much has been done by the government, back from his present high plane to the level of the Canadian farmer. Mr. Reynolds maintained that the export business did not fix the American prices of grain to any considerable degree, though the Canadian price is always fixed by it, and cited the export business in last year's corn, wheat and oats crops as illustrative of his point.

Mr. George Phillips of Chicago also spoke against Reciprocity, stating that the farmer's only protection has heretofore been in grain, and it were unwise and unfair to take that away from him.

Mr. Henry Goemann of Toledo also opposed Reciprocity, declaring that it would force prices to the very lowest basis, and questioning the contention that it would lower the cost of living to the ultimate consumer.

THE PURE FOOD AND DRUG ACT.

Following this discussion the Hon. Henry M. Dowling of Indianapolis delivered an address entitled: "The Pure Food and Drug Act, as it relates to the Grain Trade." He said:

The privilege of attending an annual convention of your Association and of meeting your members is one which I heartily appreciate. The assembling of

HON. HENRY M. DOWLING.

any considerable body of our prominent business men to consider the condition and requirements of their calling, is always an occasion of interest; but a conclave of those who, on so large a scale, are the general purveyors of our basic food supplies, and the distributors of our harvests, is of especial interest. If the words of an eminent American orator are true, that if we destroy our farms the grass will grow in the city streets, equally true is it that both farm and city would suffer from an interruption of your business, since producer and consumer alike are dependent upon, and profoundly interested in, the branch of commerce of which you are representatives.

In addressing grain men on the subject of grain, I am tempted to adopt the plan of a clergyman who divided his discourse into two parts, his first head being, "those things which relate to my text," and his second, "those which do not." He explained that he would not insult the intelligence of his audience by speaking about the first, for these they were already acquainted with; he would therefore proceed at once to the second branch of his subject, namely, things which had nothing to do with it.

However, the subject assigned for discussion at this stage of the program is, "The Federal Food and Drug Law as it Relates to the Grain Trade"; and I dare not depart from it, lest I bring down upon the Program Committee the imputation of having "misbranded" their program, or "adulterated" it with extraneous and irrelevant matters.

This Act, now only five years old, finds its progenitors in the remote ages of history. Adulteration and misbranding are well nigh as old as trade itself. They were rife among the ancient Greeks and Romans, and the comedy writers of those early days had their fling at the "doctored" stale fish, sold as fresh upon the market.

Six hundred years before the United States passed its Pure Food and Drug Law, England passed an act directed against the adulteration of wine and beer, beef and bread; but it was not until the London "Lancet" in 1851 commenced a campaign of education and agitation on the subject of food supplies (not unlike that conducted by some modern American weeklies against patent medicine vendors) and published analyses and the names of the delinquent dealers, that a general statute against adulterations was adopted in 1860.

Today every civilized country has its laws upon this subject; and among those governments which but recently acted is our own. For more than seventeen years the project of correcting the abuses in food preparation and sale was launched in Congress; but during all that period it never reached port. Honest and sinister attacks were made upon it; one house would pass and the other defeat it. Finally, after bills in substantially the form of the present law had been pending four years, had twice passed the House and been twice defeated by the Senate, the matter was brought to a climax by the energetic methods of President Roosevelt, and the bill became a statute.

Whatever objections to the measure may have been entertained prior to its passage, the overwhelming weight of public opinion is in its favor. It is recognized, not only by the United States, but by practically every state in the Union, that food adulteration or misbranding is, or is likely to be, injurious to the health of the consumer; that it occasions a waste of money which is paid for an honest product but which buys only an inferior one; that it subjects the conscientious dealer to unfair competition; that it degrades the character of the man who practices adulteration or mislabeling, and unjustly damages the reputation of an upright dealer who sells products poor in quality and who is immediately open to the suspicion of fraud. From pecuniary, sanitary and moral standpoints, public opinion anu the public conscience cry out in favor of the Pure Food Law.

But it is this statute as it bears upon the grain trade which directly interests us. In two possible respects, a sale of grain may fall under its ban, the grain may be adulterated or it may be misbranded. The law defines its own terms and declares that "an article shall be deemed adulterated, in the case of food, first: If any substance has been mixed and packed with it so as to reduce or lower or injuriously affect its quality or strength; second: If any substance has wholly or in part been substituted for the article; third: If any valuable constituent of the article has been wholly or in part abstracted."

The act also defines misbranding, this being declared to occur to a food product, first: If it be in imitation of or offered for sale under the distinctive name of another article; second: If it is falsely labeled or branded so as to deceive or mislead the purchaser; third: If in package form, and the contents, stated in terms of weight or measure, are not plainly and correctly so stated; and fourth: If the package or its label bears any statement, design or device regarding the ingredients or substances contained in the package, which statement, design or device is false or misleading in any particular.

The violation of this law is a criminal offense, but in one important particular it differs from most of the criminal statutes of which we hear. If there be a charge against a man of having committed larceny or arson or assault and battery, there must not be only a merely accidental infliction of injury, explainable upon the ground of mistake; there must be the guilty mind, the felonous intent to steal, burn or strike; otherwise there is no crime. Not so with the class of offenses defined by the pure food and drug act. These belong to the list of crimes known as "statutory offenses" in which no element of actual guilt need be present in order to secure a conviction. If the letter of the law is violated, the law itself is infringed, even though the offender be the victim of an honest error or blunder, or even though the foreign matter added to the grain is more valuable than the grain itself, or radically improves the quality of the whole. It is the generally *damaging result* which the law aims to prevent, and this it accomplishes, not by punishing those who intentionally seek to thwart its purpose, but by throwing the entire burden upon each individual of seeing to it that, so far as he is concerned, he does not contribute to that damaging and prohibited result, either innocently or otherwise. While this is the stern mandate of the statue, it is not intended as a snare for the unwary or as means of oppression. In theory, any degree of admixture of foreign matter, whether dirt, weed seeds, chaff or grain, would be a technical violation; but the history of the prosecutions under the Law shows that where convictions have gone against dealers who have rendered themselves amenable to this act, there has been good reason to believe the presence of foreign goods was not accidental. Thus the convictions down to and including Dec. 12, 1910, showed that the most common offences were the mixing oats with shrunken and unmerchantable barley and other grains and selling the whole as "No. 2 White Oats," or "No. 3 White Oats," or "Fancy Clipped Oats," or oats of some other named grade. In these cases the percentage of extraneous matter varied from 15 per cent to 54 per cent.

Nor is it enough to use the word "oats" alone,

although no particular grade is specified; for if there is an appreciable amount of foreign grain or other matter which is not indicated in the label, there is "misbranding" within the meaning of the law, as well as an "adulteration." Thus where the sale was of "oats," but the mixture was oats and barley, the seller was fined $75 and costs.

Neither is it a safe practice to add the word "mixed," unless it be distinctly stated what are the elements of the mixture; for one dealer who sold as "No. 2 Mixed Oats" a compound of barley and oats was held liable to a fine of $100, with costs of prosecution. (See Judgment 406, U. S. Dept. of Agric.)

In practice, however, I am credibly informed that those entrusted with its enforcement judge each case under the law on its own merits, and are not inclined to prosecute those whose product shows a mere trace of inferior grain. It is recognized that a farmer may be compelled, by the failure of his wheat crop, to sow oats in the same field, and, like the grain in the parable, both are allowed to grow together until the harvest, when a scattering trace of wheat appears among the principal crop. To fine a dealer for selling a carload of grain in this condition would be a grave injustice; and while he is technically guilty, the attitude of the Federal authorities is to overlook such minor infractions, *unless it be the case of an old offender*, in which event the pound of flesh would be taken, despite the insignificance of the adulteration. In the enforcement of the Pure Food and Drug Law as to other food and drug products, as small a trace as 5 per cent of an adulterant or 2 per cent short weight has been held as a violation; and the same would probably be true in instances of persistent violators of the Act with respect to grains.

What has been said as to the sale of the original grain is true with respect to stock foods and other grain products. Here enters the additional element of stating upon the label the percentages of constituents, including protein, fat and crude fiber. If these are incorrectly given, the goods are misbranded, whether they are adulterated or not, and hence there has been an infraction of the law.

If the label purports to state the ingredients, but omits to mention any extraneous matter, whether it be an adulterant or not, there has been an offense committed, as where stock feed was sold containing rice or oat hulls, but the latter were not mentioned on the label, or where ground corn cobs entered into the combination of a "mixed bran feed." Even though otherwise correctly describing the contents, a label will render the dealer amenable to the law if it misstates the place of manufacture. (U. S. Dept. of Agriculture Judg. No. 439.)

Aside from the cases just now referred to, there is one class of cases in which the law has not as yet been fully declared; but by analogy to another similar question, the rule would seem to be obvious. I refer to the practice known to have been followed at least to a limited extent, in this state, of bleaching, dark, wet, shrunken oats so they will resemble "white oats" and selling them as such. The law has been construed by the Department of Agriculture and by the courts to prohibit the bleaching of flour and selling it as "patent flour" (Judg. No. 382, Dept. of Agriculture); and by the same token, a like treatment of oats would be similarly dealt with as "misbranding" and "adulteration."

Still another practice is open to question—the treatment of smutty wheat with a deodorizer which kills the smut odor. If smutty grain were cleaned and sold as if it were of a higher grade, and the use of the deodorizer helped to accomplish this purpose, the law would unquestionably be violated, as the label or brand might be such as would deceive the purchaser into buying a product which would make inferior flour.

We have thus far considered the law and its practical construction. It may not be inappropriate to examine the procedure by which it is made effectual.

The government inspector starts out with a fundamental premise, viz., that grains are not all of the same grade. In some instances, as he is aware, the grading has been done in an unofficial way, and had the sanction of trade custom only, or even of a private custom. Before the law was enacted, a great western elevator company, operating more than forty elevators in Kansas and Nebraska, had adopted certain standards with reference to which grains were bought and sold in that section. Where such is the case, the Federal authorities will regard the recognized trade custom as their basis of standardization.

Elsewhere the board of trade have their own standards. As is generally known, the Chicago Board of Trade has its own laboratory and force of inspectors and analysts, and where such is the practice, and the grain is sold with reference thereto, the grades so fixed are applied under the statute.

The Grain Dealers' National Association at its Twelfth Annual Convention at St. Louis, in 1908, standardized grains, specifying with minuteness the different grades of wheat, barley, oats, corn and rye. The United States government, through its Bureau of Plant Industry, has also issued bulletins on grain standardization.

Starting out with the proposition that grains are susceptible of being graded and have been graded, the inspector obtains a sample out of the suspected lot, and notes the marks, brands and tags upon the package or container, as well as any printed or written matter thereon, and the name of the vendor or his agent. The sample is then delivered to the Department of Agriculture and by it subjected to analysis. By a system of sieves and with the aid of powerful microscopes, the component parts of the mixture are separated and identified, and the proportion of each is ascertained and stated.

If there is a question as to the mis-stating of the percentages of the chemical constituents, as in the case of stock foods, there must be a chemical analysis to determine the percentages.

The results of the laboratory examination or analysis are then laid before the Department of Agriculture, and if a prima facie violation of the statute appears, the alleged violator is so notified and is furnished a copy of the laboratory findings, and a date is set when he may appear and show cause why the law should not be enforced against him. On the date set, the party presents himself, in person or by attorney, and may propound questions and submit evidence tending to show error in the conclusions of the government analyst. If the Department remains satisfied with the report originally made to it, the matter is placed in the hands of the proper United States District Attorney, with instructions to proscute under the law.

The procedure in the United States District Court may assume two different forms. It may be an ordinary prosecution for a misdemeanor with a maximum fine of $500 for the first offense, and one year's imprisonment, or both; or it may take the form of a "libel," that is, a suit against the food product itself, the title of the case being "United States of America vs. 200 sacks of oats." In the former prosecution, the extent of the penalty assessed depends largely upon the individual views of the district judge; the fines varying from $10 and costs to the maximum of $500, prison sentences not being assessed.

If the suit be in the form of a libel, the marshal seizes the property for confiscation, and if the judgment goes in favor of the United States, the property may be destroyed or sold, as the court may direct. The owner, however, may regain possession of his goods if he pays all the costs of the libel, and satisfactory bond to the United States, to the effect that the food product will not be sold or disposed of contrary to the provisions of the law. Among the common provisions of these bonds for good behavior is a requirement that the goods shall be rebranded so as to show their real nature, and until this is done, there is no redelivery to the owner. Thus oats which formerly bore the brand "No 3 White Oats," now came back to their owner branded "Barley mixed Oats," while another consignment dropped its honorable title of "No. 3 White Oats" and bore the humbling but more truthful legend: "Mixture of oats, wheat, barley, weed seeds, stems, hulls, chaff and inert matter." (Judg. Dept. of Agriculture, 650.) This reminds us of the laws passed by some indignant legislators requiring oleomargarine to be colored a bright pink before it is sold.

Nor is the execution of the bond an idle formality. The Government inspectors are commissioned to follow up the objectionable product and trace it through its first sale, and if the terms of the bond are violated, action upon the bond for the full penalty is instituted. This forfeiture of a bond has occurred in at least one instance.

To carry on the enforcement of this law in all its branches the Department of Agriculture now has a force of 260 men, operating all over the country. When the statute was first enacted, the available force was but 32; and even the present force is not adequate. Forty food inspectors are charged with the duty of securing food and drug samples, and with these and other United States authorities the food and drug commissioners and health officers of the States and Territories co-operate. As a result, over 45 judgments of the Dept. of Agriculture have been entered, up to December 12, 1910, in instances of grains and stock foods which violated the law, a number one and one-half times as great as the discovered violations during the same period by olive oil, syrups of lemon extract; approximately as great a number as the violations by vinegar, and half as great as those by milk, these products being the arch offenders against the law.

The law is therefore not a dead letter. Its general plan is recognized to be beneficial to the public, and both courts and juries are inclined to uphold the Department of Agriculture in its enforcement. Yet it is unquestionably open to grave abuses. There is no restriction placed upon the sources from which the inspector may receive his information of violations. Hence, a buyer who finds the market has fallen before the consignment has come to hand and who desires, for this or other reasons, to repudiate his bargain, can inform the inspector that the shipment is adulterated or misbranded, and if there is a technical infraction of the law, the buyer has accomplished his purpose and an innocent seller has been made to suffer. Or the information may be lodged by some unfriendly competitor, and the owner of the grain finds himself in the meshes of a criminal prosecution.

The corollary from this possible abuse of the statute is that the only secure course is to practice the eternal maxim that "eternal vigilance is the price of safety." Whether it be as to the marked weight on the sacks, or as to their contents, whether it be in regard to stated analyses or grades, the law demands that the literal facts be stated, and innocent intent is no safeguard. The Act will entail greater expense, as well as require increased caution upon the part of the grain dealer; but the alternative is the annoyance of a hearing before the Department of Agriculture, often to be followed by a criminal prosecution in one's own district and among one's own business acquaintances, by which the stigma of technical guilt will attach to the defendant, however guiltless of intentional wrongdoing he may be.

And as time goes on, the public becomes more familiar with the law and its possibilities, as inspectors become more skilled and flagrant violations become fewer, the natural tendency will be for administrative and judicial officers to be keener on the scent and draw the lines closer and view first offenses with even less consideration than they now regard them.

In the meantime, it becomes the part of wisdom for every dealer to thoroughly familiarize himself with the law and to devise such methods of self-protection, by ascertaining the exact grade of his grain, that his shipments will pass inspection by the most lynx-eyed analyst or the most reluctant purchaser.

Mr. Dowling's address provoked considerable discussion. Secretary Courcier explained the efforts of the Grain Dealers' National Association to have the Association's grade adopted as a basis of inspection under the law, and Inspector Culver called attention to the two exceptions made by the Department of Agriculture to those grades, that "Purified Oats" be labeled "Sulphured Oats," and smutty wheat so graded. Mr. Goemann called the attention of the dealers present to the fact that no matter what the individual market's rules happens to be, grain must comply with the provisions of the national law or be in violation of it. In other words grain acceptable at one market under a certain grading established by that market, might under that grading be a violation of the law. Other dealers spoke along similar lines.

Walter W. Bonner, of Greencastle, Ind., ex-president of the Indiana Bankers' Association, next talked on the subject of "Loaning Money by Grain Dealers to their Customers." Mr. Bonner spoke in happy vein but nevertheless strongly condemned the practice of loans by grain men to farmers with no security but a prospective crop, characterizing it as demoralizing to grain dealer and raiser alike. He pointed out the inevitable results of such a practice —mutual distrust and suspicion, and showed how under present day business organization, no farmer whose credit is good need go further than his bank to obtain the desired accommodation, and the mere fact that the farmer appeals to the grain dealer for a loan is evidence in itself of his bad credit. Mr. Bonner advocated the selling of good seed to farmers as a measure of great value. Mr. Bonner's views were strongly endorsed in the discussion following his address.

The last address on the afternoon's program was by Mr. A. F. Files of Evansville and was entitled "Interpretation of Trade Rules." Mr. Files briefly outlined the history of trade rules and took up a number of the points which lead to disputes and differences between dealers. The discussion on this subject was led by Mr. Frank M. Montgomery of Indianapolis and Mr. O. J. Thompson of Kokomo. Mr. Thompson dwelt on the desire of the shipper to obtain from receivers prompt notice of grade and discount on consignments.

President Foresman next introduced the question of the establishment of a Crop Reporting Bureau by the Association, and appointed a committee consisting of Messrs. E. K. Sowash, D. C. Moore and A. B. Cowee to fully consider the cost of such a bureau and the advisability of establishing it.

Recess was then taken until evening when the dealers were entertained by the local brethren.

The entertainment consisted of a vaudeville performance in the same hall, which was thoroughly enjoyed.

SECOND DAY'S PROCEEDINGS.

[By Telegraph.]

The first item on the program was a statement by F. F. Collins of Cincinnati, who gave a detailed explanation of the new weighing system of the Chamber of Commerce of that city, which he considered equal in perfection of detail to that of any market in the country. The inspection there came in for comment during the discussion.

Jas. R. Barr, Earl Park, spoke on the question, "Is the moisture test practicable for country dealers?" He plead for the necessity of more uniformity in the tester results. The paper opened up the entire moisture test question and a lively debate ensued, in which Culver, Paddock, Gardner and others, just in from the Bloomington convention where the tester was practically repudiated by resolution, freely expressed their opinions of that action. Thereupon a committee, consisting of Messrs. Barr, Thompson and Sec'y Riley, was appointed to take up the subject and make a formal report thereon.

DISCOUNTS IN NEW YORK.

Mr. P. E. Goodrich then read Mr. L. W. Forhell's address on "Discounts," as follows:

The discounting of "off grade" grain is a matter that for years has been the cause of more dissatisfaction to the shippers of grain to primary and terminal markets than almost any other feature of the grain business. These unsatisfactory conditions are bound to continue so long as the discounting is carried on entirely without system or supervision by exchange authorities.

It remained for the grain trade of the New York Produce Exchange to awaken to the fact that a more intelligent method was needed; and to this end a system was devised and put in operation a little more than three years ago that at once appealed to shippers as being so eminently fair that friction has been reduced to a minimum, if not altogether eliminated. Such recognition has it received, that upon the beginning of a new crop season our merchants are in receipt of numerous inquiries as to whether the same system is to prevail as formerly; and obtaining replies in the affirmative, they at once express their approval and proceed to enter into contracts for future delivery, secure in the knowledge that grain so shipped by them will be applied on contract, with the "off-grade" accepted at the discount fixed by the committee on the day of arrival.

In order that the working of this system may be thoroughly understood, I will endeavor as briefly as possible to explain just how it is operated.

The committee on grain is empowered to appoint three "settlement committees," one each for wheat, corn and oats; and it is provided that on each of these committees there shall be a member of the grain committee which gives to such sub-committees an official standing. It is the duty of the several committees to meet at a certain hour each day, generally at the close of the market, to receive all samples of "off-grade" grain intended to be applied on contracts and arrange their discounts.

The method of arriving at such differences is to determine what is a fair average price for the "off-grade" to be applied from sales of it in the open market on that day; and this is then compared with the average price obtained for the contract grade in question, with the result that an equitable discount is established. Should the grain offered for discount be of a quality known as "no grade," which corresponds to that of "sample grade," it is the duty of the committee then to determine as closely as possible the market value of such grain and arrange the discount accordingly. A record of all cars so discounted is filed with the secretary of the Exchange, and a copy is immediately posted on a bulletin board for public inspection. In performing their duties, the committees act with absolute impartiality, and their decisions must be accepted by both shipper and receiver.

In no case does a committeeman ever discount grain received by him on contract; and when such grain is submitted, he retires from the committee and a competent substitute is called in to act in his stead. Thus it will be seen that all interests are as carefully safeguarded as possible, and any shipper who wishes to verify returns made him, has but to write to the secretary of the Exchange and promptly receive the information.

The system was formulated on the presumption that in contracting grain for future delivery the seller would endeavor to ship only such grain as would be reasonably sure of grading in the New York market. Its practicability having been successfully demonstrated by reason of more uniform, and, to a certain extent, more reasonable, discounts than have hitherto prevailed, advantage was taken by a few shippers as an easy method to dispose of grain of very inferior quality which was not readily salable in their home markets. Their method was to sell No. 2 red wheat, steamer corn, or No. 3 white oats, which are the principal commercial grades, and then fill such contracts by shipping grain that on arrival would prove to be of the unmerchantable class and quite often out of condition.

While it occasionally happens that owing to delays in transportation or unusual climatic conditions the character of the grain may be changed while it is in transit, such excuses cannot avail to cover a shipment of wheat that is full of smut or garlic, nor will it serve to cover an arrival of corn that is hot and mouldy, when the same has been in transit barely a week during the winter months. In the case of oats, the abuse has been less frequent.

The practice of attempting to apply wheat of a character referred to was prevalent two years ago and to an extent that merchants and exporters declined to contract except with those shippers whose reputations were such that the likelihood of receiving low grade and unfit grain was minimized. The committees also aided in stamping out the practice by refusing to establish a market difference, on the ground that there was not a ready sale for such grain and therefore could be no degree of permanency to its value. To establish discounts would perhaps cause either party to the contract to endure an unnecessary hardship. Also in these cases, it was evident that the spirit of the contract had been violated.

Their recommendation to the receiver was, when possible, to handle the grain through the elevators for account of the shipper and when in condition to again present it for discount. Either do this or sell on the market at the best price possible, establishing a difference in that manner.

Happily, such shippers constitute but a small minority; for I take great pleasure in stating that the experience of the New York merchants in the main under our discount system has been a most agreeable one.

They no longer have to write long letters in justification of a certain discount made, nor are they in receipt of the same from shippers seeking an explanation. The better the system is understood throughout the Middle West, the more eager are shippers to sell their grain subject to contract conditions as to discounts under the system in vogue in the New York market.

The matter of dockage is something that we know little or nothing about, as this custom is not practiced by the railroad terminal elevators at New York.

The weighing of grain is superintended at each elevator by the inspection department of the Exchange, and a deputy is stationed in the scale room, who verifies the weights of each car of grain as it is weighed into the elevator. In addition to this, our Rules provide that the weighmaster be licensed by the Exchange only upon application to the grain committee and after an examination by the inspector-in-chief, who must certify to the fitness of the applicant to perform the duties required of him before such application is granted. Weighmasters at private elevators and track weighers are appointed in the same manner. All licenses must be renewed once a year and removal follows should charges be made and substantiated.

I wish to thank the members of the Indiana Grain Dealers' Association for this opportunity to explain in detail the workings of our discount and weighing systems, and hope that the explanations given will lead to a better understanding of such matters that will be to your distinct advantage in the future.

In the course of the discussion, Messrs. Goodrich, Fox, Paddock and Gardner commended highly the New York system.

Sec'y Riley then read a paper based on an elaborate enquiry by himself and by "An Illinois Dealer," on the cost of handling grain through a country elevator. The paper demonstrated pretty conclusively that the cost as estimated by country dealers generally is too low and that the margins taken should be greater.

Sec'y J. V. Taylor invited the convention to attend the National Hay convention at Niagara Falls.

The committee on crop reports recommended that the committee be given further time for consideration. Granted.

Sec'y Riley read the report of the committee on nominations, which recommended the election of the following:

President—Chas. A. Ashpaugh, Frankfort.

Vice-president—Mr. Scearce, Mooresville.

Directors—Fred B. Fox, Tipton; E. E. Elliott, Muncie.

The resolutions adopted thanked the officers for their services, the Indianapolis dealers for their entertainment, and the speakers for their contributions to the program of the meeting.

The trade rules were amended asking that receivers report immediately to consignors when cars fail to grade according to the contract and the discount demanded ou that account.

The Association adopted a motion to ratify the National Trade Rules as amended at Chicago in 1910.

A resolution was adopted protesting against the proposition of the Post Office department to send trade journals by fast freight trains instead of the regular mail trains.

The auditing committee reported that the financial reports were correct and should be approved. Report adopted.

The new officers were then installed, whereupon the meeting adjourned, *sine die*.

[For the "American Elevator and Grain Trade."]

THE GRAIN TRADE OF THE PAST.

VI.

BY DANIEL M'ALLISTER.

In a former letter I mentioned the reluctance with which the grain dealers who had established themselves along the lines of canals, sixty years ago, gave up their holdings there in favor of the incoming railroad system; and the fact, too, that all shipments made from this part of the country prior to that time were made by boats, through the canals, to the Lakes on the north or the Ohio River on the south. As to the amount of grain shipped in those early days, we have, of course, no accurate means of knowing; but from personal observation I should say it was much larger, relatively, than it is today—relatively, in proportion to the amount produced, I mean, because cities of our state have grown to be "consuming points" and take up nearly all the surplus the farmers have to spare. The Government report for 1910, not yet fully completed, will show the population of Ohio to be 4,767,000, and of Franklin County, including Columbus, 221,500. The same report will show that the production of wheat in Ohio, 1910, was 31,221,000 bushels, and in Franklin County, for the same period, the crop was 536,000 bushels.

Perhaps we might as well figure a little here. I find it mentioned in history that at a period longer ago (very many years) than the time of which I have been writing there used to be a "unit" of weights called "a stone," which, it seems, was used by the shepherds of Judea, in the dawning days of Christianity, as a crude balance-weight in the handling of wool. The "weight" was, in fact, a stone, a round boulder, of given size, and was afterwards decided to be of fourteen pounds avoirdupois. Perhaps the term "a stone" is in use today in some parts of Europe, as I know it was, seventy years ago, when I was a little boy, in Ireland. [It is still in use in parts of England.] "A stone of meal" was, at that time, a well-known quantity; and I think the term is in use even yet in the same place. Whether or not there be any connection between the "stone" and the barrel of flour; or between the barrel of flour and the average annual consumption per capita of population, I am unable to say; but inasmuch as the barrel of flour has been fixed in weight at one hundred and ninety-six pounds, the square-root of a "stone," and is acknowledged to be nearer to the annual consumption per capita (little and big) than any other weight, we may well imagine that the problem was discussed along the river Nile in Egypt prior to the year "One Anno Domini."

However this may be, or wherever these things may have found their origin, the best evidence we have today fixes the consumption at one barrel per annum to the individual, or thereabouts. My esteemed and scholarly friend, Mr. Warder, of Warder & Barnett, Springfield, Ohio, who manufactured and sold "The Golden Fleece" there, forty years ago, told me that he had figured it out to his entire satisfaction, that a family of six persons consumes on an average seven barrels a year—six for the family, and one for "comers and goers"; and that he estimated five bushels of wheat to the barrel, about six bushels to the individual, little and big. This, on a population of 4,767,000, would make Ohio's requirements for food 28,602,000 bushels, only 2,519,000 bushels short of its production last year; with seed for the coming year yet to be supplied. Following the same rule of estimate, this county, Franklin, requires 1,329,000 bushels for food, or about 793,000 bushels more than it produces, which, along with enough for the coming year's seed, will have to be made up by shipping in.

I had a very interesting conversation recently with Mr. Gwinn, president of the Gwinn Milling Co., here, who, by the way, is a man of large practical experience and deep scientific thought. He is not inclined to class Ohio as a wheat exporting state at all; but says of her in admonition of her people, "Ohio is the garden spot of all the states; and whenever her farmers get down to scientific principles in what they do, her crops may be increased as two to one."

The warehouses that I spoke about, down there on the canal, the wharf, the fifty wagons, waiting for their turn—where are they now? All gone; and the canal, too, filled up and used for a street. The "life is somewhere else—up at the railroad depot and at the stations of electric cars. The mill, too, named above, with just as many cars of wheat to be unloaded, waiting for their turns, as there were of wagons sixty years ago, down there on the canal. But such is progress; and the throng goes rushing on.

APROPOS THE SCALE PROBLEM.

In a recent editorial you said something about country scales and of the willingness of Weighing Department of the Chicago Board of Trade to go and "test" those out of order, whenever requested to do so. Many scales, you say, have been found incorrect; and yet you failed to say just how, or what the "make" that needs the greatest care.

The subject is not new to me, by any means. I treated of it somewhat briefly in a former letter; but like yourselves avoided mentioning the "make" of scales, or causes, other than the one of "age," or being "out of doors." There is a difference, however in the make. Those scales with bearings at the corners, pendent from the sills, when used for wagons out of doors, are very hard to keep in good repair. The constant driving crowds the sills together; then the law of gravitation does the rest. The scales will balance-up all right apparently, but the "beam" will move a little slowly because the center has been changed; or, rather, because there have been two centers created in place of one, so that the weight rests in part on each, suspended in the middle.

For instance—and without entering into scientific technicalities—suppose we take a fifty-pound "test" weight; run a piece of string through under its handle; then loop each end of the string into the hook of an accurate spring scale. The result will be fifty pounds, plus the string. Then we take the string and loop one end of it into another similar spring scale, holding the scales back-to-back. The result will be twenty-five pounds on each scale, for there are only fifty pounds of gravitation; but if we separate the scales, hold them apart, so that the pendents are forced out of plumb, then the principle of gravitation becomes lost in the obstruction and the "mechanical devices"—"The Screw, the Lever and the Wedge"—begin to act. When scales are crowded thus they always go against the buyer; they never go the other way. I got my knowledge on the subject in the costly school of experience, and through rough, hard knocks.

Let me tell you. I was young at the time; had a good run of trade, and was doing well. I was using an out-door scale in buying; but had to sell on an inside hopper scale. I soon found that my scale outside was wrong; but I did not know the why. I had no time to make a change; my trade was crowding me; I simply had to bear it—as I did, about a dollar on a sixty-bushel load.

The fact gave me occasion for much thought. I studied it both day and night—the law of gravitation, bearings, levers, beams. Finally a thought came to me: "Lengthen out the levers underneath." I thought I had found the trouble; and I thought, too, that I had a "patent" on my hands to yield a fortune. I went down in the morning quickly to ascertain how my device might be applied. To my surprise I found the new invention had been "pre-invented" long before. I found, though, that it would not work to overcome the trouble. Extension of the bearings only made the "crowding" worse. The fault was, as I discovered, at the other end; the scales must be rebuilt, and would be better if placed within the house.

No dealer can afford to use an outside scale of such a make when buying, when the scale is old. Better to throw it on the "junk" or lock it up; and then put the new one in the house, if possible, than to be constantly quarreling with oneself—and the man at the other end also—on account of discrepancies in weights.

MONTREAL CONGESTED.

Montreal during May was congested with grain, her elevators being full, with twenty vessels, on May 16, lying in the harbor with 800,000 to 1,000,000 bushels of wheat on board unable to unload. The movement of wheat during May through the city was about a million bushels a week, and all ocean-going ships sailing during the month carried their full grain capacity and all boats to sail during June and part of July had been chartered for grain space capacity.

R. E. COX DEAD.

The Kansas Grain Dealers' Association has lost a valuable and popular official in the death of its president, R. Earl Cox of Humbolt, who died of kidney disease at Kansas City on May 14.

Mr. Cox was born on a farm near Humboldt in April, 1882. His father subsequently established

THE LATE R. E. COX.

the town of Elsmore and was its chief merchant. As the schools were inadequate, R. E. Cox when a small boy saw more work than school masters, yet he acquired an education and at fifteen graduated from a high school and became quite a student of literature and music. He went into the grain business with his father about 1899. He was three times elected president of the Kansas Association.

THE LEGISLATURES.

Illinois.—The Illinois legislature did not enact more laws asked for by the grain interests than it did put on the statute book. Among the bills passed we find the following that may be of interest to dealers as such:

The Civil Service bill, which extends the existing civil service laws applying chiefly to charitable institutions, to all state departments, particularly penitentiaries, reformatories, state boards and departments, and to the executive offices. There is a list of exemptions which excludes from the operation of the law certain confidential clerks in the office of the governor and the elective state officials, as well as to the teaching staff of the University of Illinois and the state normal schools. Only residents of the state are permitted to take the entrance examinations for the classified service, except for technical positions. Full hearing upon formal charges by the state civil service commission is provided as a prerequisite for discharge. Efficiency tests and promotions are provided. Blanket protection is afforded to all employes on the lists on June 30, 1911, when the law becomes effective.

An emergency act causing the state entomologist to proceed against the chinch bug, and $8,000 were appropriated for the purpose.

A bill prohibiting adulteration of stock feeds, and placing the state food inspector in charge of the inspection.

Pennsylvania.—Among the laws enacted by the late legislature of Pennsylvania are the following:

To stimulate interest in agriculture by the holding of county agricultural exhibitions $100,000 was set aside by the legislature. This amount will be disbursed at the rate of $50,000 annually for the next two years.

Through an amendment companies formed to manufacture and sell garden and horticultural instruments and deal in seeds, plants, bulbs and flowers will come under the provisions of the law allowing the erection of buildings and the holding of real estate.

DEALERS AT WICHITA.

A sort of good-fellowship meeting of grain dealers at the invitation of the Wichita Board of Trade, was held at Wichita, Kan., on June 6 and 7. About 175 dealers, brokers, millers, etc., were present; and were duly tagged by Secretary Sherman of the Board.

In the afternoon, trading hours being over, President W. F. McCullough of the Board called the guests to order for a brief formal meeting. A welcome was extended by the Mayor, to which replies were made by T. J. Donahue of Ponca City and Geo. Hayes of Hebron on behalf of the dealers of Oklahoma and Nebraska respectively. Then J. Ralph Pickell of the "Hay and Grain Reporter" told the dealers about the "Ethics of the Grain Trade," while R. A. Haste enlightened them on the mysteries of the Campbell system of dry farming and soil culture. Then everybody bolted to talk shop among themselves.

The next day an effort was made to hold another afternoon meeting, but the baseball game was too alluring and the program was postponed until evening, when the ladies of the First Methodist Church served a banquet at the Forum. After the viands had been disposed of, and the quartet had exhausted its repertoire of classic negro melodies of the "Old Black Joe" type, there were some speeches.

As a serious interlude W. E. Clark of Sawyer, Kan., talking of the cost of handling grain through country elevators, gave it as his opinion, based on ten years' personal experience, that the manner of determining this matter is most often wrong, because elevator operators figure by their bank balance, if they have one at the clean-up end of the season, as their profits, and their losses by a lack of such balance. It is now impossible to conduct a grain business as we used to, when the farmer simply drove his wagon up to the freight car and shoveled in his wheat. Doing a business on a small margin might do then, but it will not any more. He found his business for the ten years had been 884,000 bushels, and expenses $10,165.05, something over 1.4c per bushel, making a 3-cent margin as the minimum imperative. He estimated the average life of a country elevator at less than 15 years.

E. J. Smiley of the Kansas association gave a brief history of that body, showing the difference in conditions now and fifteen years ago when dealers (thirteen years ago, holding a meeting at Wichita, demonstrated to the representatives themselves of the terminal elevators on Missouri River that the honest weigher in those houses was the exception and not the rule; and they took the 100 lbs. dockage, too!

Then there was fun making by Knute Murphy of Kansas City, W. G. Goffe of Kansas City and others.

John D. Laidlaw, once prominent in the grain trade of Toronto, Ont., died recently at Lumsden, Sask. Mr. Laidlaw was formerly in partnership with J. C. McKeggie at Toronto.

Thrashing begun in Denton County, Texas, on May 29. That county is credited with producing about one-fourth of the entire 8,000,000 bus. of wheat grown in that state this season.

NEW ENEMIES OF STORED GRAIN.

F. H. Chittenden, Sc. D., of the Bureau of Entomology, U. S. Dept. of Ag., is contributing a series of articles to the "American Miller" on some new and little known insect enemies of stored grain, which comprise a list somewhat more formidable than generally imagined. Practically all of the different species of grain and flour insect enemies that have been mentioned by the entomologists by specific name, have been described in detail in the "American Miller" or in the "American Elevator and Grain Trade" in the past; but the species which will be mentioned in the present series of papers have, with few exceptions, never been treated in a popular manner hitherto.

THE LESSER GRAIN-BORER.

(*Rhizopertha dominica Fab.*)

An important insect which inhabits granaries and storehouses, and which feeds upon dry cereals is the lesser grain-borer. There is another of these

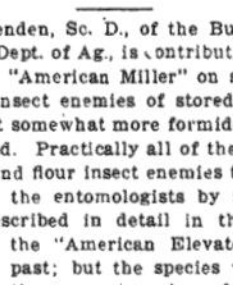

FIG. 1.—THE LESSER GRAIN BORER.

Rhizopertha dominica, Beetle with enlarged antenna at right. Beetle about 12 times natural size. (Original.)

insects and from their different sizes we may call them the lesser grain-borer and the larger grain-borer. The former is cosmopolitan and attacks cereals and many other substances; the latter is tropical and though also a general feeder, at least in its adult stage, is by virtue of its larger size apparently restricted, in the cereals, to maize.

The lesser grain-borer will receive consideration in the present paper. It has already obtained a footing in this country and is frequently brought to our shores from outside sources in stored cereals and other seeds and similar material, and is of considerable economic importance.

This is one of the smallest of beetles injurious to grain in the kernel, being considerably shorter and narrower than the grain weevils. The beetle is about one-eighth of an inch long. The form is nearly cylindrical; the head is comparatively large and prominent, and bent down under the thorax; the antennae, or feelers are prominent, as are the eyes and the mandibles. The antennæ are armed at the end with a ten-jointed club. The color is dark brown and polished throughout.

The beetle is shown in Fig. 1, with the antennæ, much enlarged, at the right.

The lesser grain borer, as previously stated, is not only cosmopolitan, but nearly omnivorous. It attacks probably all forms of grain, but has been found most abundantly in rice, wheat, corn, sorghum, pearl millet, and some prepared cereals, including bran and ship's biscuits. We have also records of the occurrence of this insect in drugs, such as rhubarb and arrowroot, dried Abyssinian banana and bread prepared by Indians from wild prairie turnip. The insect has been found apparently feeding on cork and injuring insect boxes in museums, and has been known to be troublesome in two localities by breeding in horse collars. It has been found under the bark of some trees and in dry wood and it seems probable, when we consider the habits of its kind, that this grain borer may be quite as often introduced into new localities in the wood of rice boxes as in the grain itself. This list of food habits will doubtless be extended in time. We have known of the beetles boring holes through cotton sacks while in the case of injury to the horse collars, the beetles bred in the straw and perforated the thick leather covering.

A series of experiments has been conducted with the standard fumigants, to ascertain if this species were in any degree more, or less, resistant than other insects which injure stored products, such as the grain weevils, the grain beetles, flour beetles, and others. Opportunity for experiments with hydrocyanic acid gas was offered in December, 1910, at Beaumont, Tex., where an agent of this bureau, working under the writer's special direction, conducted a series of experiments. Coincident with these experiments another series with bisulphid of carbon was being carried out at Washington, D. C. A still longer series of experiments was also carried on at Houston and Beaumont, Tex., at an earlier date, both with hydrocyanic-acid gas and with bisulphid of carbon under various conditions and strengths.

General Conclusions.—The results of the series of experiments performed with bisulphid of carbon and hydrocyanic-acid gas against the lesser grain-borer, (and incidentally against other insects) show in brief the following:

That the lesser grain-borer possesses less resistant power to both gases than do most other stored-product insects.

That fumigations in *low* temperatures, and especially below 50° F., are practically ineffective unless an excessively large amount of bisulphid of carbon or of a cyanid be used, and that it is still more desirable that from 48 hours to three days be the length of exposure in order to kill all insects in even tight inclosures.

One experiment shows that even with 10 pounds of bisulphid of carbon to 1,000 cubic feet of space in a tight receptacle only a very small percentage of grain insects were killed in an exposure of 24 hours and with a temperature of about 48° F., and another experiment shows that even with 20 pounds of carbon bisulphid to 1,000 cubic feet, or 10 times what may now be accepted as a standard, only 75 per cent of the insects present were destroyed in a 24-hour exposure.

It may be safely assumed that under ordinary conditions, in moderately high temperatures, between 65° and 75° F., 1½ pounds of bisulphid of carbon to 1,000 cubic feet of air space as generally advised, is insufficient even for a 48 hours' exposure, and that we may adopt as a general standard 2 pounds to 1,000 cubic feet for 48 hours or more, or until the odor of the gas has become entirely dissipated.

THE LARGER GRAIN-BORER.

(*Dinoderus truncatus* Horn.)

The larger grain-borer has without doubt been brought into this country from Mexico, Guatemala,

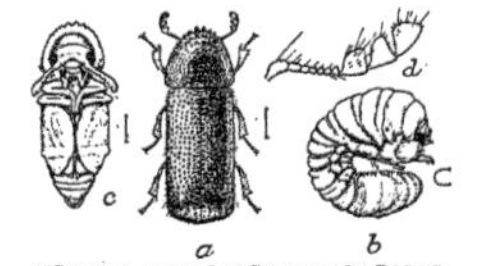

FIGURE 2.—THE LARGER GRAIN-BORER.

The larger grain-borer (Dinoderus truncatus): a, Adult or beetle; b, larva; c, pupa; d, antenna, a, b, c, about six times natural size; d, highly magnified.

and elsewhere on many occasions, but there are few published records of importation. So far as I know, it has never found permanent lodgment in the United States, but is apt to be introduced into tropical Texas as well as elsewhere. From our knowledge of the insect's habits, it differs slightly from the lesser grain-borer, preferring corn to other grain, if indeed it feeds at all on any other cereal, and it also has the wood-boring habit strongly developed. Corn in the ear is preferred to shelled corn, and edible and other tubers and roots, such as yams, serve as natural breeding places.

Attention has been called by the writer in correspondence to the difficulty of eradicating this species from a barn, if this should happen to be constructed of wood or, what is worse, adobe.

This species is elongate cylindrical in shape and dark brown in color, with paler legs and tawny antennæ. It measures one-sixth inch or less in length and is about two and a half times as long as wide. The accompanying illustration, Fig. 2, shows the characteristic structure of the beetle at *a*; *b* represents the larva which, it will be noted, strongly resembles better known bostrychids, such as the red-shouldered hickory beetle and the apple twig-borer; *c* represents the pupa, ventral view. The larva and pupa are white.

This insect was described as a new species in 1878, from specimens accidentally found in California. It was once brought to this country with corn for exhibition in the Mexican section of the New Orleans Exposition in 1885. In 1893 I found specimens in corn and edible roots from Mexico and Guatemala at the World's Columbian Exposition, held in Chicago that year. In 1894 samples of Mexican corn that had been ruined by this insect were received by me. (Fig. 3). The samples in both cases, as well as in many others that have come to my notice were fairly reduced to powder. In the case of corn, the insects bore through and through the kernels, cob and husk, and where paper wrappings and labels are used they also are perforated. Since that time this insect has been received from other sources.

The grain-feeding habit of this species is obviously

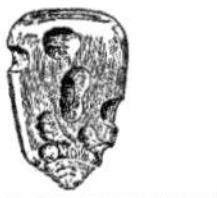

FIGURE 3.—WORK OF LARGER GRAIN-BORER.

Kernel of corn showing work of beetle of larger grain-borer.

an acquired one and with little doubt of comparatively recent times. Normally or under natural conditions, it breeds in roots and tubers. I have learned by experiment that the pupal stage varies from about 4½ days in the very hottest weather to 6 days in cooler weather during June and July, while in October the pupal period lasted 12 days. The egg was not observed but the egg period is with little doubt about the same as for the pupa under the same atmospheric conditions. By experiment I learned that the entire life cycle from the placing of beetles in corn until the issuance of the new generation, i. e., from August 25 to October 9, was 45 days, or about 6½ weeks. Temperature moderately warm during this period.

Another experiment was made with this species by confining it with some others in a superheated atmosphere, which was also very dry. As evidence of its tropical nature this species thrived better than any of the other insects exposed to the same conditions. Indeed, it appears to be the only insect that did not suffer from the extreme dryness to which it was subjected. The temperature in this case was upward of 100° F. and ran as high as 115° F.

This is of interest as bearing on the remarks made by Professor Dean, giving 116° F. as the fatal temperature.

James Hannon of Tenney, Minn., will have charge of the Farmers' Elevator at that place, succeeding William McAlpin, who resigned.

A. O. Kregan has sold his elevator interests at Belfield, N. D., and will reside at Driscoll, where he will enter the elevator business.

John Wieck, who has been manager of the Andrews Grain Co. at Detroit, Minn., for the past seven years, recently committed suicide.

Mr. Grossbeck of Chenoa, Ill., will take the position of grain buyer at the Farmers' Elevator at Weston, Ill., formerly held by Mr. Stauffer.

W. S. Tyner is manager of a new company formed at Port Arthur, Texas, to take over the J. C. Reynolds Grain Co. and the J. S. Gordon Grain Co.

J. C. Daves, a grain man of Winfield, Kan., has been appointed by the B. C. Christopher Grain Co. as its representative on the Wichita Board of Trade.

T. D. Klink, who has been in Faith, S. D., overseeing the building of an elevator, will soon take charge of an elevator at Reeder, S. D., for the summer.

THE AMERICAN ELEVATOR AND GRAIN TRADE

Published on the Fifteenth of Each Month

BY

MITCHELL BROS. & CO.

OFFICE:

Manhattan Building, 431 South Dearborn Street

CHICAGO, ILL.

HARLEY B. MITCHELL .... Editor
A. J. MITCHELL .... Business Manager

Subscription Price, - - - - $1.00 per Year
English and Foreign Subscription, - 1.75 " "

CORRESPONDENCE.

We solicit correspondence upon all topics of interest connected with the handling of grain or cognate subjects.

CHICAGO, JUNE 15, 1911.

Official Paper of the Grain Dealers' National Association and of the Illinois Grain Dealers' Association.

EMBARGO ON EXPORT CORN.

Philadelphia has achieved the distinction of having revived the Liverpool embargo on American corn sold on "certificate final" terms. This achievement, at a time when for the moment American grain exports were becoming again somewhat worth while, seems to have pleased neither Philadelphia nor exporters elsewhere; for the suspicion cast upon Philadelphia grain can scarcely be expected to cast no reflection on grain from other ports also. The grain committee of the Commercial Exchange are investigating, as is usual in such cases; but, frankly, the most valuable portion of the committee's report will be the explanation of motives.

The situation, however, is remarkable in one respect, as will be seen on reading the comments thereon by Messrs. Welsh and Siewers. Mr. Siewers formulates the faint surprise of the trade that, with so many new facilities for the estimation of corn, the inspection now at Philadelphia should so lamentably "fall down;" and Mr. Welsh in part tells us why it is so. It is all quite interesting.

When John O. Foering was grain inspector at Philadelphia, for twenty-five years, more or less, not a misgrading was recorded. This remarkable record was achieved without any extraneous aids. But Mr. Foering was individually responsible to the sufferer from a misgrading in pecuniary damages. Not that Foering's honesty needed the support of a bond; but all the world knew that blunders of inspection there would be compensated for; and no blunders were made. In those days Philadelphia had no worries about her inspection in or out; her "certificate final" terms were agreed to and consummated with no "comebacks;" the arrangement was ideal for all concerned.

But Foering, in the opinion of many, was making too much money out of his "job;" and an arrangement that may be likened unto pampering the goose that laid golden eggs came to an end, and one less responsible, more capricious and more adjustable to "the local requirements of the trade" has taken its place.

THE ACIDITY TEST.

Commissioner of Agriculture Watson of South Carolina has introduced an unexpected element into the criteria for passing on the quality of corn entering his state, which has given shippers of spoiled corn a shock, and temporarily caused some Ohio River shippers to withdraw from that market. Mr. Watson's position and procedure are referred to at length in another place in this paper.

At least, Mr. Watson has demonstrated that the last word had not been said on the scientific method of determining the deterioration of maize when the moisture test was established as a working criterion. The man who despises the moisture test as the work of the Evil One, who may be supposed to be in collusion, during certain months and under certain conditions of the market, with the man who invented the "discount for off grade," may not consider that excess of moisture may cause the development of poisonous conditions in corn; but the acidity test is able to demonstrate that fact even though the dangerous corn may be as dry as the best No. 2; and the questionable action of some inspectors, of passing manifestly rotten corn as No. 2, apparently only because it had been dried to the No. 2 requirements as to moisture, has justified Mr. Watson in bringing the acidity test to the front to render futile, and do it at once and without further argument, all differences of opinion on the part of inspectors using conventional criteria only as to the quality of corn when it is shown to be dangerous by the acidity test.

Mr. Watson has further demonstrated the sanction and wisdom of the Uniform Grade Rules, since no corn that has graded No. 2 or No. 3 under those rules has shown in his laboratory a dangerous degree of acidity.

RATHER UNUSUAL.

The action of the Illinois Grain Dealers' Association in the debate on the moisture test resolution at Bloomington was hardly up to the high standards of the Association, which in the past has been wont to give all who attended its meetings the right to be heard, if members, or the courtesy of the floor, if visitors. But in the debate on the resolution in question, in spite of its immense importance, the chair, by written communication to Mr. E. H. Culver, withdrew the courtesy of the floor, always hitherto accorded him, and by announcement gave notice to others that "as the time available for the debate was short," only members of the Association would be granted the floor.

Yet Mr. Culver was probably the most competent man on the floor, through his experience as an inspector and as a special student of the moisture problem, to say nothing of his official position as president of the Chief Grain Inspectors' National Association, to speak on this subject of the moisture test and its relation to inspection and to the National pure food act, which in the future is likely to play a more influential part in the estimation of grain than most of those who oppose the test are now ready to admit.

Whether this suppression of expert advice on this matter and the adoption of the reduction by a paltry vote of 42 (to 17 noes), in a meeting at which no doubt three times that number of country dealers were present, but were too indifferent to vote on either side of the question, can be assumed to represent the deliberate opinion of the grain trade of Illinois on the subject matter of the resolution, is a question to be respectfully passed up to the reader and to the Railroad and Warehouse Commission to answer for themselves.

FARMERS CAN SHIP.

A reader of the Nebraska Farmer asks the editor of that paper:

Can a farmer ship his grain and receive the same rates from the railroads, and get the same price for the grain that grain dealers get? If not, why not?

Instead of answering promptly in the affirmative, the editor naturally enough (for farmer-readers are presumed to prefer replies that confirm their suspicions rather than disabuse them), "hedges"—he thinks so, but isn't sure.

Farmers are not discriminated against as shippers; but there are several reasons why, even when they get a better nominal price per bushel when shipping their own grain, they do not usually make as much net money as by selling to the local grain buyer. These may all be summed up in the one statement, that as shippers they must assume all the shipper's risks and must do so without being advantaged by the professional shipper's technical knowledge of the business.

Farmers are not disposed to admit that there is such technical knowledge; they assume that all the money grain dealers make out of their business is so much money arbitrarily taken from them without rendering them a service. But the fact is that the grain dealer renders a service to the farmer and to the consumer alike, which is real, though not always visible to one who does not want to see it or understand it; and for this service he is entitled to compensation. And as competition in the grain business is so sharp that the opportunities to earn profits without the exercise of technical skill are very few, only the most competent dealers are those who make any considerable amount of money handling grain, and even they do not take it all from the farmer.

THE BILL OF LADING.

The finding of a New York court, the other day, holding the bank that handled a fraudulent cotton bill liable for the loss incurred by the transaction, has not improved the bill of lading situation. Rather, it has greatly emphasized the still pressing need of national as well as uniform state legislation to establish the character of order bills as commercial paper. Law, of course, will not entirely put an end to forged bills of lading any more than it has to other forms of forgery; but it may make the crime less common by throwing around the making of bills of lading a legal sanctity that they do not now seem to have. When office clerks may make with a lead pencil and act as custodians of bills of lading representing large sums of money, it is not to be expected that the bill of lading will ever be issued and safeguarded as property of such magnitude should be.

The authority of the Carmack amendment having been sustained by the Supreme Court, the bill is now protected against arbitrary disavowal of responsibility for loss and damage to the property represented by it when the loss occurs on the connecting line. The Commerce Commission ruling in the Shaffer case against the Rock Island, mentioned on another page, is another point apparently settled; and about half a dozen states have enacted the bankers' bill holding carriers responsible to bona fide holders for the truth of the recitals in their bills of lading; but what are these six among so many that have no such state law! Yet Mr. Paton, counsel for the American Bankers' Association, says that in this record "the commercial and financial community has cause for congratulation" as a sign of beneficial progress which has only been possible by organized effort and by an energetic "campaign of education" by the bankers' and other associations—such is the inertia of business men and legislators!

THE EFFECT.

The supporters of the resolution of the Illinois Association on the moisture test disclaim any desire to abolish the test but ask only to have it set aside as the determining factor of the grading. This is a distinction without much difference; for the resolution's proponents ask in substance that corn not otherwise objectionable shall be passed to a higher grade in spite of its excess of water.

But why exempt water and not dirt? Is water less objectionable? Both must needs be removed to make the grain a safe commodity to ship or carry; both are objectionable to the buyer, who by no sort of inspection hocus-pocus can be made to pay one penny more for the grain than it is worth as a raw material for conversion into finished products of various sorts. Of course, to the grain man, as to the farmer also, grain is a finished product, but it is so to them only, not to any other handler; and that fact makes it impossible for these producers to put prices on grain or dictate the manner or the character of its estimation in the markets where it is bought as raw material.

What is inspection, anyway? Simply a system of umpiring between buyers and sellers. It adds nothing to the intrinsic value of the grain nor does it detract from it. It simply establishes certain ranges of quality that by common consent consumers are willing to accept as basic classifications of general, not specific, quality for the convenience of the primary seller rather than the buyer who may be the consumer or the man next the consumer; the ultimate price is made by the consumer who may or may not buy by grade. Since absolute conditions of quality become more imperative as the grain gets nearer the consumer, nearly all the grain shipped by the country must be conditioned, or is conditioned, by the intermediary shippers, who as buyers pay only what the grain is worth to them to be conditioned for a subsequent buyer. If the general quality of the grade is lowered by widening the range of the grade, the average price of the grade must fall to equalize; so that the ultimate effect of any successful effort to inject more moisture into the grade will be to lower the price of all of it instead of raising the price of some of it.

It seems useless to say it to some people, but the fact remains that prices cannot be regulated by law or ordinance; only a downright monopoly can exercise such control.

INDOOR INSPECTION.

All objectors to Mr. Cowen's system of indoor inspection of grain must "show me" now, in view of the performance of the Illinois Inspection Department at Chicago during May. During that month the total number of cars of grain inspected was 18,743, of which 2,621 were inspected in a single day, May 29. This feat was the more remarkable from the fact that the entire number of cars was on May 29 inspected and placed on the tables of the Board of Trade in ample time for trading on that day, a circumstance of considerable moment to shippers of wheat in particular.

Now, this immense single day's work (never equaled in the history of grain inspection) was possible only by the indoor system of inspection put into practice at Chicago by Mr. Cowen; and it was a rather interesting coincidence that this remarkable exploit in grain inspection should have come nearly at the close of about seven years of his management of that important office.

This May record, the greatest in at least six years, is further distinguished (thanks to the indoor system) by 148 errors only in the inspection of 18,734. You can figure out the percentage at your leisure.

COST OF PRODUCING WHEAT.

Prof. A. E. Chamberlain of South Dakota bombarded the senate finance committee on May 27 with "an elaborate array of statistics" to prove that the production of wheat in South Dakota costs 57c per bushel; whereas in Canada it costs but 40c; *ergo*, South Dakota cannot compete with Canada in wheat growing, and the reciprocity agreement must be rejected in order to save the industry in South Dakota.

Prof. Chamberlain is in good company—Adam Smith made the same blunder in his "Wealth of Nations," as his friend David Hume pointed out when the first edition appeared. The cost of production of "corn" as Hume pointed out, had then no relation to its market price; and it has quite as little today. The repeal of the "corn laws" in Great Britain did not destroy wheat growing in England, as predicted, but it did improve the English farmers' method of wheat culture so that they have largely increased their yields per acre; and go on growing wheat as in the past. South Dakota ought to be able to grow wheat more cheaply than Pennsylvania, yet Pennsylvania farmers compete with South Dakota and make money growing wheat and will continue to do so, for who knows how long. Manifestly the problems of reciprocity cannot be solved by Prof. Chamberlain's method, which is warranted neither by theory nor by experience.

THE CALL.

The thought has been expressed more than once of late that some country shippers seem to be getting into the farmers' habit of "seeing things." Now, it does not necessarily follow that all one does not fully understand is necessarily dangerous, any more than that what one sees is always just what he thinks it is. The farmer has notoriously been of the sort to shy at a bogey. Illogical as it is, he has not been a searcher of the occult, although engaged in an occupation in which the unseen is always an evidence. So, too, the grain dealer has been treating some things as dangerous because he doesn't quite understand them.

The "call" is just now under suspicion. The dealer himself has been and still is striving for uniformity—equalization of "conditions" over more or less wide areas; but when he sees all his bids to arrive from a given market are alike, he jumps to the conclusion that something is wrong. And probably the farmer jumps to the same conclusion when he, too, sees that the prices offered him are always the same on a given day by all buyers in the same rate territory.

The objection to the "call," when it was first put into operation, was that made to their trade by the elevator men, who said (and some still say) that if they were but permitted by the Board rules to do so, they might make different and higher bids than they actually did; but they neglected to say that on not that day only but on every day the bids to arrive are made by the open competition of all buyers on 'change who want to bid for grain to arrive, and the highest price bid must be bid by all that day. It might be that the necessities of an elevator man today might induce him to outbid his neighbors; but that could hardly be the case every day in the year; so the card bids—the call price for grain to arrive—are made daily by the bidding of all those whose necessities as shippers compel them to bid the country the highest price they can afford in order to get the grain needed by them to fill their cash contracts. Such being the case, it is manifest that the "call" effects a more stable and closer bidding to ultimate value, of which the country gets the entire benefit.

There are some other benefits to the country of the call, that would relieve it of all hobgoblin color, if only dealers would but study it closer.

Association work is cumulative and emulative. Illinois and Indiana establish claims bureaus and make equitable arrangements with the carriers, and the shippers in other states and localities take notice and follow along the same profitable lines. Iowa establishes a system of scale examination, and Illinois, after some delay, arrives at the state of mind to follow in the same way. And that was the best piece of work the Illinois association did at Bloomington. If followed up, as it no doubt will be, that resolution should be found to be one of exceeding potential value to the careful country dealer who wants his scale to treat him as honestly as it should treat his patron.

EDITORIAL MENTION

Lightning continues to knock out elevators whose owners don't believe in the efficacy of rod protection.

New carload minimums will be in effect on in Western Trunk Line territory on July 1. Ask for Supplement 3 to Circ. 1-F.

The actual date of issue of this number of the "American Elevator and Grain Trade" is June 17, the number having been held two days to include the proceedings of the Illinois and Indiana conventions.

The Philadelphia grain men have not yet been able to adjust their market's "local requirements" to the Uniform Grade Rules; but the Liverpool grain trade association's embargo may help them smoothe out a kink or two.

The man who has been harping on the "gambling system" of the Chicago Board of Trade should tell us just what kind of a "gamble" is involved in the delivery of about eleven million bushels of May wheat.

The publishers of the "Hay and Grain Reporter," Chicago, are to be congratulated on their "Grain Exchange" number, which contained a large amount of very interesting news matter, which, no doubt, the trade thoroughly appreciated.

June 13, fatal day for the "forestaller," has gone by and Lichtstern is still solvent and said to be master of most of the storage space in Chicago open to wheat, to which the elevator men will make no objections, seeing that an outsider paying carrying charges on 12,000,000 bushels of wheat is rather unusual.

The Council of Exchanges continues to grow in strength, numbers and influence. During the past few days the Peoria Board of Trade and the San Francisco Merchants' Exchange have become members, and their delegates and representatives will take part in the interesting program at Milwaukee on the 28th and 29th inst.

The Richmond, Va., Grain Exchange has adopted the Uniform Grade Rules, moisture and all, and Brown of Tennessee, who inspects in that state by virtue of his position as executor of the pure food and feed acts, has also consented to be guided in his work by them, adding the acidity test requirement when he deems that essential to a final estimation of maize deterioration.

The Iowa seeds dealers, at a meeting at Des Moines a few days ago, commended the action of the state pure seeds law because it has improved the quality of the seeds offered for sale and has also put a curb on the "irresponsible" dealer. Such laws, when properly framed, always do benefit the honest tradesmen, who are always the majority, by taking away the dishonest dealer's opportunity of monopolizing trade with his cheaper, dishonest goods. But so long as the mail-order business continues to hold its own, there must be something more than state pure seed laws, as they offer no impediments to the distribution of adulterated seeds by mail, a fact that dishonest dealers have been only too eager to seize upon and make good use of.

The barley men of two coasts are looking forward to the completion of the Panama canal as to the route by which the barley of the Pacific may find its way to the maltsters of New York. In the meantime barley has been traveling between these coasts *via* England, apparently at a cheaper rate than *via* any transcontinental route.

The editor acknowledges receipt of the old, familiar, and indispensable "Price Current's Statistical Annual" for 1911, compiled by C. B. Murray, Cincinnati; also of the Minneapolis Daily Market Record's Statistical Year Book for 1910, a little different in scope from the Price Current's Annual, but most useful to grain men everywhere.

The Philadelphia Commercial Exchange is not talking much out loud about the rejection by the Liverpool corn trade of their grain inspection certificates; and no one can quite blame them, because it is not nice to be "called down" in that way by foreigners any more than by Southern pure food and feed inspectors rebuking the shipping of sophisticated stuff.

The Texas dealers settled the question of paying drafts in about the only way it could be settled—by dropping it; although the most rea sonable way suggested was that offered by Messrs. Early and Keel, that the seller of the grain should be paid the money due him net at the place where it is due—at home if sold f. o. b.; at destination if sold delivered.

The Illinois grain dealers repeat the demand that everywhere comes up from shippers of "3 or better," that they be given a premium on the "better," or that the building be made specific. The last alternative is the proper one; and dealers can compel such bids to be made if they unite to demand it and refuse to sell on track unless bids are made specific. But it is rather inconsistent to knowingly make a contract to deliver "3 *or better*" and then ask compensation for something different.

The lamentable state of the law of Illinois, which authorizes the collection of agricultural statistics, was a year ago called to the attention of the Illinois Association by Mr. P. S. Goodman, in a paper that probably surprised those who knew there is a law providing that assessors shall collect the data to be compiled by the county clerks and forwarded to Springfield, and had supposed at that time that it was enforced; but Mr. Goodman was rather more than corroborated by Secretary Dickirson of the Board of Agriculture at Bloomington in an address summarized in another place in this number. Mr. Dickerson did more; he showed how hopeless is any effort at reform unless those interested directly in the collection and recording of these statistics unite to create a public sentiment in favor of amending the law to require the assessors as a part of their duty to use the blanks provided and to compel farmers to answer under oath the questions put to them. The refusal of most farmers to answer the questions is founded on an absurd misconception of the uses of the statistics; but that is no reason why the law should not require them to answer in order that the state's statistical records may be made complete and accurate and put on a line with similar work by all first-class civilized governments.

Claim Attorney Bach of the Illinois association repeats again his suggestions of a year ago to shippers who want to protect claims. In a nut-shell they amount to this: Act. from the beginning on the assumption that a loss will occur in the shipment being prepared. The wise man will take every precaution to prevent a leak; he will cooper and line his car with paper or burlap or other cheap lining, but he will make a record of every detail of the loading, so that when, if it so happens, his consignee reports a loss all he has to do is to write up his record of the shipment, send it with the proper affidavit to Mr. Bach, if a member of the Illinois association, and in due time get his money.

In spite of the backward movement on the moisture test question, as shown by the record, the Bloomington meeting of the Illinois Association was one of much accomplishment and genuine pleasure to those present. Although the convention adopted a resolution aimed at the moisture rule in inspecting 3 corn, the test itself came out of the contest more firmly seated in its place as the most dependable device invented in recent years for the use and benefit of the business of a country grain dealer. It removes uncertainty in his business and places him in a position to make money, that he never occupied before the test was conceived of, but it puts it up to him to use it—it won't work itself nor is it proof against carelessness and slovenliness.

Mr. Bonner's address at Indianapolis, on loaning money to farmers by dealers, should not be charged with a professional coloring, Mr. Bonner being a banker, but estimated on the merits of his argument. Loaning money on the credit of a "next crop" is not part of a grain man's business *per se*, and the dealer should not try to break into the banker's territory. True, some grain men do have money to loan, and there can be no objection to their loaning it in the way and to whom they see fit; but fairness to themselves and the trade should dictate the policy of loaning money as a transaction apart from their business as grain dealers, on note with two names or security, real or personal. Such action would relieve the dealer of all necessity of making personal loans as a dealer where it would not be considered desirable, and it would take from the trade a most objectionable and unsafe form of competition.

It is reported that leaky cars are more numerous than for some time past. There is a substantial reason for this. The number of cars in use is increasing and that means that many old cars are coming into action. It so happens that in a period of idleness, no matter how well cared for, cars deteriorate with great rapidity. Moreover, during the last period of depression and car idleness, the railroads did not take care of their idle cars as well as they might have done; few repairs have been made except when they became imperative, and shippers are therfor being served with such derelicts as promise to answer the immediate purpose and such as grain men will consent to use.

The little dinner at Bushnell, Ill., the other day, given to his neighbors and competitors in the grain business by Mr. Geo. Cole, was a happy affair. Mr. Cole inaugurated this sort of practice at Bushnell a year ago, and found that the fellowship feeling created in the trade in that neighborhood by it had made it well worth while to all of them. This year he had about thirty-five guests, all of whom voted the entertainment a delightful one and Mr. Cole a royal host.

Prof. L. H. Bailey, of Cornell, is one of the ablest teachers of agriculture in this country; but he cannot, somehow, as is the manner of the times, get away from the idea that every farmer ought to have a conservator as his "next business friend"; and so he wants the Government to "protect the people." Why not give "the people" credit for some ability to protect themselves? All laws to "protect" somebody from somebody else, who is not particularly dangerous in any event, amount, as a rule, not so much to "protection of the people" as to interference with their commercial liberty.

The elongation of the corn belt this season has been more marked than usual, and it now extends practically from the Canadian (Manitoba) line to the Gulf of Mexico. While corn is grown from the Atlantic almost to the foot of the Rockies, the longitudinal lines of the belt are generally limited to the Scioto river in Ohio to the black plains of Kansas and Nebraska on the west. Within this area the grain business is more distinctively important than elsewhere in the country, showing that after all it is corn and oats, rather than wheat that are the great characteristic crops of the Nation.

Mr. Julian Kuné completes with this number his articles on the Chicago Board of Trade, which have pleasantly revived some, perhaps, forgotten facts of the history of that great institution. It is good testimony to the probity of that great institution and its leaders and chief men, among whom Mr. Kuné moved so many years as one of them, that after more than a generation's connection with the Board he could retire, holding still to his faith in its usefulness to the world of commerce and trade as well as to the producer and consumer of cereal and meat products, and in the essential honesty and equity of its leaders and its methods.

Mr. Forbell, of New York, has told the Indianians how the New York Produce Exchange has solved the discount problem, and it sounds good. There must needs be discounts, for shippers are both unlucky and something else, according to circumstance and necessity; but any arrangement or system that takes away from the discount the appearance of arbitrariness can hardly fail to make friends for the market that has it in operation. The fuss over the moisture out in Illinois is the unscientific and illogical way some shippers have of trying to get away from the apparently arbitrary way in which the discount is taken at Chicago, a market that might, perhaps, take a hint from New York, notwithstanding the fact that where the off-grade stuff is as heavily concentrated as it often is at Chicago, there the discount must necessarily be the heaviest, as that is only the evidence of the price adjustment of supply and demand.

It is hoped and believed that no reader will overlook the eminently readable articles Mr. Willet has been sending us from time to time on cotton and cotton seeds and the legumes of the South. The topics as handled by Mr. Willet have quite an intimate relation to the business of the grain man of the North in more ways than one, pointing, as they have, to agricultural readjustments in the South that may have far-reaching results. Moreover, the articles are so well written and the writer has so firm a command of his facts, that they are very readable, even if one were to fail to see how apposite they are to the outlook of a Northern grain man.

The May wheat deal does not seem to have made any money for the bull side. Indeed the most interesting feature of the history of the affair, as it now appears in reviewing it all from the safe side of the past, is the facility with which the yellow papers both at Chicago and St. Louis shifted the misinformation they were handing out to their readers from the bulls with their millions of profit on May 29 and 31, to the other side, with an equally sizeable deficit on June 1. The fact would seem to be that what the yellow crop reporter doesn't really know about such a campaign when in progress is in inverse proportion to the confidential way in which he assures the public that he does know all about it and is giving them the "inside facts" from day to day. The one substantial fact, however, that does remain is this: That those farmers and shippers who were able to get contract wheat into Chicago in time to unload it were handsomely profited by the deal, as they always are by the bull campaigns that the farmers so invariably howl about as "gambling."

Eugene Funk, in his brief address to the Illinois dealers, confirmed as a corn-breeding expert the fact, admitted in these columns a year or more ago by Prof. Holden, that the big corn of the experts, so popular now with progressive farmers, is not a grain that matures in this climate, and hence is not a dependable article of commerce. Why, then, continue to grow it? Unfortunately, it is profitable to the grower, especially if he be, as to a large degree he should be, a feeder of corn. Its slowly-arriving maturity and its unfitness for winter shelling and movement to consuming markets as corn is no drawback to its use as a feed for cattle and hogs which take on fat with it faster even than they do when fed on matured, hard and dry corn. That being the fact, the dealer is up against it; and he will be, until he forces the farmer who sells corn to grow a kind that will mature and cure and go into commerce dry. Most farmers know well enough in the spring whether they will feed in the fall or winter and how many head. The dealer may, therefore, force them to plant accordingly, by paying them prices based on the quality of the corn they sell and no more. As Mr. Hubbard says, the only way to teach a man anything in trade is to go right straight at his pocket-book. So dealers never will get control of this moisture trouble until they abandon their present cowardly position of non-interference and adopt a policy that will force the growing of a commercial type of corn. And in doing that they will be doing the public also a substantial service.

Daniel McAlister has revived on p. 659, some interesting notes of the oldest grain men's association in the country—the Ohio, which will hold its 30th annual meeting on June 21 and 22. A glance over the records of the meetings of those old days serves as a reminder of the fact that eternal vigilance is the price of more things than liberty. Some of the live topics then are still live wires, different today only in degree. These trade problems seem like dead weights, sometimes, that no effort may move permanently go out of one's way to forget; yet we do find that by "keeping everlastingly at it" some of the annoyances and impediments of trade and commerce may be gotten rid of after many days, only, perhaps, to find that others unknown in the past arise to take their places. It is a necessary condition of a progressive civilization that our wants never cease; may we not add also, that should our trade problems all cease to trouble progress also would come to an end and life and trade alike become stagnant, tasteless and morally profitless?

Those who think the last word has been said on inspection, even in the face of no "national inspection," are recommended to read the address of Hon. Mr. Dowling before the Indiana dealers on the operation of the pure food act in its relations to whole grain. It has been the belief of this paper for a considerable time, watching the actions of the pure food officials of the Agricultural Department, that while Senator McCumber and his fallacious national inspection bill will never arrive, yet practical Government control over grain in interstate commerce has already been achieved and in a way not contemplated by either the makers of the pure food act or the grain trade. As the Government in this fight for such control has already won out in the Hall-Baker case, it is not likely to let loose its grip, more particularly because, if the Hall-Baker decision is permitted to stand, it accomplishes all that the millers ask for in the protection of wheat against sophistication and all the corn millers and the feeders of corn and oats in the South ask for the estimation of corn, oats and corn products. There remains, then, in this unexpected development of a system of examination (not "inspection") of grain by the pure food inspectors, the creation of Government standards therefor; and we have had the statement made to us that next winter will see a bill for that purpose introduced in Congress. Even if no bill appears then, there is nothing to prevent the Agricultural Department from making such standards by regulation as it pleases. And when the Department does this, the moisture content of 3 corn, we may be sure, will not be put at 19.25%; indeed, it has been said on excellent authority that the limit will not exceed 17%.

TRADE NOTES

The National Gas and Gasoline Engine Trades Association will meet at Hotel Pontchartrain, Detroit, Mich., June 20-23, a program of unusual interest will be given and a number of entertainments and water and land trips will help make the convention a success.

The Knickerbocker Company of Jackson, Mich., has just issued a fine new booklet entitled "Dust Collectors." It contains descriptions of the "New Cyclone 1905," the "Morse Rarefied" and the "Turret Cyclone," handsomely illustrated in two colors and is well worth having.

Moulton & Evans, contractors of Minneapolis, Minn., have been awarded the contract for building a storage elevator of 200,000 bushels' capacity for the Crowell Elevator Company at Omaha, Neb. The building is now under construction and will be completed in time for the new crop.

The list is constantly growing of users of the Automatic Dump Controller, made and sold by L. J. McMillin of Indianapolis, Ind. Some elevator owners are users of as many as five of these machines which goes to show their convenience. They have become a necessity today in the equipment of a modern elevator.

An illustration of the S. Howes Co.'s "Eureka" Sample Taking Machine is shown on their June calendar. The machine, manufactured by this well known Silver Creek, N. Y., house is for taking samples of flour or feed automatically every hour or more if desired. Its convenience in the elevator or mill is apparent and it has proved a useful adjunct in many plants, to the machinery equipment.

The latest Bulletin from the Hess Warming & Ventilating Co. of the Tacoma Building, Chicago, illustrates and describes the Hess Cold Air Conditioner and Cooler for all kinds of grain or seeds. It renovates and preserves grain, arrests heating and fermentation and makes cool and sweet any grain treated by it, one of its special features is its simplicity. It goes together without trouble and any millwright or handy man can set it up. It requires no expert knowledge or skill to operate it.

A neat little folder has been published showing the Revolving screens manufactured by the Weller Mfg. Co. of Chicago. This firm builds screens of every description for mines, starch works, cement plants, oil mills, rock crushers, coal, sand, gravel, etc. A part of the folder also calls attention to their perforated metal suitable for cottonseed oil mills, glucose and sugar works, linseed oil mills, rice mills and breweries and malt houses. The same quality of workmanship is put into these machines as in their well known Weller-made lines of elevating, conveying and power transmitting machinery.

Some 33 illustrations of various machines of the Sidney Line appear on a wall hanger just issued by the Philip Smith Mfg. Co. of Sidney, Ohio. They include such popular machines as the Sidney Combined Corn Sheller and Cleaner, Sidney Revolving Screen Corn Cleaner, Sidney Chain Dry Feeder style H., Sidney Safety Man-lift, Sidney Dustless Warehouse and Elevator Separator, etc. The list includes boots, spouts of different construction and will be useful to the grain elevator man as a glance will show the style and quality of so many machines. Every machine or article manufactured by us, the hanger states, has our guarantee.

Among the firms which had attractive exhibits at the Industrial Exposition in connection with the annual meeting of the Fraternity of Operative Millers of America, held at Detroit, Mich., June 5-10, were, The Huntley Mfg. Co. of Silver Creek, N. Y.; Invincible Grain Cleaner Co., Silver Creek, N. Y.; Richardson Scale Co., New York City; Sprout, Waldron & Co., Muncy, Pa.; The American Machinery Co., Port Huron, Mich.; S. Howes Co., Silver Creek, N. Y.; Richmond Mfg. Co., Lockport, N. Y.; Strong-Scott Mfg. Co., Minneapolis, Minn.; Barnard & Leas Mfg. Co., Moline, Ill.; Nordyke & Marmon Co., Indianapolis, Ind.; Fairbanks, Morse & Co., Chicago, Ill.; The Wolf Co., Chambersburg, Pa.; Allis-Chalmers Co., Milwaukee, Wis.

[For the "American Elevator & Grain Trade."]

MOIST CORN DANGERS AND THE LIVERPOOL EMBARGO.

EDWARD R. SIEWERS.

The "Liverpool Grain Embargo" and the ban placed upon all Philadelphia inspection certificates of corn, which is still puzzling the Philadelphia Commercial Exchange, the grain men, the railroad authorities, the steamship officials, the financial companies and leading trade organizations and business concerns, is now in special charge of a strong committee of some of the ablest and strongest members of this association; and what the fates will decree will be known later on, while for a month or more the foreign blockade at this port has been as effective and complete in the corn line as was ever maintained by the United States government against the southern ports of entry during the darkest days of the great Civil war. And now comes the information from abroad that satisfactory corn shipments have not been received for some time from any of the Atlantic seaboard terminals.

Now this state of affairs, which seems to be widespread and a matter of the most dire importance, has raised the almost unanimous, and exceedingly interesting inquiry in many grain circles throughout the East, is the faulty condition increasing or lessening of Western corn that reaches Philadelphia at all seasons of the year, and particularly in the winter and early spring and approaching the beginning of "the good old summer time," and is the trouble with bad, unfit, or moist corn a continuing one, and is it possible to ascertain just where the difficulty originates and when is it at its height?

Several things are universally conceded, towit, that the corn yield was a big one of the season of 1910; that the arrivals, as they began coming in from the West, as to general appearances, looked 'good' to the average and experienced grain man, though nearly all agree that moisture in the corn as developed later on was unusually great; that, besides the Western corn shipments arrived much earlier than in former years.

The opinion of some of the most experienced and shrewdest grain experts in this vicinity, whose authority in such matters was ever held high, both at home and abroad, leads to the belief that corn conditions at Philadelphia normally are and were about the same as elsewhere throughout the East, but that export corn has not been so carefully looked after as heretofore, and that for some reason the same supervision has not been quite so rigid; and those in charge, from the grain committee to the inspectors, including the receivers and exporters, have not drawn the lines as closely as might have been done to prevent any possible complaint from European buyers as to the condition of corn arriving at the foreign ports during the uncertain and trying period of the germinating season.

Faulty corn may at any time be expected in shipments that reach the Eastern terminals from the West from May 15 up to July 15. Just at this point let it be said that it is the growing belief among some of the "wise men" here, that the seed corn selection and plantings of recent years, with the eyes of the farmers dazzled with the big specimens of fancy show corn that has been handed out in the corn belt as high as a dollar per cob, has had much to do with increasing moisture conditions; for they say the larger the grain of corn the more moisture it contains; and they aver that the plain and modest old style corn, with a long, thin berry, not only matured earlier as a rule but certainly dried out quicker; and there was scarcely any difficulty on complaint by foreign receivers, when this character of corn came in from Nebraska, Kansas and Iowa during former years, and crossed the ocean for the export trade. Now, if this is so, would it he well to go back to the old-time seed selections, or would it be considered as taking a progressive step backward, when new ideas and ideals prevail and are regarded as the "proper caper?" The old "Smoke-house" apple, and the Rambo, and the Russet were the great keeping apples; but outside of the Baldwin and one or two other varieties, all of the new comers are extremely fancy, high colored and of good size, but must be handled very gingerly, and when exposed soon come to naught. Might it be so with the corn as with some new fangled varieties of potatoes that decay often from the inside under any conditions?

The moisture condition of corn moving through Philadelphia during the winter is regulated by the temperature, which is more or less cool, but when the grain is exposed to higher temperatures the dampness is soon attracted to the outside of the kernels and increases unless properly handled and the temperature reduced without delay to approach the normal. It is a well known fact that when warm weather approaches all nature is on the sprouting bench, and the germination of corn is greatly facilitated, which seems to be the prevailing basic cause for bad turn-outs of shipments of corn for export during the germinating season, and these peculiar conditions at times are apt to mislead the judgment of the most expert.

In bygone days the inspecting authority who graded grain, and especially corn, did not have the facilities that are now afforded by the moisture testing apparatus to assist him in forming his judgment as to the keeping and carrying qualities of corn that was to be shipped abroad from Philadelphia, or even to other Eastern ports, and was forced to depend upon the correctness of his honest and painstaking decision, on the skill and knowledge of grain derived from his years of experience; and it would seem that notwithstanding the most modern appliances for moisture testing are now available, more complaints are made against the export shipping markets than ever, of the unsatisfactory condition of corn oeing cargoed from this port. Surely there must be some definite and satisfactory reason for these unfortunate changes of conditions. Either the various commercial bodies have been of late too lax or derelict in keeping up the standards they have adopted for the guidance of the inspection department, or there has been a very material change by Nature, unknown to the human mind, in the maturing of the corn crop, that offsets the better judgment of the experts who have for years made a specialty of watching crop maturing conditions.

When corn was carried from Philadelphia on sailing vessels, shipments started in December and virtually not the least attention was paid to the germinating period. It was sold as 'sail" mixed, white or yellow corn, and when loaded in the vessels it was supposed to be able to stand a voyage of from ten to ninety days, inasmuch as sailing craft had no stipulated time for arrival at foreign ports. Later on, when steamships began to carry grain, the "steamer" grade was adopted, which was corn slightly damp and, in judgment of the inspector, suitable to endure a twenty-five days' voyage, if necessary, and arrive on the other side of the water in acceptable condition. About that time the grades were made "sail corn" and No. 2 corn, and this grade was supposed to carry well either by sailing vessel or steamship and arrive in Europe in satisfactory condition, and was invariably sold without recourse under Philadelphia and other seaboard port certificates, the former being regarded as second to none in standard and integrity; and, therefore, it seems extremely strange and almost unaccountable that No. 2 corn, should, with the increased speed and better accommodations of steamships, arrive in the condition that the foreign ouyers complain of.

It is indeed a subject of mystery to all those who feel that they are in a position to know the true conditions as they actually exist, for from their past experience corn loaded at any of the Atlantic ports for foreign markets should be expected to reach Europe in good condition; and with the fast going freight steamers of the present day, loading corn under similar conditions as to grade, it certainly is a surprising piece of news that cargoes of corn have been arriving from Philadelphia in such bad order.

Some years ago, under the old inspection system, a good sized cargo of corn was loaded here about the middle of May, right in the midst of the usual germinating period, and it was shipped to Cairo, Egypt, entering the tropics in the hottest of weather and was reported by the foreign receivers as having arrived in first class condition. This inquiry is now being daily made, why were former Philadelphia inspection certificates regarded so highly, that they were practically an insurance on the bill of exchange?

Since this embargo at Liverpool, every bushel of grain, and corn in particular, going from Philadelphia for export, will be scanned more critically than ever, when it reaches the other side of the Atlantic, upon the principle and time worn adage of "once detected, always suspected," even if it could be said of the Commercial Exchange, as of the English ruler, that "the king can do no wrong"; and even though things in dispute are in the end adjusted by the authorities, it will be a long time before absolute confidence will be entirely restored in relation to the standing of Philadelphia grain inspection certificates.

There is a general feeling here, as well as at all of the terminal grain markets of the East, that the coming grain conventions will take up this matter of unsatisfactory grain and corn conditions with relation to the shippers, exporters and receivers, as well as the farmers who grow the corn, and some profitable and interesting development may result therefrom. As it now is, the great corn exporting trade of this country, which has always been its boast and pride ever since that important food product ruled as king among the cereals, has gradually grown less, and through circumstances which have occurred recently, is threatened with a temporary or partial extinction; and it behooves every grain man throughout the land to be up and doing and use his best efforts to stay the hand of any further embargoes.

EXPORTS AND IMPORTS.

The following is a statement of the exports and imports of various cereals, seeds, etc., for the month of April, 1911, and for the ten months ending with April, 1911, as reported by the Bureau of Statistics, Department of Commerce and Labor (quantities only unless otherwise stated):

ARTICLES.	April, 1911.		TEN MONTHS, ENDING MARCH	
	1910	1911	1910	1911
Exports—				
Barley, bu.	11.217	334,019	4,169,037	9,138,359
Buckwheat, bu	....	23	155,037	216
Corn, bu	3,627,898	5,373,553	32,674,279	55,396,911
Corn Meal, bbls	27,721	51,981	274,863	392,778
Oats, bu	149,979	175,485	1,172,713	1,328,091
Oatmeal, lbs.	669,375	3,826,325	14,427,885	25,516,185
Rice, lbs	1,334,329	3,298,761	3,484,819	10,275,146
Rye, bu.	16,765	96	219,756	2,543
Rye Flour, bbls	166	391	3,071	5,666
Wheat, bu.	2,953,131	1,315,085	43,507,565	21,741,986
Wheat Flour, bbls	828,330	872,553	7,990,343	8,390,999
Bran, Millfeed, etc., tons	3,112	6,439	43,720	47,603
Dried Grains, etc. tons	6,212	7,884	50,335	57,487
Rice, bran, meal, etc. lbs.	254,550	67,400	19,433,029	14,028,081
Total Breadstuffs	$8,925,435	$9,990,353	$120,299,938	$106,995,297
Glucose and Grape Sugar, lbs	12,620,460	17,876,754	120,421,657	154,772,531
Hay, tons	3,130	3,880	47,603	46,307
Oil Cake and Oil-Cake Meal:—				
Corn, lbs.	2,438,728	7,192,729	39,391,409	68,793,346
Cotton Seed	48,211,333	75,339,608	567,435,937	706,682,902
Flaxseed or Linseed lbs.	62,520,443	43,915,004	542,286,317	479,276,122
Vegetable Oils:—				
Corn, lbs.	566,756	2,630,384	9,611,265	19,383,984
Cotton Seed, lbs	19,367,283	29,674,364	192,450,148	182,786,328
Linseed, gals	9,434	21,506	192,844	142,640
Clover Seed, lbs	204,187	105,439	6,787,685	4,291,895
Cotton Seed, lbs.	6,132,998	231,235	23,845,875	9,653,207
Flax Seed, bu.	331	55	65,118	445
Timothy Seed, lbs	2,902,827	289,952	26,391,863	9,207,083
Other Grass Seed, val.	$18,451	$20,627	$585,002	$312,176
Beans, etc., bu.	20,534	18,998	325,535	255,405
Imports—				
Oats, bu.	40,006	7,941	883,632	101,783
Wheat, bu.	2,934	569	42,276	508,139
Wheat Flour, bbls	15,952	2,999	113,620	124,504
Rice, lbs.	10,081,340	9,467,869	70,558,607	63,684,603
Rice, Flour, Meal, etc. lbs.	13,450,553	10,198,629	115,041,057	107,097,944
Castor Beans, bu	26,902	34,793	622,672	473,815
Clover Seed, lbs	1,821,435	875,398	12,633,486	23,887,249
Flax Seed, bu.	1,395,247	751,219	3,148,836	8,211,593
Beans, etc., bu	83,692	48,748	921,434	937,478

EXPORTS OF FOREIGN MERCHANDISE.

Oats, bus.	5,794	....	215,436	4
Rice, lbs.	602,421	631,434	6,792,597	4,908,749
Rice Flour, lbs.	....	....	10,470	27,290
Wheat, bus.	....	....	12,918	1,361
Clover Seed, lbs	....	....	....	93,862
Other Seeds, value	$73	$1,407	$6,702	$7,587
Beans, bus	1,569	1,965	61,839	11,355

NEW ORLEANS — Reported by H. S. Herring, Secretary of the Board of Trade.

Wheat, bushels	65,000	5,000	24,674	....
Corn, bushels	443,333	695,000	220,612	315,003
Oats, bushels	179,000	161,000	25,984	1,309
Hay, tons	905	2,325	37	67
Flour, bbls	135,783	65,250	69,109	36,122

RECEIPTS AND SHIPMENTS.

Following are the receipts and shipments of grain etc., at leading receiving and shipping points in the United States for the month of May, 1911:

BALTIMORE—Reported by James B. Hessong, Secretary of the Chamber of Commerce.

Articles	Receipts		Shipments	
	1911	1910	1911	1910
Wheat, bushels	1,221,728	926,642	633,848	882,879
Corn, bushels	367,350	256,833	347,390	248,245
Oats, bushels	333,599	205,377	40	140
Barley, bushels	2,500	....	....	....
Rye, bushels	11,303	2,549	....	....
Timothy Seed, bus	677	....	....	820
Clover Seed, bus	....	503	....	....
Hay, tons	7,600	4,542	1,395	1,002
Flour, barrels	204,974	160,755	76,648	70,126

Mr. Wm. B. McGroarty, Agent Southern Railway, was elected to membership. Certificate in name of Mr. Geo. R. Needham was transferred.

BOSTON—Reported by James A. McKibben, Secretary of the Chamber of Commerce.

Flour, barrels	135,938	139,724	50,944	53,724
Wheat, bushels	1,107,409	949,425	874,746	765,208
Corn, bushels	941,985	370,221	568,195	483,964
Oats, bushels	380,670	427,680	50,440	32,333
Rye, bushels	2,482	2,000	....	....
Barley, bushels	3,190	37,927	16,765	8,519
Flax Seed, bushels	....	700	....	....
Peas, bushels	1,374	5,171	....	....
Millfeed, tons	733	2,295	52	177
Corn Meal, barrels	2,330	1,915	1,845	206
Oat Meal, cases	6,534	24,016	1,770	12,525
Oat Meal, sacks	3,215	11,220	5,310	10,040
Hay, tons	11,330	9,930	2,144	962

BUFFALO—Reported by Secretary of the Chamber of Commerce. From opening of navigation to June 1.

Wheat, bushels	10,999,000	9,076,000	....	....
Corn, bushels	7,915,000	3,003,000	....	....
Oats, bushels	1,465,000	2,534,000	....	....
Barley, bushels	1,349,000	1,902,000	....	....
Rye, bushels	....	25,000	....	....
Other Grass Seeds, lbs	....	....	....	....
Flax Seed, bushels	102,404	892,000	....	....
Flour, barrels	709,730	1,015,116	....	....

CHICAGO—Reported by George F. Stone, Secretary of the Board of Trade.

Wheat, bushels	3,582,000	2,099,600	1,571,700	453,600
Corn, bushels	9,054,200	3,007,800	9,128,425	6,043,500
Oats, bushels	8,873,500	6,430,800	8,284,700	6,286,600
Barley, bushels	1,243,600	1,248,800	347,700	422,500
Rye, bushels	57,500	88,000	15,000	38,500
Timothy Seed, lbs.	106,100	645,200	159,100	427,300
Clover Seed, lbs	363,600	1,800	185,300	....
Other Grass Seeds, lbs.	463,000	412,900	962,400	1,127,500
Flax Seed, bushels	41,400	74,000	11,200	11,450
Broom Corn, lbs.	909,500	570,600	1,004,600	398,100
Hay, tons	20,937	24,565	2,147	4,209
Flour, barrels	443,376	490,069	500,610	457,425

CINCINNATI—Reported by W. C. Culkins, Superintendent of the Chamber of Commerce.

Wheat, bushels	344,320	249,104	327,718	218,214
Corn, bushels	1,068,762	765,972	695,704	659,165
Oats, bushels	733,274	509,620	537,534	398,990
Barley, bushels	5,000	13,000	260	1,048
Malt, bushels	124,005	174,040	44,540	49,500
Rye, bushels	41,202	41,172	25,372	11,060
Timothy Seed, lbs	12	102	724	1,513
Clover Seed, lbs	225	1,369	1,145	1,951
Other Grass Seed, lbs	8,573	6,938	4,922	6,541
Hay, tons	11,883	13,611	8,245	13,615
Flour, bbls	163,080	85,712	78,575	60,686

CLEVELAND—Reported by M. A. Havens, Secretary of the Chamber of Commerce.

Wheat, bushels	48,317	....	22,999	....
Corn, bushels	313,305	....	210,312	....
Oats, bushels	398,328	....	180,477	....
Barley, bushels	42	....	....	....
Rye, bushels	250	....	....	....
Flax Seed, bushels	....	....	....	....
Hay, tons	6,728	....	479	....
Flour, bbls	49,254	....	7,976	....

Rec'd by Lake, May—Corn, 189,000; oats, 1,760,000; wheat, 100,000.

DETROIT—Reported by F. W. Waring, Secretary of the Board of Trade.

Wheat, bushels	154,591	31,439	10,286	6,685
Corn, bushels	350,652	155,370	222,345	84,153
Oats, bushels	264,189	216,043	8,125	18,675
Barley, bushels	18,283	32,609	1,074	1,393
Rye, bushels	5,654	4,645	3,911	....
Flour, barrels	21,805	23,895	18,404	15,124

DULUTH—Reported by Chas. F. MacDonald, Secretary of the Board of Trade.

Wheat, bushels	1,096,577	950,774	2,901,972	4,003,940
Corn, bushels	165,229	90,460	570,665	35,000
Oats, bushels	414,380	588,069	645,346	1,772,311
Barley, bushels	13,401	704,326	147,572	634,624
Rye, bushels	885	17,874	1,175	21,000
Flax Seed, bushels	17,664	148,195	85,457	165,932
Flour, bbls	302,550	365,750	....	....
Flour Production	60,380	50,975	357,485	387,406

KANSAS CITY, MO.—Reported by E. D. Bigelow, Secretary of Board of Trade.

Wheat, bushels	1,274,400	1,073,600	2,120,400	1,196,800
Corn, bushels	1,386,000	1,164,950	1,732,400	1,545,600
Oats, bushels	467,500	307,500	268,600	369,000
Barley, bushels	21,000	4,400	25,200	6,600
Rye, bushels	7,700	2,200	4,400	3,300
Kaffir Corn, lbs.	4,000,000	1,500,000	3,600,000	....
Flax Seed, bushels	....	....	....	....
Bran, tons	980	640	5,480	6,660
Hay, tons	17,712	17,772	9,660	5,064
Flour, barrels	12,750	5,000	95,750	151,250

MILWAUKEE—Reported by H. A. Plumb, Secretary of the Chamber of Commerce.

Wheat, bushels	710,670	206,690	792,270	62,992
Corn, bushels	475,730	248,600	405,950	736,810
Oats, bushels	1,214,330	687,650	1,056,126	804,575
Barley, bushels	763,100	695,500	543,842	275,003
Rye, bushels	94,800	69,870	44,720	32,220
Flax Seed, bushels	....	15,600	....	10,800
Hay, tons	3,838	2,170	792	24
Flour, bbls	280,390	269,660	278,696	269,306

MONTREAL, QUEBEC, CANADA—Reported by George Hadrill, Secretary of the Board of Trade.

Wheat, bushels	4,733,191	5,223,626	2,872,776	2,811,388
Corn, bushels	1,660,658	309,459	808,229	171,505
Oats, bushels	2,215,998	1,988,021	1,188,080	971,948
Barley, bushels	113,887	122,050	21,484	17,815
Rye, bushels	....	....	....	....
Flax Seed, bushels	51,305	90,347	....	47,002
Flour, bbls	339,829	97,593	294,769	105,536

MINNEAPOLIS—Reported by John G. McHugh, Secretary of the Chamber of Commerce.

Articles	Receipts		Shipments	
	1911	1910	1911	1910
Wheat, bushels	4,995,440	4,395,010	2,045,940	1,455,580
Corn, bushels	595,600	648,770	277,940	360,270
Oats, bushels	719,940	735,860	1,128,040	1,155,150
Barley, bushels	859,280	1,199,710	890,270	1,289,660
Rye, bushels	80,500	81,600	59,500	124,120
Flax Seed, bushels	118,270	232,140	78,420	148,710
Hay, tons	5,040	2,270	1,280	870
Flour, bbls	29,026	22,720	1,154,928	1,109,569

NEW YORK—Reported by H. Heinzer, Statistician of the Produce Exchange.

Wheat, bushels	2,470,800	1,366,500	2,251,074	1,084,586
Corn, bushels	1,376,725	275,025	1,110,821	229,958
Oats, bushels	2,211,250	1,695,275	84,681	42,840
Barley, bushels	344,276	183,600	....	111,230
Rye, bushels	20,550	11,500	....	....
Timothy Seed, lbs } Clover Seed, lbs } Other Grass Seed, lbs }	bgs. 1,602	.... bgs. 2,406	.... bgs. 638	bgs. 1,851 " 688 ....
Flax Seed bushels	586,078	754,730	....	....
Hay, tons	26,628	28,022	b'ls 2,367	b'ls 3,537
Flour, bbls	743,000	584,508	351,182	223,464

OMAHA—Reported by F. P. Manchester, Secretary of the Omaha Grain Exchange.

Wheat, bushels	870,000	150,000	794,000	486,000
Corn, bushels	2,486,400	1,756,700	2,030,000	1,653,000
Oats, bushels	583,100	659,200	747,000	684,000
Barley bushels	172,200	42,000	33,000	4,000
Rye, bushels	4,400	....	2,000	4,000

PEORIA—Reported by John R. Lofgren, Secretary of the Board of Trade.

Wheat, bushels	75,198	38,000	78,434	14,000
Corn, bushels	1,493,056	1,130,727	980,044	857,528
Oats, bushels	885,893	1,141,200	1,070,791	1,356,200
Barley, bushels	142,600	184,400	47,445	44,658
Rye, bushels	13,200	23,100	3,384	13,529
Mill Feed, tons	2,771	2,995	6,507	4,281
Spirits and Liquors, bbls	12,437	13,291	44,246	44,801
Syrups and Glucose, bbls	550	11,000	5,560	7,455
Seeds, lbs	60,000	150,000	55,000	150,000
Broom Corn, lbs	15,000	....	150,000	75,000
Hay, tons	2,781	3,090	1,170	1,128
Flour, bbls	188,200	230,750	189,637	208,840

PHILADELPHIA—Reported by Frank E. Marshall, Secretary of the Commercial Exchange.

Wheat, bushels	1,388,385	1,245,865	1,114,768	1,005,471
Corn, bushels	128,631	107,862	....	16,965
Oats, bushels	703,331	427,926	....	....
Barley, bushels	1,000	23,000	....	....
Rye, bushels	1,600	1,600	....	....
Timothy Seed, bags	....	....	....	....
Clover Seed, bags	....	822	....	....
Other Grass Seeds, bags	....	....	....	....
Flax Seed, bushels	....	47,200	....	....
Hay, tons	7,271	6,688	....	....
Flour, bbls	297,782	189,041	95,763	70,986

SAN FRANCISCO—Reported by Wm. B. Downes, Statistician of the Merchants' Exchange.

Wheat, centals	308,066	....	890	....
Corn, centals	5,282	....	661	....
Oats, centals	52,242	....	235	....
Barley, centals	443,111	....	182,365	....
Rye, centals	2,060	....	....	....
Broom Corn, bales	....	....	....	....
Hay, tons	12,776	....	2,357	....
Flour, bbls	86,750	....	22,408	....

ST. LOUIS—Reported by George H. Morgan, Secretary of the Merchants' Exchange.

Wheat, bushels	914,100	583,000	746,705	796,045
" bags	3,305	477	....	300
Corn, bushels	2,502,000	2,289,100	1,190,780	1,431,470
" bags	4,548	1,505	10,980	10,555
Oats, bushels	1,611,600	1,792,000	904,880	981,045
" bags	4,250	66	20,555	26,650
Barley, bushels	21,000	14,300	12,320	6,300
" bags	12	....	....	....
Rye, bushels	12,000	13,000	13,370	17,050
" bags	52	....	....	....
Hay, tons	18,819	13,609	11,025	4,865
Flour, barrels	208,665	188,250	214,050	182,500

TOLEDO—Reported by Archibald Gassaway, Secretary of the Produce Exchange.

Wheat, bushels	94,000	223,000	355,200	141,000
Corn, bushels	424,600	348,650	174,400	292,600
Oats, bushels	258,000	177,000	344,500	175,800
Barley, bushels	....	....	....	....
Rye, bushels	....	8,000	....	6,600
Clover Seed, bags	340	515	1,240	191

RECEIPTS OF WHEAT AT PRIMARY MARKETS.

Receipts of wheat at winter and spring grain markets for 49 weeks, since June, with comparisons, in bushels, compiled by the Cincinnati Price Current:

	1911	1910
St. Louis	19,133,000	21,846,000
Toledo	4,480,000	4,349,000
Detroit	2,046,000	2,157,000
Kansas City	37,261,000	35,543,000
Winter Wheat	62,920,000	63,895,000
Chicago	28,116,000	27,518,000
Milwaukee	9,647,000	8,455,000
Minneapolis	86,192,000	90,896,000
Duluth	27,255,000	57,346,000
Spring wheat	151,210,000	184,215,000
Aggregate 49 weeks	214,130,000	248,110,000

Total receipts of winter and spring wheat at primary markets 49 weeks since June, 1910, with comparisons.

	Winter	Spring	Total
1910-11	62,920,000	151,210,000	214,130,000
1909-10	63,895,000	184,215,000	248,110,000
1908-09	61,213,000	162,944,000	224,157,000
1907-08	56,357,000	144,891,000	201,248,000
1906-07	63,030,000	173,109,000	236,139,000

ELEVATOR AND GRAIN NEWS

ILLINOIS.

John Lieb & Son are erecting an elevator at Edgewood, Ill.

An elevator will be erected at Marengo, Ill., by J. C. Hattendorf.

Claudon Brothers are remodeling their grain office at Ludlow, Ill.

F. G. Supple is rebuilding his elevator at Ogden, Ill., which burned last March.

The proposition of erecting another elevator at Chadwick, Ill., is being agitated.

The Yuton Grain Co. of Yuton, Ill., has increased its capital stock from $4,000 to $6,000.

The A. L. Bartlett Co. will rebuild its elevator at Rockford, Ill., which was destroyed by fire.

The Neola Elevator Co. has purchased a new gasoline engine for its elevator at Stoner, Ill.

The new elevator of Shearer & Miller at Sibley, Ill., was recently completed and put in operation.

Work has been begun on the $7,000 improvement to be made on the farmers elevator at Minonk, Ill.

The Farmers' Elevator at New Holland, Ill., has been leased by J. A. McCreery for the coming year.

A small addition has been built to the office of the elevator of the Davis Grain Co. at Laura, Ill.

John Karcher & Son have taken over the grain and coal business of Karcher & Jackson at Herscher, Ill.

Horton Brothers & Co. have installed a new automatic grain weigher in their elevator at Tolono, Ill.

Ed. Pendelton recently sold his elevator at Hersman, Ill., to Montgomery, Morris & Means of that place.

A concrete grain elevator will be erected at Springfield, Ill., by Frank Weidlocker, on the site of the old Enos property.

Rich & Blankenbaker are overhauling their elevator at Sidney, Ill. A new shipping room and concrete engine room have been built.

W. J. Rosenberger has opened the elevator of the Pinckneyville Milling Co. at Pinckneyville, Ill., and will do business there during the coming season.

The Meredosia Farmers' Grain Co. of Meredosia, Ill., has increased its capital stock from $10,000 to $20,000, for the purpose of erecting a new elevator.

The De Long Brothers' Elevator at Blue Ridge, Ill., has been torn down and a new one is being erected. The new structure will be larger than the old one.

The Carhart, Harwood, Code Co. of Chicago, has been incorporated with a capital stock of $40,000, by George T. Carhart, Arthur N. Harwood and Daniel J. Phenix.

Secretary S. W. Strong, of the Illinois Grain Dealers' Association, reports that Stice & Sand succeed S. A. Hendee, at Swan Creek, and H. E. Jewell succeeds Surface & Ensign at Magnolia.

The Winchester Farmers' Elevator & Mercantile Co. of Winchester, Ill., has been incorporated with a capital stock of $10,000 by James T. Wilson, Claude Thomas and Ornsby Dawson.

A new elevator will be erected at Middletown, Ill., by the Middletown Grain Co. on the site of the one recently burned. An insurance of $6,000 was carried on the building and $1,000 on the grain. The total loss was $9,500. The officers of the company are: S. R. Kirby, president; Ed. Anderson, secretary and Charles Zinsmeister, manager.

The Barry Milling & Grain Co. of Barry, Ill., has sold its property, including the grounds, the railroad track, the elevator site, the office building and the Hadley Elevator, to the M. D. King Milling Co. for a consideration of $4,000. The new owners will not rebuild the mill but will put up an elevator.

MINNESOTA AND WISCONSIN.

A new elevator is proposed for New Prairie, Minn.

A. Brooks has opened an elevator at Varco, Minn.

T. S. Chittenden & Co., are planning to erect an elevator at Ripon, Wis.

The Benson Grain Co. of Hills, Minn., has opened its elevator for business.

A new elevator will be erected by the Cargill Elevator Co. at Hawick, Minn.

Charles Scleicker is installing new machinery in his elevator at Millville, Minn.

The Hunting Elevator at Mankato, Minn., is being repaired and a new building erected.

S. S. Smith & Son, who have been in the grain and feed business at Excelsior, Minn., for a number of years, have erected a six-bin grain elevator on the site of the old M. & St. L. Round House at that place.

The farmers have organized a company and purchased the Matson Elevator at Sherburn, Minn.

A meeting of those who had subscribed stock for the new farmers' elevator at Clarkfield, Minn., was held recently.

The Van Dusen Co. intends to tear down the old elevator at Canby, Minn., and erect a modern 50,000-bushel house.

The Cargill Elevator Co. will tear down its elevator at Northtown, Minn., and build a new one in time for this year's crop.

The big elevators of the Peavey Grain Co. of Superior, Wis., situated in the east and west ends of the city, will be opened August 1.

The Farmers' Elevator Co. of Spicer, Minn., has been organized with a capital stock of $20,000 and will probably build a new hollow brick elevator.

A 40,000 bushel elevator will be erected at Clearbrook, Minn., by the farmers on a co-operative basis. C. K. Bergland is president and Alfred Henderson, secretary.

The Oconto Farmers' Equity Produce Company of Oconto Falls, Wis., has been incorporated by Robert Hall, A. J. Schoenbeck and Frank Nevenhausen, with a capital stock of $2,500.

H. J. Waddell of Aberdeen, S. D., and Ralph Waddell of Danville have rented the Spaulding Elevator at Mapleton, Minn., and will do business under the name of Waddell Brothers.

The Interstate Grain Co. of Minneapolis, Minn., has been incorporated with a capital stock of $3,000,000, by O. S. Ostrom, C. S. Hulbert, H. K. Halverson, G. W. Sherwood and George E. Skinner.

Linzay Pankake has purchased the elevator of the New London Milling Co., at Dassel, Minn., for a consideration of $4,000. Mr. Pankake has been local agent for the house for the past thirteen years.

The Wirtz Grain Co., a new concern at Milwaukee, Wis., has engaged in the grain and feed business with offices in the Mitchell Bldg. A. C. Wirtz, formerly connected with the Wissbeck-Grunwald Co., is the head of the new firm.

OHIO, INDIANA AND MICHIGAN.

The Twining Gleaner Elevator Co. of Bay City, Mich., is now ready for business.

A grain and bean elevator will be erected at Byron, Mich., in the near future.

The Stiefel Grain Co. of Albion, Ind., is putting an unloading dump in its elevator.

Jones & Sheldron have purchased the plant of the Pierce Elevator Co. at Daleville, Ind.

The new elevator of the Farmers' Grain & Feed Co. of Grelton, Ohio, was completed early in June.

J. J. Jasper is putting up an elevator at Madison, Ind., which will have a capacity of 10,000 bushels.

The new elevator at Deshler, Ohio, will be owned and operated by the Wadsworth Feed Co. of Warren, Ohio.

The new plant of the Farmers' Co-operative Elevator Co. at Sandusky, Mich., is being rushed to completion.

Morrison & Thompson are equipping their elevator at Kokomo, Ind., with a Hall Signaling Grain Distributor.

Horr Brothers, grain and feed dealers of Portsmouth, Ohio, will erect a three-story warehouse at that place.

The Farmers' Co-operative Co. is being organized at Gibsonburg, Ohio, for the purpose of erecting an elevator there.

An addition is being erected at the north end of the Farmers' Grain & Hay Co.'s elevator at Applegate, Mich.

The Eureka Milling & Elevator Co. has installed two Hall Signaling Distributors in its elevator at Brown City, Mich.

The Farmers' Grain Co. of Sheldon, Ind., has purchased the elevator of C. F. Davison for a consideration of $4,250.

The Irvin T. Fangboner Co. of Bellevue, Ohio, has been incorporated with a capital stock of $50,000, by Irvin T. Fangboner and others.

The old Pierson Cider Mill at Van Wert, Ohio, owned by R. P. Pierson, will probably be purchased as a site for the erection of a grain elevator.

The Farmers' & Gleaners' Elevator Co. has been organized at Elkton, Mich., with a capital stock of $30,000, and will erect a large elevator at that place.

A. Waller & Co., grain dealers of Henderson, Ky., recently purchased a building site in Johnson, a new town west of Owensville, Ind., and will erect a grain elevator at once. The Henderson Elevator Co. is also desirous of obtaining a site at that place.

The Indianapolis Elevator Co. of Indianapolis, Ind., has installed an Ellis Grain Drier capable of handling 500 to 600 bushels per hour, in its plant at that place.

Babcock & Hopkins will rebuild their elevator at Rensselaer, Ind., which burned a few weeks ago. The new house will probably be constructed of cement blocks.

J. E. Flora, J. W. Campbell and others are the incorporators of the newly organized Farmers' Grain & Supply Co. of Camden, Ohio. The capital stock is $20,000.

The Cavett Grain & Produce Co. of Cavett, Ohio, has been incorporated with a capital stock of $15,000, by F. D. Brandt, W. W. Border, D. L. Pugh, W. E. McQuown and A. H. Thayer.

The Dayton Grain & Hay Co. of Dayton, Ohio, has been incorporated by Levi H. Thompson, H. L. Thompson, Elihu Thompson, George L. Lane and John W. Finfrock, with a capital stock of $20,000.

The two grain elevators and a malt house at Sheboygan, Wis., owned by the Conrad Schreier Brewing Co., which were recently destroyed by fire, will be rebuilt.

Two new elevators are being erected by the firms of Middleton & Dolle and Wharton & Co. at Yale, Mich., which will be about the same size as those already owned by the firms.

Thomas, Kinder & Co., who purchased the Shirley Elevator at New Castle, Ind., a few years ago, have disposed of it to John La Vallee. J. F. Taylor will be retained as manager.

The elevator of the Farmers' Elevator Co. at Hogener Station, Ind., on the C. B. & Q. R. R., will have to be moved about twenty feet, as the railroad desires to double track that part of its road.

Walter Snyder, formerly associated with J. B. Seymour in the grain and onion business in Kenton, Ohio, has retired from the firm. Mr. Seymour will continue to operate his grain and onion elevators in Kenton and vicinity.

An effort is being made to combine the hay and grain elevators at Cincinnati, Ohio, into a single corporation. The houses involved are the Union Hay & Grain Co., the Early & Daniels Co., the Gale Brothers Co., the Cincinnati Grain Co. and August Ferger & Co. The new corporation will be known as the Cincinnati Grain & Hay Co., and will have a capital stock of $1,500,000. The elevators involved will have a capacity of 900,000 bushels and the hay warehouses, 1,200 cars of hay.

The New Haven Elevator Co. has been organized by J. A. Heath at New Haven, Mich., with a capital stock of $30,000. The new company takes over and combines the business of Jay Baldwin and William Kurshals, valued at $300,000. A large bean elevator will be built at once. Branches are operated at New Baltimore and Fair Haven. The directors are: W. H. Acker, A. A. Bennett, Jay Baldwin, William Kurzhals, W. D. Begrow, J. A. Heath, T. K. McGinnis, W. E. Harting and Charles Schwanebeck. The officers are W. H. Acker, president; A. A. Bennett, vice-president; J. A. Heath, secretary, and Jay Baldwin, treasurer and general manager.

IOWA.

An elevator will be erected at Simstown, Iowa, by the Turner Brothers.

S. White is remodeling and adding to his elevator at Highland, Iowa.

An elevator will be erected at Olaf, Iowa, to take the place of the one destroyed by fire.

The Wells-Hord Grain Co. recently sold its business at Toledo, Iowa, to the farmers.

The Pomeroy Co-operative Grain Co. has purchased the Western Elevator at Pomeroy, Iowa.

The Farmers' Elevator Co. recently purchased the east elevator of Charles Doyler at Templeton, Iowa.

The Farmers' Elevator Co. has been organized at Bayard, Iowa, with Charles Maxwell as president.

John Gray recently purchased the Trans-Mississippi Elevator at Onawa, Iowa, which he formerly owned.

The Dedham Grain, Stock & Lumber Co. of Dedham, Iowa, has been organized with a capital stock of $10,000.

A contract has been let by the Farmers' Elevator Co. for the erection of a 10,000 bushel elevator at Ericson, Iowa.

The farmers of Grandmound, Iowa, have organized an elevator company and will either buy or build a house.

The Farmers' Elevator Co. of Alvord, Iowa, has purchased a 1,000-bushel Richardson Automatic Scale for its elevator.

The Imperial Milling Co. and the Van Wickle Grain & Lumber Co. have completed their 150,000 bushel elevator at Council Bluffs, Iowa, and have opened offices in the Brandeis Bldg., in Omaha, Nebr.

The interests of the Blanden Grain & Lumber Co. at Blanden, Iowa, have been purchased by the Farmers' Elevator Co.

The Trans-Mississippi Grain Co. has equipped its elevator at Correctionville, Iowa, with a Hall Signaling Grain Distributor.

The Farmers' Grain & Live Stock Co., whose plant at Stanton, Iowa, burned some time ago, has purchased the business of Turner Brothers.

Joe Tierney and Henry Ahmann have purchased the Peoria Elevator at Remsen, Iowa, buying back the interest of Peterson & Hendrickson.

The Stuhr & Reesy Grain Co. will erect an elevator at Minden, Iowa, on the site of the one destroyed by fire. The new house will be a little larger than the old one.

The plant of the Updike Grain Co. at Blencoe, Iowa, which burned a short time ago, will be rebuilt. The new elevator will have a capacity of 25,000 bushels.

Sufficient stock has been subscribed for by the farmers around Flugsted, Iowa, to insure the erection of an elevator. Work will be commenced as soon as possible.

The Hunting Elevator Co., which has been in business at McGregor, Iowa, for forty years, has moved its offices to the Flour Exchange Bldg., in Minneapolis, Minn.

The newly organized Farmers' Elevator Co. of Hancock, Iowa, will probably purchase the Des Moines Elevator at that place. George R. Warner will probably be manager.

The elevator of the Nye-Sneider-Fowler Co. at Carroll, Iowa, has been purchased by the Farmers' Elevator Co. for a consideration of $8,000. C. D. Hart will continue as manager.

The Farmers' Elevator Co. of Marshalltown, Iowa, has increased its capital stock from $5,000 to $12,000. The number of shares to be held by any one person is limited to ten.

W. S. Kichner, Joseph Wacha, F. W. Dostal, William Held and J. C. Child are the incorporators of the Toledo Farmers' Elevator Co. of Toledo, Iowa. The company has a capital stock of $10,000.

The elevator of the Farmers' Elevator Co. at Lake City, Iowa, will be enlarged. The capacity will be increased by 8,000 bushels and the engine power will be doubled. Work is to be completed July 1.

The Farmers' Elevator Co. of Dysart, Iowa, has purchased the elevator of the Iowa Grain Co. at that place for a consideration of $9,250. Herman Schroeder, the former manager, will be employed by the new owner.

The New Providence Co-operative Co. of Lawnhill Sta., New Providence P. O., Iowa, is lowering its driveway thirty inches and putting in a controllable dump, new pit, boot and leg and an automatic scale to take care of its increased business.

The Davenport Grain Co. has been incorporated at Davenport, Iowa, with a capital stock of $100, by M. Rothschild, R. E. Beebee, W. J. Martin, J. F. Dow and Bert Dow. M. Rothschild is president; R. E. Beebee, vice president; Bert Dow, secretary, and W. J. Martin, treasurer.

WESTERN.

An elevator is being built at Beaverton, Mont.

An elevator is being erected at Cache Junction, Utah.

The erection of an elevator at Ryegate, Mont., is being talked of.

The Hanson-Barzon Elevator Co. will erect an elevator at Plentywood, Mont.

The elevator of Douglas, Mead & Co., at Glendive, Mont., partly planned for last year, will be erected in a short time.

The Elevator Construction Co. has the contract to build a 20,000-bushel cribbed elevator for J. W. Jenks at Cozad, Wyo.

An eight concrete tank elevator with a capacity of 240,000 bushels will be erected at Great Falls, Mont., by the Royal Milling Co.

A. E. Aiken and the Lowe Brothers have formed a partnership for the erection of an elevator with a capacity of 40,000 bushels at Glendive, Mont.

K. K. Lequinn of Wilsal, Mont., and K. S. Williams of Cedar Rapids, Iowa, will erect a grain elevator at Wilsal, a new town in the Shields Valley.

The hay and grain business and warehouse of J. A. Byrne of White Salmon Falls, Wash., has been purchased by the White Salmon Valley Fruit Growers Union.

The Perkins Grain & Milling Co. of Perkins, Cal., completed a two-story frame addition to its warehouse, 50x96 feet in size, about July 15. C. Best is manager of the company.

The California & Oregon Grain & Elevator Co., a subsidiary corporation of the Globe Grain & Milling Co., will erect a $30,000 steel grain elevator on land leased from the Southern Pacific Railway Co., at Wilmington, Cal. A rental of $600 a year will be paid for the land and the lease has been obtained for thirty years.

The Hupfer Hay & Grain Co. of Salt Lake City, Utah, has been incorporated with a capital stock of $15,000. The officers are: A. R. Pintro, president and J. J. Hupfer, secretary-treasurer.

The Johnstown Milling & Elevator Co. of Johnstown, Colo., is making extensive improvements on its elevator and dump for unloading grain. Rolls for grinding feed and making corn meal have been installed.

A warehouse 100x50 feet in size is being erected at Madras, Ore., by the Balfour, Guthrie Co. A wheat platform has been constructed at Vanora and warehouse facilities are being provided at Mecca and Gateway.

By-laws and articles of incorporation were recently drawn up for the Dennis Elevator & Transportation Co. of Dennis, Mont., at a meeting of the farmers of that vicinity. William O'Brien was elected president and T. J. Bushell, secretary.

MISSOURI, KANSAS AND NEBRASKA.

A farmers' elevator may be erected at Ashland, Nebr.

A farmers' elevator company has been organized at Chalco, Nebr.

The Lincoln Grain Co. will remodel its elevator at Milligan, Nebr.

An elevator will be erected at Wentzville, Mo., by the Kaneubrock Milling Co.

The Lord Milling Co. of Wamego, Kan., is enlarging its elevator at Delphos, Kan.

The erection of an elevator at St. Libory, Nebr., is being agitated by the farmers.

R. M. Van Ness of Hampton, Nebr., has purchased a Hall Signaling Grain Distributor.

An elevator will be erected at Pollard, Kan., by the N. Sauer Milling Co., of Cherryvale, Kan.

An attempt is being made to secure a 20,000-bushel elevator by the citizens of Zenith, Kan.

The Albion Elevator Co. of Albion, Neb., is erecting a lumber shed with a concrete foundation.

The Gooch Milling & Elevator Co. has purchased the grain elevators at Cheney and Emerald, Nebr.

W. D. Fulton has sold his elevator at Talmage, Kan., to the Rock Island Mill Co. of Hutchinson, Kan.

Perry Frazier has installed a Hall Signaling Grain Distributor in his elevator at Chapman, Kan.

John Rothmuller has purchased the grain and coal business of the Ewart Grain Co. at Crete, Nebr.

The Platte Grain Co. will install a Hall Signaling Grain Distributor in its elevator at Glenville, Neb.

The North Bend Grain Co. of North Bend, Neb., will equip its elevator with a Hall Signaling Grain Distributor.

The Hutchinson Mill Co. is building an elevator at Elmer, Kan., which will probably be ready by harvest time.

The Ellsworth Mill & Elevator Co. will erect an elevator at Bunker Hill, Kan., and remodel its house at Ellsworth.

The elevator of Moses Brothers at Spearville, Kan., has been purchased by the Dodge City Milling & Elevator Co.

An elevator having a capacity of 20,000 bushels will be erected by the Farmers' Grain & Live Stock Co. at Bruno, Neb.

The Morrison Grain Co. of Kansas City has purchased the elevators at Barnard and Milo, Kan., from Welsh Brothers.

J. D. Curtis has leased the elevator connected with the electric light plant at Stella, Neb. The house has been closed for a year.

A Hall Signaling Grain Distributor has been installed in the elevator of the Verona Grain & Lumber Co. at Prosser, Neb.

Bert H. Lang of the Lang Commission Co., grain dealers of St. Louis, Mo., recently purchased a site at that place for an elevator.

The Rock Milling & Elevator Co. is erecting elevator at Belpre, Lewis, Talmadge and Barnard, Kan., on the Santa Fe Railroad.

Two large new steel grain storage tanks are being added to the elevator equipment of the Pratt Mill & Elevator Co. of Pratt, Mo.

E. G. West, whose elevator at Gothenburg, Nebr., is to be torn down, has purchased the house of the Omaha Elevator Co. at that place.

A Farmers' Co-operative Elevator Co. has been organized at Nickerson, Kan., for the purpose of erecting an elevator in the near future. A. H. Bressler is president of the company and J. S. Brooks, Joe Chesky, Pete Detgen, Hubert Jossey, C. J. Shuyler and R. Eubanks are the directors.

Bert Finch, M. Finch, M. Bach, Henry Bethke and J. H. Vogle are the stockholders in the newly organized Stuttgart Elevator Co. of Stuttgart, Kan.

A grain elevator to be operated by electric power will be erected at Omaha, Neb., for the Crowell Elevator Co. It will have a capacity of 250,000 bushels.

The plant of the Terminal Elevator Co. at Lewiston, Nebr., has been purchased by O. Vanier of Fairbury, who will overhaul it and cover it with iron.

John Campbell recently sold his interest in the La Harpe Grain & Milling Co. at La Harpe, Kan., to his partners. Mr. Campbell will continue in the employ of the firm.

The R. E. Roberts Elevator Co. has obtained control of one of the elevators at Gretna, Nebr., and will improve the house. This company now operates five elevators.

The Cavers Elevator Co. intends to construct a 150,000 bushel addition to its 200,000 bushel elevator at Omaha, Nebr., which is situated on the Council Bluffs side of the river.

The Rogers Elevator at St. Louis, Mo., has been declared regular and used for the storage of much of the grain which was in the Burlington Elevator which was recently wrecked by a storm.

Henry Wacker of Greensburg, Kan., is planning to build an elevator on the Rock Island Railway between Greensburg and Mullinsville, provided a switch can be secured from the Rock Island.

The Natoma Mill & Elevator Co. intends to erect a new mill and elevator at Natoma, Kan., if crops improve, and the Shellabarger Mill & Elevator Co. will improve its elevator at the same place.

The Tilden Elevator Co. of Tilden, Neb., has been succeeded by the Tilden Farmers' Elevator Co. under the management of the following officers: N. E. Graves, president; Man Giebler, secretary, and Hiram Marble, manager.

SOUTHERN AND SOUTHWESTERN.

Bill Thomas is rebuilding the elevator at Wakita, Okla., which burned some time ago.

James Barracks has purchased an interest in the Baton Rouge Mill & Elevator Co. at Baton Rouge, La.

A 40,000 bushel grain elevator and warehouse will be erected at Lynchburg, Va., by the Lynchburg Milling Co.

The Western Grain Co. is behind the project to organize a new mill and grain company at Birmingham, Ala.

P. M. Shields & Co, a new firm at Wellington, Texas, will probably build a grain elevator at that place this year.

A Hall Signaling Grain Distributor is being installed by the Star Mill & Elevator Co. in its elevator at Amarillo, Texas.

The Chattanooga Feed Co. of Chattanooga, Tenn., will erect a warehouse and store building and will install a small grain elevator.

A six-story warehouse and storage building will be erected by William G. Scarlett & Son at Pratt St. and East Falls Ave., Baltimore, Md.

The Marquis Grain Co. of Enid, Okla., has been incorporated with a capital stock of $5,000, by T. D. Marquis, S. Marquis and Gus S. Manatt.

The plant of the Bewley Mill & Elevator Co. at Keller, Texas, was recently entered and the scales, engine and machinery stripped of the brass fittings.

Messrs. Huff and Cook, millers of Roanoke, Va., have commenced work on a grain elevator at that place. The house will be of brick and three stories high.

The Grove Feed & Storage Co. of Elkins, W. Va., has been incorporated by W. A. Grove, H. R. Allen, B. W. Taylor and others, with a capital stock of $10,000.

The J. C. Reynolds Grain Co. and the J. S. Gordon Grain Co. have been taken over by a company formed at Port Arthur, Texas. W. S. Tyner is manager of the new concern.

The R. A. Smith Grain Co. has been incorporated at Fayetteville, Tenn., by D. C. Sherrill, R. A. Smith, L. E. Cowden, W. S. Moore and J. S. Poindexter, with a capital stock of $12,000.

The brick warehouse and steel elevator at Nashville, Tenn., owned by the William Miller Estate, was recently sold at auction to the American National Bank for $8,500 by the executors.

Owing to the bumper crop of grain expected in that region the report comes from Americus, Ga., that a granary 60x100 feet is being erected on the Sumter County farm by Sumter commissioners.

Articles of incorporation were recently filed by the Iron City Grain Co. of Iron City, Ala. The company will have an authorized capital stock of $10,100, though it will start business with only

$5,100. The officers are: H. Kockritz, Jr., president; J. W. Foster, vice president, and C. F. Allgood, secretary-treasurer.

The Hanna Cotton & Grain Co. of Hanna, Okla., has been incorporated with a capital stock of $7,000. The directors are R. B. Moore, J. M. Henderson, C. A. Helf and John R. Doss, all of Hanna, and J. H. Bellis of Cushing.

An elevator will be erected at Perry, Okla., on the site of the elevator formerly owned by the Donahoe Brothers, by E. J. Miller, who has operated cotton gins and grain elevators in northern Oklahoma for many years.

The business of the Miller Grain Co. of Orange, Texas, established a few years ago, and operated by Max Miller as manager, was recently sold to A. B. Goodman of Beaumont, who will conduct the business under the name of the Orange Grain Co.

The Hannifin Mill & Elevator Co. of Broken Arrow, Okla., will probably install cob burners in its corn elevators as there is no market for the cobs.

The Katy Mill & Elevator Co. of Caddo, Okla., has increased its capital stock from $7,500 to $15,000.

EASTERN.

J. K. Hornley & Sons of New Brighton, Pa., have purchased a warehouse, having sold the Star Flour Mills.

The Grosvernordale Grain Co. of Thompson, Conn., has changed its name to the Thompson Grain Co.

The Potter Grain Elevator at Greenfield, Mass., is now occupied by the firm of Luey & Abercrombie, a grocery firm.

The Erie Railroad Company has purchased the elevator properties of the Erie Elevator Co., at Jersey City, N. J.

The Ogden Grain Co. of Utica, N. Y., has been incorporated with a capital stock of $50,000, by F. C. Ogden, W. A. Soper and R. R. Davis.

A grain elevator will be erected by Charles Slosberg at Norwich, Conn., at the rear of the old building of Winters, Swift & Co., which will be used in connection with the elevator. The machinery will be on the first floor and the grain bins with a total capacity of 18,000 bushels of grain will be above. A mill for cracking corn, provender and meal will be installed. The machinery will be operated by two 15-horsepower motors. The cost will be about $8,000.

THE DAKOTAS.

A co-operative elevator company was organized at Bisbee, N. D.

The new Atlas Elevator at Rockham, S. D., has been completed.

Ole J. Baker has purchased the Mel Davis Elevator at Flandreau, S. D.

Plans for the erection of several new elevators are being made at Flasher, N. D.

The erection of two elevators and other buildings at La Moure, N. D., is being talked of.

A 30,000-bushel elevator is being erected at Wasta, S. D., by the G. W. Van Dusen Co. of Minneapolis.

The Farmers' Elevator Co. has purchased the Minneapolis & Northern Elevator at Hillsboro, N. D.

An elevator will be erected at Burnstad, N. D., by the Farmers' Elevator Co., which is being organized.

A Farmers' Elevator Company has been organized at Kampeska, S. D., and an elevator will be erected.

The books of the Grain Producers' Elevator Co. of Minto, N. D., are $2,500 short and the agent is missing.

The Farmers' Elevator Co. at Grand Forks, N. D., will rebuild its elevator at that place, which burned recently.

The Dempster Co-operative Grain Co. of Dempster, S. D., will erect a 25,000 bushel grain elevator at that place.

The Atlas Elevator at Turton, S. D., is nearing completion and will have a capactiy of about 50,000 bushels.

A modern elevator will be erected on the site of the old house at Wessington, S. D., by the Atlas Elevator Co.

A warehouse and office building will be erected by Martin Braatelien for the Farmers' Elevator Co. of Ambrose, N. D.

A meeting was held recently at James, S. D., to decide on either buying or building an elevator for the coming season.

The Cargill Elevator Co. will dismantle its elevator at De Villo, Fairmont, P. O., N. D., and will erect a modern house.

Gottfried Sperling has become sole proprietor of the old Lyon Elevator at Jud, N. D., owned by John Klein and others.

The Occident Elevator Co. of Minneapolis, a part of the Russell Miller Milling Co., recently purchased the elevator of O. A. Krugan at Belfield, N. D. Mr. Krugau purchased the elevator about a year ago from F. H. Shepard & Co.

The Frankfort Farmers' Elevator Co. will build an 80,000-bushel cribbed elevator at Frankfort, S. D.

The old McCaull-Webster Elevator at Butler, S. D., is being torn down and a new one will be built on the old site. J. L. Barry is the owner of the property.

The recently incorporated Mose Elevator Co. at Mose, N. D., has bought the elevator of B. C. Phipps and will open for business August 1, with H. B. Omdal as manager.

The farmers in the vicinity of Hickson, N. D., are contemplating the erection of a farmers' elevator. The capital stock will probably be between $10,000 and $15,000.

George C. Ostrander and his son W. D. recently purchased and took possession of the Atlas Elevator at Watertown, S. D. The business will be conducted under the name of the Feed & Fuel Co. as the new owners intend to install feed grinding machinery and to handle feed as their chief business.

An organization has been formed at Devils Lake, N. D., to be known as the Farmers' Grain Dealers' Association. Fifty or more elevator companies throughout the state were represented at the meeting. W. A. Pitkin of Sawyer was elected president and L. W. Unkenholtz of Mandan, secretary-treasurer.

The Courtenay Farmers' Elevator at Courtenay, N. D., which was recently purchased by S. M. Posey for a company of stockholders at a mortgage foreclosure sale, will be operated by a new company organized for that purpose. The new by-laws to be enacted by the shareholders will probably restrict the number of shares any stockholder may have, and eliminate the system of voting or having a voice by proxy. The proposition of bonding the manager in order to insure the carrying out of orders, will also be discussed.

CANADIAN.

Steps are being taken for the erection of an elevator in Brooks, Alta.

An elevator is being erected at Wadena, Sask., by the Goose Lake Elevator Co.

The Goose Lake Grain & Lumber Co. is building an elevator at Kindersley, Sask.

The Indian Head Farm Elevator Co. of Indian Head, Sask., has sold out to Dewar & Kendrew.

The Manitoba Elevator Commission intends to remodel the elevators at St. Claude and Oakville, Man.

The Boston-Newell Syndicate will erect a private elevator five miles west of Brooks at Cassils, Alta.

An elevator with a capacity of 20,000 bushels will be erected at Herbert, Sask., by the Herbert Rolling Mills Co.

The Farmers' Elevator Co. of Estevan, Sask., has become insolvent and the business will be wound up.

A meeting of the grain growers was held recently at Radisson, Sask., at which an elevator company was formed and it was decided to build an elevator.

Bids for erecting a grain elevator at Brocket, Alta., were received by J. D. McLean, secretary of the Department of Indian Affairs at Ottawa, Ont., up to June 15.

The elevator at Miami, Man., recently purchased from the Miami Farmers' Elevator Co. by the Manitoba Government Elevator Commission, will be moved to Grosse Isle, Man.

A new storage elevator is to be built by the Harbor Commissioners at Windmill Point, Montreal, Que., with a capacity of a half million bushels. John S. Metcalf & Co. have the contract.

The work on the grain elevator being erected by the Harbor Commissioners opposite the Bonsecours Market at Montreal, Que., is progressing rapidly. Concrete is being used in its construction.

The Manitoba Elevator Commission is remodeling its elevators at various points throughout Manitoba. The new elevators have an increased number of bins and are fitted with better cleaning machinery, besides having more motive power and weighing-out scales.

The Harbor Commissioners are endeavoring through injunction proceedings to prevent the Grand Trunk Railway from constructing grain tanks on Windmill Point, Montreal, as they claim that they leased the land to the railway for the purpose of building a million bushel grain elevator and that the construction of the tanks is a violation of the lease.

New York is importing European rye to be ground in that city.

After July 1 "top sampling" will be against the law in Nebraska. The new statute, effective on that date, specifically states that grain tests must be made by taking a vertical section from top to bottom of the bulk to be tested. Under this provision it will be necessary to "plunge" wagon as well as car grain bought or sold by test in the state of Nebraska.

THE EXCHANGES

The Philadelphia Commercial Exchange has adopted a rule requiring purified oats to be so branded.

All appropriations by the St. Louis Merchants' Exchange must be approved by the order of the members.

The Buffalo Chamber of Commerce sent a large delegation to Washington, during the Senate hearing, to advocate the reciprocity agreement.

The St. Louis Merchants' Exchange has decided that the doors of the trading floor shall be closed on Saturdays at 12:30 p. m. and on other days at 1:30.

The officers of the Buffalo Corn Exchange have been re-elected as follows: President, H. D. Waters; vice-president, S. M. Ratcliff; treasurer, L. S. Churchill; secretary, F. E. Pond.

The Kansas City Board of Trade has amended its rules to permit a majority, instead of three-quarters, of the membership to ratify a building contract approved by the directors.

W. C. Culkins on May 15 assumed his duties as Superintendent of the Cincinnati Chamber of Commerce. C. B. Murray, his predecessor, remains with the Chamber, at least for some time, as statistician.

The Chicago Board of Trade has adopted a new commission rule on future business, making the rate $7.50 on each closed transaction of 5,000 bushels, an increase of $1.25; one-half that amount to members; in effect June 13.

The Wichita Board of Trade has ordered the strict enforcement of the rule that only members of the Board (limited to 50) or accredited representatives of members in the absence of the latter, shall be permitted to trade on the floor.

The St. Louis feed men have attempted to fight the position of Merchants' Exchange members on the weighing at team tracks, and have threatened to "buy in the country direct;" but they are paying all the fees except $1 per car paid by the receiver on 'change.

The Davenport Grain Exchange has been incorporated at Davenport, Ia., with the following officers: President, M. Rothschild; vice-president, R. E. Beedee; treasurer, W. J. Martin; secretary, Bert Dow. These four, with J. F. Dow, compose the board of directors.

Memberships in the Minneapolis Chamber of Commerce are strong and a recent quotation of $3,850, making a new high record on this advance, which since the crops began to look good has added $800 to $900 to membership values. Eventually it is believed memberships will sell again at the high record of $5,000.

W. A. McCoy has been indefinitely suspended from the Chicago Board of Trade under the rules of the board providing for the suspension of members at the instance of creditor members. McCoy several weeks ago left for parts unknown, leaving a good many claims against him. Since then he has not been heard from. He was only a small trader.

The editor of these columns should last month have acknowledged receipt of the Fifty-third Annual Report of the Milwaukee Chamber of Commerce, compiled by Sec'y H. A. Plumb. It covers the year ended April 3, 1911; and besides the completeness of the report, it is unusual on account of the promptness of its appearance after the close of the Chamber's fiscal year.

Members of the Milwaukee Chamber of Commerce have organized the Chamber of Commerce club for social and educational purposes. The following officers were elected: President, Harry M. Stratton, of the Donahue-Stratton Co., flour and feed; vice-president, L. R. Fyfe; second vice-president, T. Corcoran; secretary-treasurer, Walter L. Kassuba. The organization is modeled largely after the Chicago Board of Trade club.

The Omaha Grain Exchange is hunting new quarters, and has appointed a committee headed by N. B. Updike to confer with Dr. H. Gifford relative to the erection of an Exchange building on his lot at the northwest corner of Seventeenth and Douglas streets. Two propositions are under consideration, it is said, one for the Gifford building and another for the Exchange to buy the lot and erect a building of its own. The Exchange has about $100,000 cash on hand.

The election of officers of the New York Produce Exchange was held June 5 with the following results: President, Edward R. Carhart; vice-president, John Aspergren; treasurer, Edward C. Rice; managers, two years, Lyndon Arnold of Rohe & Bro., George T. Hay of J. F. Whitney & Co., Louis G. Leverich of Shaw & Truesdell Co., John R. Wood of N. Y. P. Exchange bank, O. H. Montgomery of N. T. Sweezey's Sons & Co., Winchester Noyes of J. H. Winchester & Co.; trustee of gratuity fund, John V. Jewell.

NEW CLEARING HOUSE PLAN.

The special committee appointed by the Chicago Board of Trade directors about a year ago to devise a new method of clearing trades has made its report to the board of directors.

Chairman S. P. Arnot says: "The new plan is composed of what is known as the Hosford plan, the present plan in operation on the Open Board of Trade and of the corporate method of clearing trade differences. Under the new plan traders will be able to have their books evened up every day, and do away with the present plan of ringing trades."

BEAN RULES AT DETROIT.

In framing up a program to increase the bean trade of Detroit, the Board of Trade of that city, on May 23, adopted rules calculated to eliminate the effect of the trade of the exchange of the local railway rules that beans handled in Detroit shall pay local rates in and out instead of a through rate. The new rules are as follows:

"A carload of beans shall consist of 250 new, unmarked cotton bags, no charge for bags, aggregating 41,250 pounds net. More or less adjusted at market price.

"Weights are guaranteed within a quarter of one per cent on arrival at destination. Claims for shortage or damage must be presented within five days after arrival of cars and accompanied by itemized weights with sworn affidavit attached.

"Detroit Board of Trade certificates of weight and inspection shall be final between buyer and seller, unless otherwise specified.

"Commission shall be two cents a bushel where delivery is made on contract, one cent per bushel where deals are closed before delivery.

"Ten cents a bushel may be called from either buyer or seller, and margins kept good, and in case this is not advanced immediately deals may be closed without notice.

"Buyers must furnish shipping instructions within 48 hours after written or wired request of seller for same or the beans may be sold for account of the buyer. The seller has option to ship any time during the month of the option. In case of default the buyer may buy them in for account of the seller.

'Delivery shall be by bill of lading with draft on arrival with interest at 6 per cent from date of shipment, or draft payable on presentation without interest. Buyer shall state with his shipping orders how to make draft.

'The basis for sales and purchases of beans through the Detroit Board of Trade shall be f. o. b. shipping points, taking 28½ cents a 100 pounds in car lots to New York City, N. Y., 13 cents to Chicago, Ill., or 17 cents to Louisville, Ky. Points taking more than the above rates, the seller must allow the buyer the difference. Points taking less the buyer must pay the difference.

"Where beans are sold without specifying rates the buyer has option to order beans shipped where he pleases. The seller must protect the above rates, but seller may designate when trade is made which rate he will protect.

"Eastern or New York territory based on 28½ cents a 100 to New York shall be defined as all points from Baltimore on the south to Portland, Me., on the north.

"Southern or Louisville territory based on 17-cent rate to Louisville, Ky., shall be defined as points from Virginia cities on the east to St. Louis on the west inclusive.

"Western or Chicago territory based on 13-cent rate to Chicago, Ill., shall be defined as points north of St. Louis, Mo., to Duluth, Minn.

"All sales of beans whether cash or future shall be of what is known as "new beans" on or after October 1 of each year.

"In case of dispute about quality a sample shall be taken by a reliable and disinterested party from at least 10 per cent of the bags sealed and sent to the secretary of the Detroit Board of Trade and the bean inspection committee shall decide the grade, which grading shall be final and the difference adjusted accordingly by the committee. In case of misdelivery shipper shall have the right to tender other deliveries provided the time of shipment and conditions of the contract are fulfilled. Other disputes shall be adjusted by the bean inspection committee of the Detroit Board of Trade, whose rulings shall be final.

"Choice handpicked pea beans must be good average color of the year's crop, sound, dry, well screened and must not contain more than one pound of discolored and split beans, and not more than five pounds of large and medium beans bushed of 60 pounds.

"Prime handpicked pea beans must be good average color of the year's crop, sound, dry, well screened and must not contain more than two pounds of discolored and split beans, or more than seven pounds of large or medium beans a bushel of 60 pounds.

"Choice handpicked red kidney beans must be good average color of the year's crop, sound, dry, well screened and must not contain more than one pound of discolored or split beans, and not more than two pounds of sports or blue beans a bushel of 58 pounds.

"Prime handpicked red kidney beans must be fair average color of the year's crop, sound, dry, well screened and must not contain more than three pounds of discolored and split beans and not more than three pounds of sports or blue beans per bushel of 58 pounds.

"Sample beans: All beans that will not pass into the above grades. The inspection committee shall give reasons and state the amount of pickage."

CHANGES IN EXCHANGE MEMBERSHIP.

Chicago.—Sec'y Stone reports the following changes in the membership of the Chicago Board of Trade during May: New members—Sanford F. Reese, Alvin H. Poehler, Rufus F. Brett, Ervin L. Roy, Arthur N. Harwood, Roland McHenry, David R. Forgan, Frank A. Hayward, Thos. P. Loney. Withdrawals—Henry H. Carr, Henry Poehler, L. B. Wilson, Allan F. Cohn, Arthur Dyer, Walter H. Wrigley, Sam'l H. Green, Chas. B. Pike, D. E. Hartwell.

Cincinnati.—Supt. W. C. Culkins of the Cincinnati Chamber of Commerce reports the following members elected on June 6: Burkitt C. Budd of A. R. Budd Coal Co., 511 First National Bank; Joseph F. Costello, with Union Grain & Hay Co., 306 W. Fourth St.; George W. Williams, vice-president Fourth National Bank, 18-22 E. Fourth St., and William C. Culkins, Superintendent, Chamber of Commerce.

Duluth.—Sec'y Chas. Macdonald reports the following changes in the membership of the Duluth Board of Trade during May: New member—O. K. Sellar, Duluth, Minn. Withdrawn—M. E. Scroggins and C. Z. Driesbach, both of Duluth.

Kansas City.—Sec'y Bigelow reports the following changes in membership of the Kansas City Board of Trade in May: E. R. Stripp admitted on transfer of membership standing in name of Issy Landa and Wm. Schrenkler admitted on transfer of membership in name of Otto Swaller.

Milwaukee.—Sec'y Plumb reports the following changes in the membership of the Milwaukee Chamber of Commerce occurred during the month of May, 1911: New members—Allen A. Breed, Frank L. Howe, W. J. Hollister, Richard D. Jones, Linus J. Beck. Transferred memberships—Henry Manegold, F. L. Wolfe, Geo. Des Forges, dec'd.

Peoria.—J. A. Speers has applied for membership on the Peoria Board of Trade.

San Francisco.—Sec'y Friedlander reports that the following were elected to membership in The Merchants Exchange during the month of May, 1911: Tong Bong, Sing Fat Company, to succeed Jay Hing, and A. W. Splivalo, A. W. Splivalo Co., to succeed C. A. Carlisle.

Toledo.—Sec'y Gassaway reports Mr. H. W. Applegate is applicant for membership in the Toledo Produce Exchange on the certificate of F. W. Rundell, deceased. With Mr. Charles C. Coe he will continue the business of W. A. Rundell Co., with Mr. James E. Rundell as special partner.

COUNCIL OF EXCHANGES.

Following is the program of the mid-summer meeting of the Council of North American Grain Exchanges, to be held in the Hotel Pfister, Milwaukee, on June 28 and 29:

WEDNESDAY, JUNE 28.

Meeting called to order, 10:30 a. m.

Roll Call.

President's Address, by Hiram N. Sager, Chicago.

Secretary's Report, by J. Ralph Pickell, Chicago.

Treasurer's Report, by W. M. Richardson, Philadelphia.

Committee Reports:—On Constitution and By-Laws, by C. F. Macdonald, Duluth; on Statistics, by Frank I. King, Toledo; on Bills of Lading, by Charles England, Baltimore; on Circular of Instructions Re Bs/L, by L. W. Forbell, New York; on Intermarket Agreement, by H. L. Goemann, Toledo.

WEDNESDAY AFTERNOON SESSION.

Committee on Publicity, by J. C. F. Merrill, Chicago.

The Relation of the Press to the Modern Grain Exchange, by Pres. W. P. Bishop, Milwaukee Chamber of Commerce.

Elimination of Split Quotations, by Bert H. Lang, St. Louis.

The Practical Working of the Council, by Ex-President James Bradley, Chicago.

Newspaper Publicity Regarding the Functions and Services of the Grain Exchanges, by H. W. Daub, St. Louis.

A Credit Association, by Frank I. King, Toledo.

Topics for informal discussion—The Regulation of Traveling Solicitors; A Federal Bucket-Shop Law; Reciprocal Demurrage; Elimination of "Corners"; Prohibition of Advances by Receivers to Country Shippers Except on Bills of Lading; Recent decision under pure food law in Hall-Baker Grain Co. case as affecting grain shipments.

THURSDAY MORNING SESSION, JUNE 29.

Meeting called to order, 10:30.

Committee on Crop Improvement, by J. C. Murray, Chicago.

Breeding and Dissemination of Pure Bred Grains, by Prof. R. A. Moore, College of Agriculture and Agricultural Experiment Station, Madison, Wis.

Improvement of American Barley, by Dr. Robert Wahl of Wahl-Henius Institute of Fermentology, Chicago.

Crop Improvement Committee work, by Secretary Bert Ball, Chicago.

THURSDAY AFTERNOON SESSION.

Unfinished Business.

Special Committee Reports.

Resolutions.

DELEGATES.

The following delegates have been appointed to attend the meeting:

Minneapolis Chamber of Commerce—J. R. Marfield and C. A. Magnuson.

St. Louis Merchants' Exchange—John L. Messmore, Edward M. Flesh; alternates, Manning W. Cochrane and N. L. Moffitt.

Chicago Board of Trade—S. P. Arnot, J. J. Stream, Th. E. Cunningham; alternates, C. B. Pierce and J. C. Murray.

Toledo Produce Exchange—F. I. King and H. L. Goemann; representatives, Pres. David Anderson, E. L. Camp, E. H. Culver.

New York Produce Exchange—E. Pfarrius and L. W. Forbell.

Kansas City Board of Trade—George H. Davis and C. W. Lonsdale.

Milwaukee Chamber of Commerce—J. A. Mander and P. P. Donohue.

Baltimore Chamber of Commerce—F. A. Meyer and Charles England; alternates, Walter Kirwan and John M. Dennis. J. Collin Vincent, Crop Improvement Committee; alternate, James T. Clendenin.

RECIPROCITY AGAIN.

Following is a brief extract from President Taft's address on the reciprocity agreement before the new Western Economic Society at Chicago on June 3:

"The only real importation of agricultural products that we may expect from Canada of any considerable amount will consist of wheat, barley, rye and oats. The world price of these four cereals is fixed abroad where the surplus from the producing countries is disposed of and is little affected by the place from which the supply is derived.

"I have been attacked on the floor of the House and elsewhere as occupying an inconsistent position. It has been said that I have urged the reciprocity agreement with the idea of lowering the cost of living on the one hand and then have asserted that the farmers would not be injured by reduction in the price at which they sell their products on the other hand. It is asked, is it possible to reduce the cost of living on the one hand and maintain the present prices of farm products on the other? My own impression is that the cost of farm products is determined by the world's supply and not by local conditions or tariff or otherwise, and that as long as the movement toward manufacturing and away from the farms continues and the supply of farm laborers is reduced, a continuance of high prices for farm products is inevitable.

"The general conditions are these: We have a people numbering 90,000,000, occupying the best part of the North American continent, with the widest variety of products and with an unexcelled fertility of soil.

"To the north of us are a people just like ourselves, in descent, in wealth per capita, in education, in traditions, in ambitions and aspirations. They have a country nearly equal to ours in area, not so fertile generally, and certainly not so rich, in the wide variety of agricultural products.

"There are 7,000,000 of people. With them we have a trade of $325,000,000 a year. We export to them $225,000,000 a year. If we deduct from our exports to Germany, which is eight times as populous as Canada, the value of cotton and the copper that we send there, it will be found that we export more of our manufacturers and agricultural products to Canada than we do to Germany and that England is the only foreign customer we have that takes more of our goods than this comparatively small population of Canada.

"If that be true, and Canada continues to grow, what may we expect to sell her if we reduce the tariff wall, introduce as near as we can free trade, and she increase her population from 7,000,000 to 30,000,000? Shall we not be flying in the face of providence to maintain a wall between us and such a profitable market as she will furnish us?"

The officers and agents of the St. Anthony & Dakota Elevator Co. had a "family party" at the Waldorf Hotel, Fargo, N. D., on May 31, to 'talk shop" and have a good time.

COMMUNICATED

[We invite correspondence from everyone in any way interested in the grain trade on all topics connected therewith. We wish to see a general exchange of opinion on all subjects which pertain to the interest of the trade at large, or any branch of it.]

CROPS IN SOUTHEASTERN OHIO.

Editor American Elevator & Grain Trade: Having just returned from a visit to "the scenes of my childhood," in Washington County, southeastern Ohio, I thought I might as well tell you that the country and the growing crops look fine. Wheat, especially, promises a good yield, and corn, although a little backward, is coming on nicely; is even in its stand; healthy in its color, and the fields totally without yellow, or "drowned out" spots.

Oats are like corn—backward, but vigorous looking, and have every appearance of producing a good crop.

Potatoes look fine; and clover hay, also, but timothy—the regular hay crop—seems not to have had much attention, the acreage for it is not there.

I rode in a buggy with a boyhood friend, a farmer, for twenty miles, and had the benefit of what he saw and thought. "The wheat," he said, was excellent; much of it promising a yield of twenty bushels to the acre; and the evenness of the straw and its freedom from rye, cockle, or other admixture, shows that farmers are giving more attention to the seed they use than formerly. Everything indicates prosperity and the farmers seem contented. I never saw the country look more beautiful.

Yours very truly,
DANIEL McALISTER.

Columbus, O.

THE TRADE NEWS OF TOLEDO AND OHIO.

Editor American Elevator & Grain Trade: On the strength of present crop prospects farmers and small elevators have been dumping their corn holdings into this market in an unexpected manner recently. Corn receipts for the week ended June 9 have been more than 114,000 bushels, and more than 115,000 bushels of oats have come in during the same period. Crop prospects all along the line are most promising; and holders feel that there is no longer anything to be gained by carrying grain stocks, while there is a grave possibility that such a policy might be ruinous. There has been a fair demand for both corn and oats recently, shipments of the former for the week just ended aggregating 45,900 bushels, and of the latter 71,400 bushels. The quality of corn coming in at present shows vast improvement. No. 2 yellow is becoming more plentiful, there being 25 cars of that grade among the past week's receipts. Of the 108 cars that came in, 47 graded No. 3, 17 sample and 19 cars No. 4. Cash corn is now selling at 57c, July at 57⅜c, Sept. at 58¾ and December at 56⅞c. Total corn stocks here are estimated at 83,708 bushels, of which 26,987 bushels grade contract. Owing to heavy receipts stocks increased last week nearly 15,000 bushels. Stocks of oats also showed a slight increase to an estimated total of 167,687 bushels, of which 77,687 bushels grades contract. Cash oats is selling at 40c, and July, September and December at 40¼c.

Reports from all over Ohio and contiguous territory are to the effect that growing wheat is growing more promising every day. Recent rains in dry sections have vanquished all danger of damage from drought, and no complaints are heard from any source. Local stocks decreased last week a trifle through heavy local consumption. Although the receipts were 48,000 bushels as compared with shipments of only 8,000 bushels, the local supply decreased more than 13,000 bushels to a total of 297,637 bushels, of which 213,124 bushels grades contract. Prices are being constantly beaten down by the universally optimistic reports of bumper crop prospects. Cash wheat is now selling at 92¾c, July at 93⅛c, September at 92⅛c, and December at 94¾c. Scattered mills are operating very light and appear to find no difficulty in securing all the wheat they need in their immediate localities. Very few have been forced to the larger grain centers recently for wheat. There has been a fair movement of wheat from first hands, but there is comparatively a small percentage of the last crop remaining in the bins of farmers. Indications point to an early harvest in this section. Export bids are still too far out of line to bring any substantial volume of foreign business. Local mills are running normally and the demand for feed is very strong.

A sigh of relief went up from the seed interests of Ohio, when the legislature adjourned without enacting the proposed Huber pure seed measure into law. The bill which passed both houses was referred back to a senate committee, where it died a natural death upon the adjournment of the lawmaking body. At least, it can not be revived until next session which will convene a year from next January. This bill which was one of the most drastic ever proposed, and which threatened to destroy the seed business of Toledo, was fought for months by Toledo dealers.

A fair delegation from Toledo will represent grain and milling interests at the coming meetings of grain men at Bloomington, Ill., on the 13th and 14th of June, and later at Indianapolis.

E. L. Camp, formerly president of the Toledo Produce Exchange, has been chosen a trustee of the newly organized Toledo Commerce Club. The Club grows out of a merger of the Toledo Chamber of Commerce and the Toledo Business Men's Club, two of the strongest commercial organizations in the city. It has a membership of more than 1,200, including nearly all the prominent grain and milling men of the city.

Fred Mayer, David Anderson and W. H. Morehouse attended the recent automobile races at Indianapolis. They report crops between here and that point as very promising.

A change has resulted in the personnel of the large grain firm of W. A. Rundell & Co., of Toledo, on account of the recent death of Frederick W. Rundell, senior member of the firm. Mr. Rundell died recently at his home on Parkwood avenue, after an illness covering a period of about a year. He had been in the grain business since 1880, and was survived by a wife and one brother, James Rundell, who has been associated with him in business. Following his death announcement was made that James E. Rundell will retire from the grain business and that the affairs of W. A. Rundell will hereafter be conducted by Wallace, Applegate and Charles Coe, both of whom have been connected with the firm for a number of years and are practical grain men. W. A. Rundell, father of Fred and James Rundell and founder of the business, was a pioneer grain dealer, having been in business before the Produce Exchange was organized. James E. Rundell retains a passive interest in the business.

Charles Burge is increasing his storage capacity materially by the erection of a large wood, concrete and brick seed warehouse at his plant at the corner of Ontario and Lafayette streets. Work is well under way on this modern structure and when completed it will add materially to the capacity of the business.

Frank Mettler, formerly connected with the grain firm of C. A. King & Co. of Toledo, died recently at his home in Chicago. Eugene Mettler, a brother of the deceased attended the funeral. At the time of his death Mr. Mettler was manager of a large baking company. Death was caused by spinal meningitis.

Kenton D. Kleinholtz, who recently made a trip through a large portion of Ohio sizing up crops, reports his surprise at the splendid showing made all over this section.

E. J. Norton, member of the field seed firm of C. C. Norton & Sons, of Greenfield, Ohio, was a recent visitor on the floor of the Produce Exchange. He says old stocks are practically cleaned up in his section, and clover crop prospect is far from encouraging.

Frank Moorman, prominent Toledo grain man, recently married Miss Opal Kenny, also of this city. The ceremony was performed at the home of the bride's parents in the presence of immediate relatives only. Following the wedding breakfast, the couple left the city on a trip up the lakes. They will be at home to their many friends after August 1, at 1027 West Woodruff avenue.

E. T. BAKER.

MINNESOTA CROPS 1909.

The Census Bureau has published its summary of Minnesota crops of 1909. Subject to later revision, they are in part as follows:

	Acres 1909.	Acres 1899.	Av. yield, 1909.	Bushels, 1909.
Wheat	3,277,039	6,560,707	17	259,021,006
Oats	2,977,264	2,201,325	32	93,885,164
Corn	2,004,007	1,441,580	34	67,777,912
Hay, etc., tons	3,944,422	3,157,690	1.5	6,041,883
Barley	1,573,836	877,845	22	34,928,545
Rye	266,604	118,869	17	4,426,208
Flaxseed	358,565	566,801	9	3,278,006

Under buckwheat there were 10,496 acres; yield, 144,773 bus. In the hay crop is counted timothy, clover, alfalfa, millet or Hungarian and other tame and wild grasses. Of the ends the following productions are reported in bushels: Alfalfa, 16; clover, 48,001; millet, 20,371; timothy, 877,042; beans, 62,939; peas, 14,990; peanuts, 15 bus. from a single acre.

On June 12 Commerce Commissioner Harlan began hearing at Memphis a complaint by the Memphis Grain and Hay Association against the I. C. R. R. Co. and others, that on grain shipped into Memphis via the defendant's lines, which is reshipped to Mississippi valley points, the Memphis shipper is compelled to pay the Memphis proper rates to such destinations, while grain dealers and millers doing business at various other points, under similar circumstances and conditions as those obtaining at Memphis, are granted proportional rates which permit them to undersell the Memphis grain dealers and millers.

ASSOCIATIONS

Sec'y J. F. Courcier concluded recently a six-weeks' visit to the Southeast on behalf of the National Association.

W. C. Brown of Beloit, vice-president, succeeds R. E. Cox, deceased, as president of the Kansas Grain Dealers' Association.

Sec'y Strong reports the following new members of the Illinois Association: Enterprise Grain Co., Champaign, brokers; Hight Grain Co., Decatur, brokers; A. D. Rockwell, Paxton, broker; Harry E. Surface, Granville, shipper; E. R. Talbott, Springfield, shipper; H. C. Vollmer Co., Lostant, shipper.

The following are new members of the National Hay Association: Lanier & Callaway, Tampa, Fla.; Herndon-Carter Co., Louisville, Ky.; H. J. Hasenwinkle Co., Memphis, Tenn.; Joseph Hunter, DeWitt, Ia.; Farmers Hay & Grain Co., Harriman, Tenn.; Early Grain & Elevator Co., Amarillo, Tex.; Graham Grocery Co., Graham, Va.

The meeting of the Hay and Grain Producers and Shippers' Association of northwestern Ohio, announced for Friday, June 16, was postponed to Tuesday, June 20, because the convention of the Tri-State Hay Shippers' Association also has been postponed to that date. All of the members of the former association who handle hay are anxious to attend at least part of the sessions of the hay convention and they want to make one trip to Toledo cover both meetings. Then, too, the Ohio Grain Dealers' Association begins its Thirty-Second Annual Convention at Cedar Point the day following, that is, June 21. As it is only a couple of hours run to Cedar Point from Toledo many are going over. Every miller and elevator operator of northwestern Ohio should attend these conventions. A fine program is announced.

INDEPENDENTS OF NORTH DAKOTA.

On May 24 there was organized at Devil's Lake, N. D., a State Co-operative Elevator Association "for the education of the farmers in the better handling of their grain."

The following officers were elected: President, F. N. Pitkin, Sawyer; secretary, S. W. Unkenholz, Mandan; first vice-president, E. A. Lee, Hatton; second vice-president, O. Dion, Grand Harbor; treasurer, E. O. Engesather, Brocket; directors, E. C. Bracken, Pekin; H. P. Larson, Hoople; E. A. Bowman, Kulm; P. G. Meby, Hatton; C. S. Inman, Antler; W. A. Hasing, Ayr; C. P. Peterson, Bisbee.

COMING MEETINGS.

June 20, H. & G. P. & S. Ass'n, Lima, O.

June 21, 22—Ohio Grain Dealers' Association, Cedar Point, Ohio.

June 23, 24—Colorado Grain Dealers' Association, at Denver, Colo.

June 28, 29—Council of Grain Exchanges at Milwaukee, Hotel Pfister.

July—Western Grain Dealers' Association, at Des Moines, Iowa.

July 21, 22—New York Hay Dealers' Association, at Syracuse, N. Y.

July 25, 27—National Hay Association, International Hotel, Niagara Falls, N. Y.

October 9, 11—Grain Dealers' National Association, Omaha.

WESTERN GRAIN DEALERS' ASSOCIATION.

The annual meeting of the Western Grain Dealers' Association will probably be held at the Savery Hotel, Des Moines, Iowa, Wednesday, July 12, 1911, says Sec'y Wells in "The Grain Improvement Advocate."

The program for the meeting has not yet been arranged, but will probably be confined to the business of the association and general discussion of the subjects pertinent to the grain trade. It has been suggested that a lunch be served at 1 o'clock and that the business of the meeting be taken up and concluded at the luncheon and that a preliminary meeting be held at 11 o'clock for the purpose of appointing committees to prepare resolutions, etc.

Letters received from a number of members indicate that there will be a very good attendance.

GRAIN DEALERS' NATIONAL.

Under date June 5, Sec'y J. F. Courcier reports the following new direct members of the Grain Dealers' National Association: J. C. Murray, Chicago; Daniel Grain Company and Cunningham Commission Co., Little Rock, Ark.; Bonacker Brothers, Consolidated Grocery Co., C. B. Witt, Miller-Jackson Grain Co., Harman & Hulsey, Snow & Bryan, Peninsular Naval Stores Co., and Pitman Grocery Company, Tampa, Fla.; F. Saussy & Company, W. A. Wiggs & Company and Lewis-Upchurch Company, Jacksonville, Fla.; Cairo Milling Company, Cairo, Ill.; Joseph Hull & Co., J. E. Vann & Co., W. N. Gramling Co., J. M. Cox Company, and Whitman Commission Co., Waycross, Ga.; Valdosta Grocery Co., Curry Grocery Co., The A. S. Pendleton Co. and Valdosta Brokerage Co., Valdosta, Ga.; Callahan Grocery Co., H. C. Draper & Co. and Maddox Grocery Co., Bainbridge, Ga.; Brandon Grocery Co. and C. W. Cooper Co., Thomasville, Ga.; Heard Grocery Co., Cordele, Ga.; and Tift & Peed Grocery Co., Albany, Ga. Also the following associate member: Hay and Grain Publishing Co., Chicago, Ill.

RESOLUTIONS OF RESPECT.

The directors of the National Hay Association have adopted and spread on their minutes, as well as sent to the families, the following resolutions:

IN MEMORIAM, F. W. RUNDELL.

Whereas, God in his divine Providence and wisdom has taken from our midst our friend and fellow member, Fred W. Rundell of Toledo, O., who by his faithful attention to the rules and regulations of the National Association and his strict adherence thereto won the respect and esteem of all its officers and members who were fortunate enough to know and come in contact with him; therefore, be it

Resolved, That in his death this Association has lost a valuable member, his firm an officer who was fitted by natural and acquired ability to fill any office within its gift with honor to his firm and credit to himself; that the members have suffered the loss of a sincere friend; the city in which he lived a splendid citizen; and his family a devoted, loving husband and brother.

IN MEMORIAM CHAS. DIEFENTHALER.

The uncertainty of life and the certainty of death have been again exemplified in the death of Charles Diefenthaler, who was born near Berlin, Germany, January 18, 1847, and came to America in 1853, residing at Oconee, Illinois, during the past thirty-five years. He was in the hay and grain business for twenty-four years and since May, 1903, a member in good standing, of The National Hay Association; therefore, be it

Resolved, That the members of the National Hay Association, feeling a personal loss, tender their sincere sympathy to his wife, children, sister and brothers, until they shall be reunited in that eternal future where God is love and suffering and death are unknown.

OHIO GRAIN DEALERS' MEETING.

Following is the program of the thirty-second annual meeting of the Ohio Grain Dealers' Association at Cedar Point on Lake Erie on June 21 and 22, with the possible exception of one or two entertainment features not yet arranged for:

JUNE 21, WEDNESDAY, 9 A. M.

1. Meeting called to order by the President, M. W. Miller of Piqua.
2. Reading of minutes of last annual and semi-annual meetings by Secretary J. W. McCord.
3. Address of Welcome by James A. Ryan of Sandusky.
4. Response by Fred Mayer of Toledo.
5. President's Address, by M. W. Miller of Piqua.
6. Report of Secretary-Treasurer, J. W. McCord.
7. Appointments of Special Committees: (a) resolutions, (b) auditing, (c) nominations, by President M. W. Miller.
8. "The Relation of the Grain Dealers' National Association to the Individual Grain Dealer." Address by John F. Courcier, Secretary of the Grain Dealers' National Association, of Toledo.
9. "Why Corners in Chicago are Detrimental to the Cash Grain Interests of the Country," by George H. Phillips, better known as "Corn King," of Chicago.
10. "Inspection and Care of Scales at the Country Elevator," by J. A. Schmitz, scale expert, Chicago Board of Trade, Chicago.
11. "Shrinkage in Corn, December to June," by E. H. Culver, Chief Inspector, Toledo.
12. Adjourn to 9 a. m., Thursday, June 22nd.

Grain men and their ladies attending this convention will be afforded an excellent opportunity to witness the airship and hydro-aeroplane flights by Glenn H. Curtiss, on the afternoons of Wednesday and Thursday. The Cedar Point Company has closed a contract with Mr. Glenn H. Curtiss for a series of flights and the first exhibition will take place, weather permitting, on the first afternoon of the convention, followed by a second flight on Thursday afternoon. In these exhibitions Curtiss will use his latest invention, the hydro-aeroplane, rising from the water in front of the Breakers' Hotel.

JUNE 22, THURSDAY, 9 A. M.

1. Calling meeting to order by President Miller.
2. "What the Individual Grain Dealer Can Accomplish for Better Quality and Yield in Ohio Agriculture," by A. P. Sandles, secretary State Board of Agriculture, Columbus.
3. "Expenses per Bushel vs. Profits in the Country Elevator," by Chas. S. Clark, Chicago.
4. "Arbitration—Its Benefits and Difficulties," by E. A. Grubbs, member arbitration committee of the Grain Dealers' National Association, Greenville.
5. Reports from regular committees.
   (a) Arbitration, by E. W. Scott, Columbus.
   (b) Legislative, by Chas. E. Groce, Circleville.
   (c) Membership, by H. G. Pollock, Middleport.
   (d) Claim Bureau, by E. C. Bear, Hicksville.
   (e) Traffic, by H. L. Goemann, Toledo.
6. General reports from everywhere, by everybody.
7. Reports of Special Committees: (a) Resolutions, (b) Auditing, (c) Nominations.
8. Election of officers.
9. Adjournment.

On Wednesday evening the grain men and ladies will be the guests of The Cedar Point Resort Co. at the Coliseum Ball Room, the official badge of the Association admitting all to the ball room floor.

The ladies attending the convention will be the guests of the Cedar Point Resort Co. on Thursday morning for a delightful ride on the lagoons. The boats will be available at 9:30 o'clock, and while the grain men are attending the business session, the ladies will be inhaling the invigorating breezes which surround this delightful watering place. Other entertainments are in contemplation.

The Cedar Point Resort Co. has made the Association a special rate of $1 per day per person, two in a room, and $1.50 per day single rooms, at the Breakers Hotel. This rate not only applies during the days of the convention, but from the time of arrival until departure and grain men and their families can make this convention their outing period as well as a business session.

TEXAS ASSOCIATION.

Sec'y G. J. Gibbs sent to his members, among other things, the following post convention information:

T. G. Moore of Fort Worth, who was elected first vice-president, declining to serve, the new executive committee elected Mr. W. W. Hanning of Fort Worth in his place.

The executive committee has selected the following to serve as the Arbitration Committee: A. B. Crouch, Temple; J. A. Hughes, Howe, and Kent Barber, Ft. Worth.

President Hunt has reappointed L. G. Belew of Pilot Point, Texas, as the Texas member of the Tri-State Board of Appeals.

The following new members were elected at the Dallas meetinb: C. W. Barrett & Son, Temple; Bell Grain Company, Crowell; M. D. Chastain Grain Co., Ballinger; Fort Worth Elevators Co., Ft. Worth; H. C. Hughes Co., Meridian; Johnson Bros., Denton; Kell Milling Co., Vernon; Meridian Grain & Produce Co., Meridian; J. W. Philpott, Miami; Plains Grain Co., Groom; Oscar J. Rea & Co., Clifton; Rhome Milling Co., Rhome; Granbury Milling Co., Granbury; Sanger Mill & Elevator Co., Sanger; and Terminal Grain Co., Ft. Worth.

The following have resigned since my last report: G. B. R. Smith Milling Co., Sherman; and McKinney Elevator Co., McKinney (out of business).

"I attended the annual meeting of the Oklahoma Grain Dealers' Association, May 23-24, and am pleased to report that our sister association had a very pleasant and profitable gathering at Oklahoma city. While before that Association I succeeded in having our arbitration plan adopted by that organization; and hereafter the Oklahoma Association will compel its members to arbitrate with others, as does our association. Heretofore that Association could not compel its members to arbitrate differences with dealers who were not members of that Association. Considerable friction has existed between the Texas and Oklahoma Associations over arbitration matters; and I now believe that this condition will not longer exist. By mutual agreement, jurisdiction will lies in the association where the contract is performable; that is, if you buy f. o. b. Oklahoma points, then any difference will be arbitrated before the Oklahoma board; if bought delivered Texas, then the difference, if any, will be subject to arbitration before our board."

A city ordinance of Seattle, Wash., requires grain, hay and feed dealers to plainly mark on each package thereof, the net weight of the contents.

The Moore Grain Co. of Kansas City, Mo., has filed articles of incorporation to carry on business in Texas with headquarters at Fort Worth. The capital stock is $10,000.

George Gillian has accepted the position of sales manager of the feed department for the Crabbs-Reynolds-Taylor Co. of Crawfordsville, Ind. He entered upon his duties June 1 with headquarters at Lafayette, Ind.

The Russell Grain Co., Kansas City, advanced several hundred dollars to W. W. Breisford, alias W. M. Green, recently, on bills of lading covering two cars of corn, which later turned out to be fictitious. The two cars represented to contain corn turned out to be empty coal cars. Green was arrested when he was receiving the money advanced on the second car.

In the late May deal in wheat James E. Bennett & Co. of Chicago defaulted on a line of 205,000 bushels. It was stated that the firm acted as principal for William Lanyon of St. Louis, but the latter could not get the wheat in Chicago to deliver the last of the month. It was understood that 115,000 of the amount was sold to Peavy & Co. The matter will be adjusted by the arbitration committee.

COMMISSION

The failure of J. M. Buckley & Co., dealers in grain and feed at Philadelphia, Pa., was announced recently.

Hon. J. Barry Mahool, late mayor of Baltimore, Md., will again engage in active business in the grain firm of Frame, Knight & Co. of which he is a member.

Lamson Bros. & Co. of the Board of Trade, Chicago, have established a branch at De Kalb, Ill. Ernest Carter will be in charge, with offices at 118 North Third street.

R. A. Smith Grain Company, Lincoln, Neb., has been incorporated with capital of $12,000, by D. C. Sherrell, R. A. Smith, L. E. Cowden, W. S. Moore and J. E. Poindexter.

James A. Begg, formerly broker in the corn pit for Shearson, Hammill & Co. of Chicago has embarked in business as an independent broker. He will make a specialty of corn and oats.

Robert Thin, who has been for several years connected with the firm of A. S. White & Co., Chicago, as junior partner, has retired from business and will make his home permanently in England.

The Oklahoma Grain & Brokerage Company of Oklahoma City, Okla., has been incorporated with a capital stock of $10,000. The directors are C. Y. Portain, Duke Stone and Watson H. Candill.

The Louisville Hay & Grain Company of Louisville, Ky., has been incorporated with a capital stock of $10,000. The incorporators are Charles B. Goff, Edna Mae Goff, L. P. Hulett and Virgil H. Hulett.

The Interstate Grain Company of Minneapolis, Minn., has been incorporated with a capital stock of $3,000,000. The incorporators are O. S. Ostrum, C. S. Hulbert, H. K. Holverson, G. W. Sherwood, George E. Spinner.

C. H. Tayer & Co. of the Continental Bank Building, Chicago, added to its force of traveling representatives the past month by engaging P. C. Taylor, formerly of St. Louis to represent the firm in Illinois and H. H. Mullin of Britt, Iowa, to travel in northern Iowa and southern Minnesota.

The firm of Mereness & Potter have succeeded the grain commission firm of Mereness & Gifford at Milwaukee, Wis. The firm has been recently incorporated with a capital stock of $15,000. The officers are W. E. Mereness, president; F. J. Egerer, vice-president, and M. H. Potter, secretary and treasurer.

B. G. Ellsworth, former president of the Milwaukee Chamber of Commerce, has retired from the firm of L. Bartlett & Son Co., Milwaukee, with which he has been connected for several years. Mr. Ellsworth expects to retire from business only temporarily because of ill-health. After a rest he will return to Milwaukee and re-enter business.

M. L. Vehon, who had been with Rosenbaum Bros. for sixteen years in charge of their cash and receiving department, has formed a partnership with L. J. Schwabacher and began a general commission business at 331 Postal Telegraph Building, Chicago, on June 15. Mr. Schwabacher is president of the L. J. Schwabacher Co. The firm has ample financial resources to take care of any volume of business.

The Mereness & Potter Co., a new firm with a capital stock of $15,000, has opened offices in the Mitchell Bldg. in Milwaukee, Wis. W. E. Mereness, Jr., is president; F. J. Egerer, vice-president; and M. H. Potter, secretary and treasurer. M. H. Potter was associated with the Glavin Grain Co. for five years as salesman and vice-president and W. E. Mereness, Jr., with the firm of Mereness & Gifford for the past three years.

On account of the death of F. W. Rundell a change was made recently in one of the older firms of Toledo, Ohio, when W. A. Rundell Co. succeeded W. A. Rundell & Co. Two new members were taken into the firm, Wallace Applegate and Charles Coe. Both are energetic young men and equipped to help push the business on to new success. James E. Rundell retains his interest but will not be actively engaged in the business.

The announcement has been made that on June 1 the grain commission business of Bogert, Maltby & Co. will be consolidated with that of Hulburd, Warren & Chandler, with offices at 130 LaSalle street, Chicago. E. V. Maltby will assume charge of Hulburd, Warren & Chandler's cash grain department while J. A. Waring, Frank Cheatle and M. M. Adrian will be connected with the firm as traveling representatives. W. B. Bogert will leave for an extended pleasure trip abroad.

L. W. Forbell & Co. have succeeded Forbell & Kipp, grain commission merchants at 342 Produce Exchange, New York city. Mr. -orbell, who continues at the head of the business, has been long and favorably known to the grain trade of the East and West which gives the assurance that his long established business will be continued by the new firm with the same energy and close attention to the interests of western shippers, as characterized it in the past, together with enlarged facilities in the way of a capable force to carry on the work.

HAY AND STRAW

An alfalfa mill may be erected at Harper, Kan.

The wheat harvest began in central Missouri on June 12.

The hay crop, both in timothy and clover in Tennessee, is good.

An alfalfa meal mill will be erected at Elko, Nev., by Texas capitalists.

Riverside County, Cal., will have about 50% of an average crop of hay this year.

J. H. Fickey of Mobutie, Texas, is reported to have purchased the alfalfa mill at Cherokee, Okla.

Work on the alfalfa mill at Orland, Cal., is well under way and is in charge of John Thomas.

The hay crop in Iowa will be light this year owing to the continued dry weather and unusual heat. Hay is selling from $12 to $14 a ton.

Dairy men in Maine will this summer experiment freely with alfalfa. The Government will supply the seed, and planting will be made in July.

The farmers of Clay County, Minn., believe that they will be able to cut three crops of alfalfa this year, owing to the ideal weather conditions.

The alfalfa mill at Hobart, Okla., began operations for the season a short time ago, on a much larger scale, due to the increased acreage sown.

The annual convention of the National Hay Association will be held on July 25-27 at Niagara Falls, N. Y.; headquarters, International Hotel.

The annual convention of the New York State Hay Dealers' Association will be held on July 21-22, at Syracuse, N. Y.; headquarters, The Onondaga.

A report from Gypsum Valley, Kan., on May 23, states that the first crop of alfalfa is being harvested. The crop is very short owing to the dry weather.

The Louisville Hay & Grain Co. of Louisville, Ky., has been incorporated with a capital stock of $10,000, by Charles B. Goff, Edna Mae Goff, L. P. Hulett and Virgil Hulett.

The Chicago Board of Trade has appointed W. R. Mumford, George S. Bridges and Henry R. Whiteside delegates to the convention of the National Hay Association, to be held at Buffalo on July 25-27.

The Dayton Hay & Straw Co. of Dayton, Ohio, has been incorporated by Levi M. Thompson, H. L. Thompson, Elihu Thompson, George L. Lane and John W. Finfrock, with a capital stock of $20,000.

Hope of an average hay crop this year has been given up by specialists, even the Northwest, where there has been abundant moisture, recently sending in complaints of a short crop, due to May drought.

The first car of wheat of this year's crop sold at Kansas City, Mo., was auctioned off on the floor of the Board of Trade on June 12. The wheat came from Wagoner, Okla., and sold for 86¼ cents a bushel.

The Hupfer Hay & Grain Co. of Salt Lake City, Utah, has been incorporated with a capital stock of $15,000. A. R. Pintro is president; W. A. Wistness, vice president, and J. J. Hupfer, secretary and treasurer.

The directors of the alfalfa mill at Chico, Cal., will increase the capacity of the plant from thirty to sixty tons by installing a new cutter, which will be ordered in the east. The mill was only recently put in operation.

The Hume Alfalfa Mill Co. proposes to erect an alfalfa mill at Hume, Cal., which will have a daily capacity of sixty tons. The stockholders have made a thorough investigation of the methods employed at the Chico mill.

The Southern Idaho Alfalfa Milling Co. of Kimberly, Idaho, has been incorporated with a capital stock of $25,000. H. M. Vanderpool of Hansen and C. T. Brown, W. S. Star and J. O. Gates of Kimberly are the directors.

Sixty cars of hay, about 650 tons, in one shipment, were received at Minneapolis on May 26. The hay was of three varieties: timothy, alfalfa and prairie, and was grown in Kansas, shipped first to Kansas City and thence to Minneapolis.

The first crop of alfalfa in Umatilla County, Ore., is 25 per cent short this year, due to the chilly spring. The shortage will be more than made up for by the increased acreage and the second and third crops promise to go above normal.

The receipts of all grades of hay, while still moderate, continue ample for the light demand and is being moved at slightly reduced prices. Low-grade timothy, also clover and clover mixed hay, is still very dull and hard to place at any price.—Pittsburg H. & G. Reporter.

Canadian hay is being exported to the United States in all directions, one firm in this city putting out 25 car loads a day, and sending them to the Eastern and Southern States, as well as to St. Louis, Buffalo, Toledo, Cleveland, and other cities in the Western states that used to ship to New York. The export demand is so great that the railways find it difficult to supply all the cars needed at country stations.

Timothy hay sold on May 29 at Chicago at $27 per ton in carload lots, being the highest price since the Civil war. "At this price," the Record-Herald reminds us, "timothy is worth almost as much pound for pound as wheat and considerably more per pound than either corn or oats."

George S. Blakeslee, retiring president of the Hay Receivers' Association of Chicago, was recently chosen as the delegate of the organization to the National Hay Convention which is to be held at Niagara Falls, July 25 to 27 inclusive. J. J. Considine has been chosen president of the Hay Receivers' Association.

Notwithstanding the large export demand from the United States for Canadian hay our farmers have a considerable amount yet to market between now and the new crop, although the best qualities are pretty well all picked up, and American buyers have now to be satisfied with second best grades, and they are very glad to get them.—Montreal Trade Journal.

Sec'y Taylor of the National Hay Association reports the following hay production in 1910 and 1909 in the five leading hay states in tons:

	1910.	Percent.	1909.	Percent.
New York	$6,351,000	10.4	5,002,000	7.7
Pennsylvania	4,433,000	7.3	3,742,000	5.8
Ohio	3,948,000	6.5	4,033,000	6.2
Iowa	3,780,000	6.2	5,983,000	9.2
Illinois	3,717,000	6.1	4,135,000	6.4
Five states		36.5		35.3

Just thirteen years ago today, on June 13, 1898, Joseph Leiter's wheat deal collapsed, with losses somewhere between $15,000,000 and $20,000,000. It was twenty-four years ago today, June 13, 1887, when the Harper deal collapsed, carrying down with it nearly a score of Board of Trade firms and causing the collapse of the Fidelity Bank at Cincinnati, and the subsequent incarceration of its president in the Ohio penitentiary. Chicago Board of Trade men trod lightly and kept a sharp watch on the corners today, the former unlucky experiences on the 13th making them a little skittish about the hoodoo date. —Record-Herald.

The general feed situation, as a result of the hottest early year wave since 1900, is one of anxiety. In 1900 and 1901 (the former hot years) the United States failed to raise above 51,000,000 tons of hay. Since 1896 the United States has consumed an annual average of around 60,000,000 tons. A 10,000,000 ton hay shortage as compared with 1910 equals 620,000,000 bushels oats in actual poundage. In 1901 oats collapsed along with hay—crop 659,000,000—25.1 bushels to acre. In 1900 oats ran 29.5 bushels and the crop totaled 809,000,000. In 1906 shortage of hay boomed a second record oats crop of 964,000,000 to the above 40 level.—E. W. Wagner.

A law passed by the Missouri legislature two years ago that a hay inspection fee of 50c a car be levied, has been ignored in both St. Louis and Kansas City. In order to come to some conclusion, the Missouri Railroad and Warehouse Commissioners met the hay dealers of St. Louis recently and it was agreed that the fee be cut to 25c. The Kansas City dealers also accepted this. Two hay inspectors are maintained in St. Louis, but the office has been unprofitable. By general acceptance of the cut fee it is expected to put the inspection on a self-sustaining basis. A test case is pending in the courts to determine whether the act passed makes the payment of the fee compulsory.

The June hay condition of 76 suggests the smallest hay crop in a decade; smallest to date—55,000,000 in 1906. In 1906 no June report was rendered, but the Government gave the following conditions in August: Kentucky, 75; Ohio, 74; Indiana, 63; Illinois, 66; Iowa, 76; Missouri, 60; Kansas, 67. One million tons of hay, approximately equal around 35,000,000 bushels of corn and 62,000,000 bushels of wheat—in actual poundage. A decrease of 5,000,000 tons in hay production will equal 175,000,000 bushels of corn or 310,000,000 bushels of oats. The hay report is vital in its relation to corn and oats. In addition, June pastures are 6 to 12 points below normal at 81. Pastures at 81 are 9 points below the ten-year average.

"Hay and forage" is the big crop of New Hampshire, the leading crops in 1909, ranked in the order of valuation having been: Hay and forage, $7,846,000; potatoes, $1,205,000; corn, $621,000; oats, $217,000; and dry edible beans, $62,800. In all these crops however there was a decrease compared with 1899. From 1899 to 1909 the acreage of hay and forage decreased 85,225 acres, or 16.1 per cent. From 1879, when its acreage was 674,440 acres, it fell to 652,722 in 1889, and then to 615,042 in 1899, finally reaching 529,817 in 1909, a constant and consistent decrease. The average yield per acre was 1.1 tons; the average value per acre, $14.80. Of the important forage crops "timothy and clover mixed" leads all others, not only in acreage but also in value. In 1909 its total acreage was 210,196 acres, valued at $3,265,000. "Other tame or cultivated grasses," with 180,611 acres, valued at $1,978,000. Next in order came "timothy alone," with 84,155 acres, valued at $1,441,000, and lastly, "coarse forage," with 12,700 acres, valued at $530,000.

The Pittsburg Grain and Flour Exchange has by resolution authorized its secretary to confer with the state Department of Agriculture in regard to the quality of hay that is being shipped into that city, which is said to contain more Canadian thistles than is allowed by law. It is the intention of the Exchange to have the state department take the matter up and have the law enforced.

Hay is Wisconsin's largest crop, the Census Bureau on May 24 publishing a report giving the leading crops of the state and the value of each for the crop year 1909 in the relative order of value, as follows: Hay and forage, $40,866,377; oats, $28,657,670; corn, $25,727,654; barley, $12,682,136; potatoes, $7,915,763; tobacco, $3,855,033; rye, $3,163,520, and wheat, $2,585,188. Hay and forage were reported by 161,248 farms, or 91 per cent of the whole number in the state in 1909, as against 88.9 per cent in 1899. The number of acres harvested was 3,079,101 in 1909, as compared with 2,397,982 in 1899, 2,232,317 in 1889, and 1,484,920 in 1879. The quantity produced was 5,002,642 tons in 1909. Of the improved farm land in the state, 25.8 per cent was devoted to this crop in 1909, as compared with 21.3 in 1899. The per cent of increase in the number of acres in hay and forage, between 1899 and 1909, was 28.4. The average yield per acre was 1.6 tons and the average value per acre, $13.27 in 1909.

MINNEAPOLIS HAY EXCHANGE.

The annual election of officers of the Minneapolis Hay Exchange was held on May 27, at which the following officers were elected for the ensuing year: President, Guy Carleton; vice president, E. L. Phelps; treasurer, J. C. Miller; secretary, H. L. Elliott. The vice president and treasurer succeed themselves. Board of directors—John McGregor, W. F. Cleveland, Will Tierney; board of arbitration —W. F. Cleveland, H. L. Elliott, J. C. Miller, Nels Olson, T. Kerwin.

HIGHEST MARKET PRICES.

The following table shows the highest prices, also prices for No. 3 timothy hay in the markets week of June 10:

	Choice.	No. 3.
Boston	$25.00	$16.00
New York	28.00	20.00
Jersey City	28.00	21.00
Brooklyn	28.00	19.00
Philadelphia	26.00	20.50
Pittsburg	24.25	19.00
Pittsburg prairie	13.50	....
Providence	26.00	17.00
Baltimore	25.00	23.00
Richmond	25.50	21.50
Washington	25.50	20.00
New Orleans	26.50	20.00
New Orleans prairie	11.00	....
Kansas City	18.00	10.50
Kansas City prairie	14.00	....
St. Louis	22.00	15.50
St. Louis prairie	15.00	....
Chicago	24.50	18.00
Chicago prairie	17.00	....
Cincinnati	25.00	21.50
Minneapolis	20.00	15.00
Minneapolis prairie	15.00	....
St. Paul	20.50	13.75
St. Paul prairie	14.50	....
San Francisco	14.50	....

—Hay Trade Journal.

TEXAS PREMIUMS FOR BEST AGRICULTURAL PRODUCTS.

Probably no other state surpasses Texas in the number and value of premiums offered for the largest and best yields of various farm and garden products raised in the state this year. From reliable sources the Texas Industrial Congress has received reports that indicate a total of $30,000 in cash prizes, and additional premiums, consisting of merchandise, seed, etc., amounting to $5,000, to be awarded. These prizes are being given by the Texas Industrial Congress, local commercial clubs, merchants, banks, and individuals. Premiums are offered on a variety of farm and garden products, but corn and cotton are the principal crops for the best yields of which prices are to be given. In value, the $10,000 in cash offered by the Congress heads the list, while a number of counties are each offering premiums that aggregate from $500 to $1,000. Including the members of the boys' corn clubs, there are perhaps 10,000 contestants for these prizes, and the results are certain to be apparent in the total agricultural production of the state for 1911.

Capt. Wm. Selden has entered upon his duties as inspector of mixed feedstuffs in North Carolina under Commissioner of Agriculture R. F. Kolb.

COURT DECISIONS

[Prepared especially for the "American Elevator and Grain Trade" by J. L. Rosenberger, LL.B., of the Chicago Bar.]

Constitutionality of Weight and Board of Trade Regulation by States.

The Supreme Court of the United States (House vs. Mayes, 31 Supreme Court Reporter, 234) holds constitutional the Missouri statute of 1909, which provides that: "Every sale of grain, seed, hay, or coal shall be made on the basis of the actual weight thereof, and any purchaser of grain, seed, hay, or coal, who shall deduct any amount from the actual weight or measure thereof under claim of right to do so by reason of any custom or rule of a board of trade, or any pretense whatsoever, shall be deemed guilty of a misdemeanor, and shall be subject to a fine of not less than $10 nor more than $100 for each and every offense," etc.

The court says that the Supreme Court of Missouri well observed that the object of the statute was to prevent the enforcement of a rule of a board of trade, under the ordinary operation of which unfair and fraudulent practices occur, or would most probably occur, in the sale of grain and the other commodities named. Reference was made to the fact that the Board of Trade of Kansas City is a voluntary association of individuals who perform great service to the public, and that its purpose is to enforce, as between its members, a high standard of business dealings. Let all this be granted, and yet it must be held that the Board, in the management of its affairs, has such close and constant relations to the general public that the conduct of its business may be regulated by such means, not arbitrary or unreasonable in their nature, as may be found by the state necessary or needful to protect the people against unfair practices that may likely occur from time to time. Such regulations do not, in any true sense, interfere with that "liberty of contract" which the individual members of the Board of Trade are undoubtedly entitled under the constitution to enjoy without unnecessary interference from Government; for the liberty of contract which that instrument protects against invasion by the state is subject to such regulations of the character just stated, as the state may establish for the protection of the public and the promotion of the general welfare. If such state regulations are not unreasonable, that is, not simply arbitrary nor beyond the necessities of the case, they are not forbidden by the Constitution of the United States.

Validity of Board of Trade Margin Transactions.

In an action by a grain broker on the Chicago Board of Trade against a Milwaukee company to recover $618.75, alleged to have been expended by the plaintiff in the purchase of corn on the Board of Trade in Chicago at the request of the defendant, where the defense was, in substance, that it was a gambling transaction and not an actual purchase of corn, the Supreme Court of Wisconsin reversed a judgment obtained by the plaintiff and remanded the case with directions to enter judgment on the verdict for the plaintiff in accordance with the prayer of the complaint.

The court says (Wagner vs. Engel-Millar Co., 129 Northwestern Reporter, 392) that the question was whether these board of trade transactions were valid transactions or mere gambling contracts, and this depended upon the intention of the parties. If both parties intended no actual delivery, but merely a wagering contract to be settled by the payment of differences, then the whole transaction was a gambling contract and void, and there could be no recovery. If, on the other hand, either party intended in good faith that the contracts of purchase should be performed by delivery of the corn or warehouse receipts therefor (which was the equivalent thereof), the transaction was a valid one, and the plaintiff was entitled to recover.

The question whether there was such good-faith intent on the part of either party was not settled by the statement of the parties themselves, although such evidence was to be considered, but all the facts and circumstances throwing light on the intent were to be considered. The fact that the transactions were margin transactions, and the further fact that they were board of trade transactions, were entitled to be considered, because of the well-known fact that very many, if not a large majority, of such transactions are wagering transactions entered into with no intent to deliver the actual grain, but only to settle by the payment of differences. Nevertheless these facts were not conclusive. The intent to make actual delivery may exist in such transactions. There was direct and very positive evidence that it did exist on the part of the plaintiff in the transactions under investigation here; and the court cannot say that it is incredible, or that all the reasonable probabilities and the overwhelming weight of the evidence were against the existence of such an intent. Hence the question was for the jury.

The Planters' Bank & Trust Co. of Hopkinsville, Ky., has filed a suit against the Acme Mills & Elevator Co. to foreclose a mortgage on its plant and property, which was given to secure an issue of bonds.

Wendling & Co., grain dealers of St. Louis, Mo., recently filed a voluntary petition in bankruptcy. Its liabilities are $12,015.28, of which the payment of $1,525 is secured, and the assets are $4,240.89, most of which is due to open accounts.

Damages to the amount of $2,650 were recently awarded Mrs. Emily Bacon in the suit brought by her against the Peoria & Eastern Railway for the loss of her elevator at Lilly, Ill., by a fire, alleged to have been caused by sparks from a locomotive.

W. C. Marsh, a grain dealer of Adair, Iowa, recently went into involuntary bankruptcy with liabilities amounting to $35,000 and assets at $25,000. The farmers in the vicinity are creditors to the extent of $15,000 for grain delivered which was to have been paid for at the prices determined by future markets.

Wilton Snowden, Jr., was recently appointed receiver for the Baltimore Grain Clearing House Co., of Baltimore, Md., under a bond of $5,000. The appointment was made on petition of Howard C. Kaufman who claims that he is a creditor to the extent of $183.50 and that the company is indebted to many others and is insolvent.

A verdict of $1,479.14 was awarded the grain commission firm of Turle & Co., Duluth, Minn., for loss of flaxseed by the M., St. P and S. Ste M. R. R. Co., while the latter was hauling a carload from a point in North Dakota to Duluth. The plaintiff claimed that the car contained only 10,420 pounds of flaxseed when received, out of the 66,470 pounds which it contained on starting.

The Reinhardt Grain Co. of McKinney, Texas, has filed a complaint with the Interstate Commerce Commission against the Oklahoma Central and the Texas & Pacific Railroad Companies, asking reparation on a shipment of snapped corn sent from Blanchard, Okla., to Terrell, Texas. A rate of 29½ cents was charged while three days later a rate of 23½ cents was put into effect, although there had been no change in conditions.

A decision was recently rendered in favor of the Colorado Milling & Elevator Co. by Federal Judge R. E. Lewis of Denver, Colo., in the suit brought by the Union Mutual Fire Insurance Co. of Cincinnati, Ohio, to obtain $5,000 for assessments levied by the Ohio courts on application of the trustees of the company, which went into the hands of receivers after a life of three years, showing heavy loss. The Colorado Milling & Elevator Co. took out policies for $50,000 through J. K. Mullen some time ago, but as the insurance company had violated the state laws by doing business unauthorizedly it was not allowed to collect the assessments.

A case in the court of Clay County, N. D., in which the Atwood-Stone Co. of Minneapolis was the plaintiff, was recently decided in favor of that company, thereby upholding the legality of the purchase and sale of grain for future delivery as transacted under the rules of the Minneapolis Chamber of Commerce. The plaintiff alleges that it had contracted for 20,000 bushels of wheat to be delivered the defendant in December, 1910, and had received $500 as security on margin for the fulfillment of the contract, but owing to a decline in the market the security was exhausted and the defendant declined to furnish further security. To secure themselves against further decline, the sale was contracted by the plaintiff, involving a loss of $1,400, which the defendant refused to pay, claiming the transactions to be illegal.

THE INCREASING DEMAND FOR COW PEAS.

This favorite fertilizing legume of the Southern states is widening its market every year as its merits as a fertilizing plant become better known. It is surprising to note that even as far north as Cairo and even up into some parts of Indiana and southern Illinois the cow pea is said to do extremely well, although red clover seems to be the dominant fertilizing plant up in those latitudes.

The general and very successful use of cow peas as a fertilizer in Louisiana is attracting attention out in the tropics and efforts are making to secure supplies of these peas, or of their equivalent leguminous plants, to be used for fertilizing tropical sugar cane lands wherever sugar cane is grown. The prominent flour, grain and feedstuff house of George B. Matthews & Sons advised us recently that they had just received an order for one hundred bushels of cow peas to be shipped to Suva, Fiji Islands, in the distant Pacific, a thousand miles or more beyond Queensland in eastern Australia, and nearer by a shipment was made to Ceiba, Honduras.—*Louisiana Planter.*

OBITUARY

E. W. Cook, a member of the Milwaukee Chamber of Commerce, died recently.

J. F. McAuliffe, a pioneer in the grain sampling business at Minneapolis and a member of the Chamber of Commerce Sampling Company, died recently.

Arthur M. Sitley, head of the firm of Sitley & Son of Camden, N. J., died May 13. Deceased was a member of the Chamber of Commerce of Camden.

Claude A. Levis, a member of the New Orleans Board of Trade, died May 25 in that city at the age of 68. Mr. Levis was a representative of the firm of Ballard & Ballard for the past twelve years.

A. W. Gilbert, a former member of the Minneapolis Chamber of Commerce and at one time official grain sampler, died recently in Boston, aged 65. Mr. Gilbert sold his Chamber of Commerce membership two years ago.

E. E. Underwood, manager of the Independent Elevator at Omaha, Nebr., died recently in the hospital, following an illness due to kidney trouble. Mr. Underwood was 50 years old, and is survived by his wife and four children.

Frederick W. Rundell, senior member of the grain commission firm of W. A. Rundell & Co. of Toledo, Ohio, died recently at that place, aged 49 years. Mr. Rundell had been in the grain business at Toledo since 1880. Deceased is survived by his wife and brother.

Col. Charles A. Burt, a retired grain merchant, died recently at his home in New York City. Mr. Burt was born in Kinderhook, N. Y., sixty-nine years ago. During the Civil War he served with the Ninth New York Regiment. Deceased is survived by a widow and three children.

C. W. Sidman, who formerly had charge of the Cargill Elevator at Dassel, Minn., died recently at the age of 59. For the past few years Mr. Sidman had made his home at Spiritwood, N. D. He was a charter member of the Masonic Lodge of Dassel. Deceased is survived by his wife, one daughter, two sons and two brothers.

A. C. Merrill Bosworth, a member of the firm of Bosworth Brothers, grain dealers of Putnam, Conn., died recently at his home in that place, after less than a week's illness of pneumonia. Mr. Bosworth was born in Woodstock Valley, March 10, 1857, going to Putnam when a young man. He was married in 1880, and is survived by his wife, a son and three brothers.

William Buchheit, a member of the Milwaukee Chamber of Commerce, died May 21 at Watertown, Wis., after a brief illness. Mr. Buchheit was born in Zweibrücken, Bavaria, in 1827, and came to this country in 1851. For thirty years he was president of the Bank of Watertown, Wis. In 1889 he established the William Buchheit Malting Co. in Watertown, continuing in this line until 1897. Deceased is survived by his wife, five sons and five daughters.

George W. Simpson, a wealthy retired grain merchant, died recently in St. Louis, Mo., at the home of his son-in-law. Mr. Simpson was born in Gustavus, Ohio, 81 years ago, and lived in Jackson, Mich., Alton, Ill., and Hickman, Ky., before going to St. Louis in 1860. In St. Louis he engaged in the grain business, was connected with a flour milling company and the old Gratiot Street Warehouse Co. Deceased was a member of the George Washington Lodge, A. F. and A. M. and the Bellefontaine Royal Arch Chapter. He is survived by three children.

John H. Wrenn, a well known broker of Chicago, died recently at the home of his son in Los Angeles, Cal., from hemorrhage of the brain. Mr. Wrenn was born in Middletown, Ohio, in 1841, coming to Chicago when a young man. He was in turn connected with the firm of Tyler, Ullman & Co., Tyler, Wrenn & Co., Wrenn & Brewster, Walker & Wrenn and lastly, the firm of J. H. Wrenn & Co. At the first of the year he retired from active business. Mr. Wrenn was a member of the Baptist Church, and many clubs. Deceased is survived by a son and two daughters.

Thomas A. Bone, a well known grain man of Decatur, Ill., died recently at his home in that city after a long illness due to Bright's disease, having been confined to his bed since January. Mr. Bone was born in Christian County June 19, 1851. After gaining an education he engaged in the stock raising business. In 1874 he moved to Ottawa, Kan., and continued in that business there for nine years. He then returned to Macon County and engaged in stock raising for five years also becoming connected with the Decatur Coal Co. About 1890 he became manager of the Hatfield Milling Co. but five years later he went into the grain business with the late B. S. Tyler. For the last five years he had conducted the business alone, also operating several country elevators. Mr. Bone was married twice and is survived by his second wife and three children. Deceased was a Mason and a member of the First Presbyterian Church of Decatur.

CROP REPORTS

The following table summarizes the conditions of the leading crops of the country, based on the June government report, with indicated yields compared with the final harvest last year:

Grain.	Acreage. 1911	Acreage. 1910	Condition. June 1911	Condition. May 1911	Condition. June 1910	Condition. 10 yr. Av.	Crop. Indicated yield.	Bushels. Harvest. 1910
Winter Wheat	31,867,000	29,044,000	80.4	86.1	80.0	81.6	479,915,000	464,044,000
Spring Wheat	20,757,000	19,742,000	94.6	....	92.8	93.6	284,370,000	231,339,000
Totals	52,124,000	48,786,000	....	....	....	....	764,285,000	695,443,000
Oats	35,250,000	35,288,000	85.7	....	91.0	88.4	966,425,000	1,126,765,000
Barley	7,038,000	7,057,000	90.2	....	89.6	90.9	175,206,000	162,227,000
Rye	....	2,155,000	88.6	91.3	90.6	90.2	....	33,039,000
Pastures	....	....	81.8	81.3	88.5	90.7	....	....
Hay	....	....	76.8	84.7	86.1	....	....	....

A bumper oat crop is being harvested in Monroe County, Ala.

B. W. Snow, the crop expert, reports that there is a moisture deficiency in all the winter wheat and oats states.

Secretary Smiley of the Kansas Grain Dealers' Association estimates the wheat crop of that state at 65,000,000 bushels.

The acreage of kaffir corn in Butler County, Kan., has been increased one-third over last year, being this year 97,457 acres.

J. F. Zahm & Co. say the opinion prevails that the intense heat in the Central States has caused a marked deterioration in the oat crop.

George A. Wells, secretary of the Western Grain Dealers' Association, states that the condition of all the crops in the state of Iowa is nearly perfect.

Indiana will probably have a bumper grain crop this year though the acreage of wheat has fallen off to some extent, and some damage has been done by fly.

Owing to the cold and rain during the early spring and the recent hot weather experienced in Tennessee, the hay has burned up and the oats and wheat have been badly damaged.

A. H. Bewsher of the Bewsher Co. says the Nebraska winter wheat crop will aggregate more than 50,000,000 bushels, or 10 to 25 per cent more wheat than was raised last year.

There is an increase in wheat acreage of 25 per cent in Saskatchewan and 5 to 15 per cent more in Manitoba and Alberta. Crop conditions are more favorable than at any time during the past ten years.

The condition of wheat in Michigan for June is 91 per cent as compared with 93 in May and 87 last June. Oats condition is 88 as against 92 last June and rye 92 as against 91. The condition of corn is 91, last June it was 81.

The June crop report from Kentucky places the condition of corn at 85, wheat at 95, as against 82 last June and oat condition at 82 in comparison with 93 a year ago. Rye is 91 per cent. Corn is in need of rain and rust has appeared on some of the wheat.

The crop of oats shows a big decline according to the Missouri June crop report, the condition being 62 per cent as against 89 last month and 91 a year ago. Corn is 85.6 against 67 a year ago and wheat 85 as compared with 90 last month and 69 a year ago.

The foreign crop prospects are fair. The season has been backward in almost all Europe and a partial failure of the corn crop in Argentina and Uraguay is reported. Heavy rains in Australia have interrupted the seeding of winter wheat and decreased the acreage.

G. J. Gibbs, secretary of the Texas Grain Dealers' Association, estimates that there will be 8,000,000 bushels of wheat and 15,000,000 bushels of oats produced in Texas this year and 6,000,000 bushels of wheat in Oklahoma. Texas has not suffered so much from drouth as Oklahoma.

The condition of wheat in Oklahoma according to the June crop report is 53 against 65 a month ago and 88.3 a year ago. Corn is 82 against 88 a month ago and 93 a year ago. Oat condition 53 against 88 a month ago and 83 a year ago. Chinch and green bugs and Canadian thistles are causing some damage to wheat.

The Ohio June crop report makes the wheat condition 88 per cent, against 87 last month and 93 last June, the crop harvested being 31,000,000 bushels. Oat condition is 76 per cent against 100 a year ago and rye 85 per cent compared with 91 per cent a year ago. Wheat shows the serious effect of the long continued drouth.

The wheat crop in the Northwest is reported to be promising though not far enough advanced to withstand adverse conditions. Corn in general will be far above previous years though reports come from southern Minnesota stating that untold damage is being done by cut worms. South Dakota, west of the Missouri River, has suffered severely from drouth but only a small amount of grain is produced in that territory.

Southern Kansas and northern Oklahoma will have one of the largest oats crops ever seen in that section, if nothing serious occurs to hinder its growth.

[For the "American Elevator and Grain Trade."]

SOUTHWESTERN GRAIN AND FEED NOTES.

BY L. C. BREED.

T. E. Buckner of Steelville, Mo., announces that, owing to ill health, he intends to close out his mill property.

The elevator of the Smalling Grain Company, Chickasha, Okla., was recently destroyed by fire, causing a loss of $4,000, which is covered by insurance. The part of the elevator containing the machinery was saved. The fire appears to have started at the top of the structure, and it is thought that a small pulley was responsible for it.

The Farmers' Union Clearing House Association of Grayson County, Texas, has been incorporated. The capital stock is $2,000. The incorporators are W. T. Francis, W. S. Gilbert, A. Brackett and others.

The Union Seed Company of Bristol, Tenn., has sold out its business to John M. Fain and N. P. Lawrence. Mr. Fain was formerly the postmaster of Bristol and N. P. Lawrence has been doing business as a mercantile broker.

While grain men are aware that glucose is a product of corn, not many have heard that it is liable to be found in their shoes, or rather in the leather out of which their shoes are manufactured. This statement, however, refers to the lower quality of footwear, and as grain men like to go well shod, it is hardly probable that many of them will suffer from getting wet feet because of the fact that leather is being quite extensively loaded down with glucose, according to Dr. Wiley, the chemist of the Department of Agriculture.

It seems that the crop of hogs has not kept pace with the production of "humans." According to the U. S. census records, the statistics are as follows:

Year 1840: Hogs, 26,301,293; people, 17,069,453.
Year 1910: Hogs, 47,782,000; people, 92,000,000.

Reasoning from the basis of the law of supply and demand, it would seem that right here is some explanation of the advance in the price of hog products in recent years. It is suppose that the reasons for the relative difference in growth are, first, the increase in the cost of corn, and second, the decrease in the free range of hogs as the land has been taken up for cultivation. Maybe a third reason lies at the door of the packers' combine, if such a "trust" really exists.

The Kansas State Board of Health has recently, through its secretary, Dr. J. S. Crumbine, been busying itself in an investigation of the business of grain mixing which it claims is in direct violaton of the food and drug laws. According to Dr. Crumbine, any foodstuff must be sold, under the Kansas laws, for just what it really is, and that any practice by which a foodstuff is treated so as to make it appear better than it really is, without being branded as mixed, is a violation of the pure food laws. The department states that they expected the grain grading commission and the state grain inspector would take up the matter and stop the practice, but this not being done, the State Board of Health will take steps to prohibit misbranding of wheat, if it is found that their position in the premises is correct. This ruling is likely to be stoutly contested by elevator men, as a part of their profits have been earned by working over, cleaning, mixing and grading grain. This new departure may also make trouble for Kansas millers. At times, when the grain grown in some localities is not generally up to a high milling standard, it is necessary for millers to ship in choicer wheat from other localities and mix the two to obtain a satisfactory grade. Some of these millers brand their output, "made from the highest grade of Kansas hard wheat." The position taken by Dr. Crumbine is that this practice is outside the Kansas law, which prohibits "misbranding," and he claims that such branding is "misbranding."

E. E. Billings has retired as a member of the Billings grocery firm of Marshalltown, Iowa, and has purchased a half interest in the Bowles Elevator at that place, assuming entire charge of the business. Mr. Bowles will continue to operate his elevator at Wellsburg, where he resides.

FIRES-CASUALTIES

The Smith-Hippen Elevator at Pekin, Ill., was recently unroofed by a cyclone.

The elevator of Alice L. Potts at Cadmus, Mich., was slightly damaged by fire recently.

A fire on May 30 destroyed the elevator of the Duluth Elevator Co. at Thompson, N. D.

On May 31 the elevator of the Monarch Milling Co. at Mt. Sterling, Ky., was totally destroyed by fire.

The hay and grain warehouse of Charles Longcope of Philadelphia, Pa., was burned a short time ago.

The Monarch Elevator Co.'s building at Cashel, N. D., was destroyed by fire May 16, with a loss of $10,000.

A small fire was caused by an over-heated exhaust pipe in the elevator of the Wharton Co. at Yale, Mich.

An elevator at Watson, Minn., is reported to have been blown over by a severe hurricane which visited that section.

The elevator of the Security Elevator Co. at Young America, Minn., was slightly damaged by fire May 22.

George Howard recently fell down a shaft at the Ellison's grain elevator in Bradford, Mass., and suffered a broken thigh.

Lightning on June 7 destroyed the grain elevator at Coweta, Okla., owned by the Trowers & Hammers, causing a loss of $5,000.

A corn crib at Napoleonville, La., which contained 200 barrels of corn was recently struck by lightning and destroyed.

Fire, supposed to have originated from locomotive sparks, recently destroyed the elevator of William Ralston at Willow Island, Nebr.

Part of the iron coping on the Washington Avenue grain elevator at Philadelphia, Pa., dropped recently from the upper part of the building.

On May 21 the grain elevator of the Wall Brothers at Lizton, Ind., was destroyed by fire with a loss of $5,000, partly covered by insurance.

A vacant elevator at Fairfield, Nebr., once the property of the Ferguson Grain Co., was burned to the ground on May 21. No insurance was carried.

The Acme Elevator at Barlow, N. D., was blown over and demolished by a recent windstorm. The driveway of the Powers Elevator was blown away.

Two elevators at Conger, Minn., together with other buildings, were badly damaged by a wind storm which swept over that section of the country.

The elevator of the Atlantic Elevator Co. at Gardena, N. D., was burned on June 5. It contained about 8,000 bushels of wheat. The loss is $13,000; insured.

The dust house of the Inter-State Grain Co.'s elevator at Minneapolis, Minn., was badly damaged by fire believed to have started from spontaneous combustion.

John H. Larimore recently fell into one of the large bins at the Farmers' Elevator at Green Valley, Ill., and is suffering from a sprained wrist and other bruises.

Two grain elevators and a malt house at Sheboygan, Wis., owned by the Conrad Schreier Brewing Co., were destroyed by fire on June 2, with a loss of $300,000.

About $25,000 worth of lumber and a shed belonging to the Miller Grain Co. at Vassar, Mich., were destroyed recently by a fire caused by sparks from a locomotive.

Two elevators containing 100,000 bushels of grain were destroyed by the fire which swept away the main portion of Lake Wilson, Minn., a village seventeen miles east of Pipestone.

The elevator of Bird Brothers at Bonair, Iowa, was recently burned when struck by lightning. The loss on the building is $2,500 and on the grain 1,800, partly covered by insurance.

The buildings of the Stewart Hay & Grain Co. and the Bluegrass Produce Co., besides many other buildings were destroyed by a fire which started May 16 in the village of Carlisle, Ky.

An over-heated journal in the elevator of the Golden Grain Co. at Crary, N. D., recently caused a fire which was extinguished by H. A. Nicholson, the proprietor, before any damage was done.

Damage to the amount of $250,000 was done to the grain elevator of Demarest & Carr in New York City, N. Y., by a recent fire. Several firemen were injured. The fire is believed to have been caused by spontaneous combustion of grain dust.

The elevator and mill at Port William, Ohio, owned by J. E. Spurling of Blanchester, were recently destroyed by a fire caused by locomotive sparks. The building was erected twelve years ago by L. H. Starbuck, who conducted the business until his death, when it passed into the hands of the Gordius, who disposed of it to J. E. Spurling. The loss is estimated at $10,000, with no insurance.

The fire department was unable to save either the Neola Elevator Co.'s building or the Milwaukee Pump House at Cambridge, Iowa, when recently attacked by fire. The cause of the fire is not known.

A fire caused by a lighted match dropped in some gasoline-soaked shucks recently destroyed the elevator of Bendles & Co. at Durant, Okla., together with a car of flour, a car of wheat and sixty bushels of shucks. The loss is $8,000, with $6,100 insurance.

The old Wilson Flour Mill at Monticello, Ind., one of the old landmarks of the Tippecanoe River, was burned recently. It was built in 1849, and was the first mill in northern Indiana to use water-power. For the past two years it had not been in operation.

A portion of the mill building in which were stored some of the products of the A. Mowry Co., hay and grain dealers, of Woonsocket, R. I., recently fell into the river. It is thought that lightning caused the collapse. The building was scheduled to be torn down.

A fire of incendiary origin destroyed the elevator of the Columbia Elevator Co. at Oakland City, Ind., on June 8. Two thousand bushels of wheat were burned making the loss $10,000 with $5,000 insurance. J. T. Wilson and W. C. Miller were the owners of the building.

The co-operative elevator at Prosser, Nebr., which had a capacity of 75,000 bushels, was destroyed by a fire of unknown origin on May 22. The house was owned by the Verona Grain & Supply Co., and contained 3,000 bushels of grain. Loss is $14,000, with $7,000 insurance.

The Northwestern Elevator at Edinburg, N. D., was recently burned to the ground by a fire of unknown origin. Between 3,000 and 3,500 bushels of grain were in the elevator, none of which could be saved as the fire was beyond control when discovered. Some insurance was carried.

A fire of unknown origin was recently discovered in the elevator of H. L. Marsh at Newport, R. I., and extinguished before it gained much headway. The stock was damaged by the large amount of smoke which filled the building. During the past year the elevator has been on fire twice before.

A gasoline engine is supposed to have been the cause of the fire which destroyed the elevator at Elk Point, S. D., owned by the Crill Seed Co. Five corn cribs, a potato warehouse and other property was destroyed. Loss on the elevator is about $8,000, with no insurance. About $1,000 worth of seed corn was stored in the house.

The Farmers' Elevator at Mondak, Mont., was completely destroyed by a fire June 6, which is supposed to have started from a hot box in the top of the building and had been smoldering for some time. The building was valued at $6,000, partly covered by insurance as were also the 6,000 bushels of grain which it contained.

George Felsenhelter, aged 35, an employe of the Kentucky Malt & Grain Co. of Louisville, Ky., was seriously injured a short time ago by being crushed between a wall of the company's plant and some cars on the Pennsylvania Railroad. Both his legs were broken, several ribs were fractured and he suffered internal injuries.

The elevator at Lucerne, Ind., ten miles north of Logansport, owned by O. Gandy & Co., was destroyed by a fire which also burned the station and other buildings and might have destroyed the town had it not been for the assistance rendered by the Logansport firemen. Loss on the elevator and station is about $20,000.

The grain store house of William K. Kimball at Rochester, N. H., containing over a hundred tons of grain and other property, was totally destroyed by a fire which originated on the roof from locomotive sparks. The loss, which amounts to about $1,000 on the building and $2,000 on the grain, is partially covered by insurance. Other property of Mr. Kimball was also damaged.

A fire which threatened the entire village of Payne, Ohio, on May 16, totally destroyed the elevator of C. E. Hyman, which contained 30,000 bushels of corn and 82,000 bushels of oats, and a nearby residence. Loss on the building and contents amounts to $25,000, covered two-thirds by insurance. A hand engine was the only means of fighting the fire, as the village has no waterworks.

The building of J. G. Sawyer & Co., hay and grain dealers of Norfolk, Va., was recently damaged by fire. The upper floors were burned out and the stock on the lower floors ruined. The $2,000 damage done to the stock is covered by insurance, while the $1,500 worth of insurance carried on the building only partly covers the loss.

John W. McClatchie, of the firm of E. L. Welch & Co. of Minneapolis, and for twenty-two years identified with the grain trade, has decided to move to Medford, Ore. Mr. McClatchie has been a member of the Minneapolis Chamber of Commerce for fifteen years.

TRANSPORTATION

Switching rates at Atlanta, Ga., have been increased from $2 per car to $4 and $5.

Wheat charter rates from Pacific Coast to Europe for new crop wheat are advancing somewhat.

The Milwaukee Road has reinstated the reconsigning privilege on hay ou the Division Street tracks, Chicago, on the basis of $2, when the contents of the car have not been changed or disturbed outside of sampling; in other words, before delivery is consummated.

In order to give the Commerce Commission extra time in which to determine whether the conditions for shipping are so different there that New England should be granted permanently more than the forty-eight hours free time given to the receivers in other parts of the country the present demurrage rule of 72 hours free time has been continued until September 1.

The last link is now being completed between Sioux City and Ashland, Neb., in the making of a heavy roadbed for a grain carrying railroad from Canada to the Gulf of Mexico. Before this summer is over the link will have been forged in 90-pound railroad iron, and the Hill lines can take up the wheat of the north and the corn of the further south and send it by way of the Gulf for export.

The Omaha Grain Exchange has asked the Nebraska Railway Commission to issue an order extending free time for unloading grain. The demurrage rules give 48 hours, the time being calculated from 7 p. m. of the day that the car is put on the siding for unloading. As all grain must be inspected before it is sold and as this sometimes requires eight or ten hours, the exchange asks that the rules be changed so that the unloading limit will be forty-eight hours from 7 a. m. of the day on which the inspection is made.

On May 24 complaint was lodged with the Commerce Commission by Baltimore grain merchants that carload rates on grain are higher from certain intermediate points in Ohio, Indiana and Illinois than they are proportionately from Cincinnati or East St. Louis; that they are unreasonable in themselves and relatively; violate the long-and-short-haul clause and are discriminatory against Baltimore. The roads named as defendants are the Pennsylvania and Baltimore & Ohio lines and the Vandalia and the Northern Central Roads.

Advances in rates on grain and grain products asked for by carmen from North and South Dakota producing points to such ordinary grain centers as Minneapolis, Duluth, Milwaukee and Chicago, were on May 26 held by the Commerce Commission to be not unreasonable. The Commission holds, however, that the former established rates from origin to these destinations should be restored, except in instances of bona fide errors in tariffs or manifest violations of the long and short haul provisions. Advances in rates on coarse grain and wheat from South Dakota to Omaha, Neb., were condemned.

The Ohio Railroad Commission on May 20 established its own former and the railroad's demurrage rules and promulgated a new set that follow exactly the Commerce Commission rules as to 48 hours free time, and for various causes—reconsignment, switching orders, inspection, etc., 24 hours free time. The Commerce Commission is also followed on the rules for cars in bond; legal holidays and cars delivered to industrial plants. A rule not incorporated in the Commerce Commission rules is one asked for particularly by the grain men, that on cars containing freight requiring inspection, time shall not commence until 7 a. m., following the day of inspection, providing the inspection be made within 24 hours. The rules as to bunching cars are about the same as the interstate rules, and those for placing cars for loading, demurrage charges, claims, weather interference, are just the same. The Ohio Commission also adds a provision that when by neglect of the carrier, or by other acts, cars are so bunched that they are delivered in excess of daily shipments, the consignee shall have such free time as he would have been entitled to had the cars been delivered as they should have been.

COMMERCE COMMISSION RULINGS.

On June 6 the Commission announced its power to suspend a reduction in freight rates.

HALF-HOLIDAY IN DEMURRAGE TIME.

The Commission has ruled that the counting of Saturday (half-holiday) afternoons as a part of free time, under the uniform demurrage rules, is "not shown to operate in an unavoidable or unlawful manner in Philadelphia," etc. (Commercial Exchange v. Pa. R. R. Co., No. 3530; op. 1557.)

VALUATION IN BILL OF LADING.

The Commission has ruled that, the provision in the uniform bill of lading that, "The amount of any loss or damage for which any carrier is liable shall be computed on the basis of the value of the property (being the bona fide invoice price, if any, to the consignee, including the freight charges, if prepaid) at the place and time of shipment under this bill of lading, unless a lower value has been represented in writing by the shipper or has been agreed upon or is determined by the classification or tariffs upon which the rate is based, in any of which events such lower value shall be the maximum amount to govern such computation, whether or not such loss or damage occurs from negligence," is not found to have operated in an unreasonable or unlawful manner in connection with the shipment involved. (J. C. Shaffer & Co. vs. C., R. I & P. Ry Co., No. 3609 op. 1559.)

NEW TRANSIT RULES.

The transit rules going into effect at Chicago on June 1 in their most important features provide that "transit privileges will only be accorded shippers and grain house owners or operators who keep record in a manner acceptable to the carriers of all grain handled, including non-transit, how received and forwarded—i. e., by rail, boat, wagon or otherwise—and who will make affidavit when required as to the accuracy of such records, and who will permit inspection of their records by the chief inspector of the Joint Rate Inspection Bureau or his deputy.

"Transit houses shall make a daily report to the Joint Rate Inspection Bureau of all grain handled and surrender for cancellation in-bound freight bills to the end that at no time shall there be on hand live freight bills representing grain not actually in possession of the transit house.

"At the end of each calendar month transit houses shall also make report of the invisible loss, if any, and surrender for cancellation freight bills to cover the tonnage. It is understood that the invisible loss shall be determined as accurately as possible for the purposes of this rule, it being impossible to determine the actual invisible loss until such time as all of the grain in the transit house is weighed. Whenever the grain in the transit house is weighed a report of such actual weight shall be furnished the Inspection Bureau, and bills in excess of grain on hand, if any, shall be cancelled.

"When grain is reshipped from transit houses shippers will be required to present to the Joint Rate Inspection Bureau the inbound carrier's legally representative freight bills in duplicate, and shipping directions in duplicate, bearing shipper's certificate.

"It is not expected that the identity of each carload of grain can or will be preserved, but it is not permissible to make any substitution that impairs the integrity of the through rate; substitution, however, is not accomplished under this rule when grain is mixed or blended at the transit point for milling or grading purposes and charges are adjusted as provided herein."

KEYSTONE ELEVATOR CASE.

The Interstate Commerce Commission, by Franklin K. Lane, on June 6, resumed its inquiry into the relations of the Pennsylvania Railroad, the Keystone Elevator and Warehouse Co. and the firm of L. F. Miller & Sons, grain brokers, at Philadelphia. Mr. Marble, representing the Commission, is acting on the complaint that grain going through the Keystone Elevator pays export rates in, but ships out the grain to domestic points, a difference in favor of the grain of 1 to 3c. per cwt. in the domestic trade.

It was testified that the railroad pays the elevator 20c per ton for "elevation," and that the elevator gets ½c per bushel from the consignee for the same service; that the Miller Drying Machine Co. has drawn about one-third of the elevator's annual earnings for the use of the drier; but the railroad men denied emphatically that Miller & Sons were allowed export rates when the grain was shipped to domestic markets.

Mr. Marble put on the stand also F. C. Dickson, president of the Kentucky Public Elevator Co. of Louisville, who declared that the Kentucky Elevator had the same capacity as the Keystone, 500,000 bushel, but that it had been run twenty-two years at a profit and not one cent of "allowance" had been paid it. Mr. H. Todd, representing the Keystone Elevator Co., said the cases are not a parallel movement as the Keystone Elevator is operating the Miller drier and that more than 80 per cent of the business done in the elevator is curing and that this machine does it. He said that this places the Keystone Elevator in a class by itself, inasmuch as "no other elevator in the country is used for such a purpose." Both Mr. Marble and Commissioner Lane combated this statement. The Commissioner said rather caustically: "Philadelphia is a comparatively small market. It is a wonder that Chicago, the biggest grain market in the country, has not discovered this wonderful Miller system of cleaning. But, as a matter of fact, Mr. Todd, in Chicago and all over the West, there are elevators, large ones, where 100 per cent of the grain received is dried and cleaned. But, is that any reason for the railroads paying any one of them twenty cents a hundred drawback?"

J. J. Overholtzer, manager of the Farmers' Elevator Co. of Alcester, S. D., has been elected mayor.

FIELD SEEDS

It is said that a seed house is to be built at Wallace, Mont., in the near future.

The flaxseed crop of North Dakota should be a larger one, as all conditions to date seem perfect.

At the Iowa State Seed Dealers' Association meeting at Des Moines on June 6 the present Iowa state seed law was approved.

The Massachusetts Corn Show has issued its premium list for the 1911 show, on November 7-9, at Springfield. Professional seedsmen are not eligible in the competitions.

The United States Seed Co. of Shelby County, Tenn., has been incorporated with $500, by F. D. Craig, R. Warmly, W. E. Rhodes, John A. Crafford and John W. Apperson.

Minneapolis has finally abandoned the attempt to land the National Corn Show, having no interest in a possible deficit, a guaranty of $40,000 being required by the show's managers.

A Chicago seed house about the middle of May bought 400 bushels of seed corn in Grundy County, Ill., paying $3 per bushel. It was Madison Yellow Dent, and considered very fine.

A farmer near Stamford, Texas, after watching the performance of wild flax on his place, seeded two acres as an experiment, and anticipates a yield of probably eight bushels per acre.

The T. H. Cochrane Co., Portage, Wis., will increase capital to $100,000 and build a seed house to cost $15,000. T. H. Cochrane is president of the company; L. W. Hettinger, treasurer and R. L. Cochrane, secretary.

The directors of the Maine Seed Improvement Society at the May meeting adopted a resolution pledging the Society "to exhibit seed products at the annual meeting of the Seed Improvement Association, the Maine Dairymen's Association, the Maine Corn and Fruit Show, the State Pomological Society, the State Grange, the Annual Farmers' Week at Orono and such other places in the state as the funds will permit."

A seed swindler has been operating in Kansas, selling sorghum seed at $1,500 a bushel (in packages). Prof. Leidigh of the Kansas Agricultural College has been co-operating with C. R. Ball of the United States Department of Agriculture, in charge of the grain sorghum investigations, in trying to run down the swindlers, and they ran down a company in Oklahoma that has been selling seed by the packet. As a good grade of the seed sold by this company can be bought for $1.20 a bushel, the attractiveness of their prices can be estimated. The sorghum is called Shallu.

MARSEILLES BEAN TRADE.

Considerable quantities of beans are occasionally shipped to the United States from Marseilles, says Consul General A. Gaulin, but the trade is largely dependent upon home crop conditions. During the last calendar year the total declared value of these exports was $175,583, against $1,103,008 in 1909, and $1,107,908 in 1908; the figures for 1907 and 1906 were $15,167 and $300,762, respectively. No American purchases were made in Marseilles in 1905 and 1904.

The beans, which come chiefly from Roumania (Moldavia and Braila districts) and Russia, are sorted and repacked in Marseilles. Lima beans are imported almost exclusively from Madagascar, but this variety holds an insignificant share of the trade.

Prices have been ruling rather high since the beginning of the current trading season, owing partly to a keen demand from the interior of France, where floods and unfavorable weather practically destroyed last year's crop. A few important sales were made, however, to Boston firms early in October. During the first quarter of the present year the aggregate value of the declared shipments to the United States from this district amounted to only $17,216. The shipments consisted mainly of Giant beans from Roumania, which were invoiced at an average of $9.25 per 220 pounds c. i. f. American ports. Pea beans averaged $8.18. The market is firm, and there is no prospect of business of any consequence in this line with the United States until next season.

NEW SEED AND SEED CORN ELEVATORS.

Geo. F. Fielding & Sons at Manhattan, Kan., have but recently completed the erection of the elevators shown in the picture, one for field seeds generally and the other for seed corn in particular.

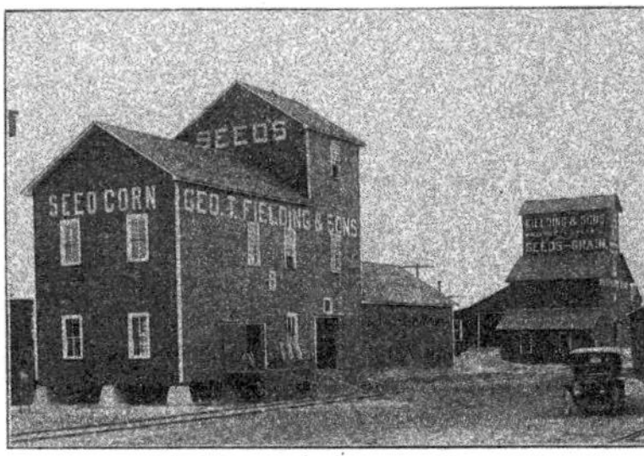

GEO. F. FIELDING & SONS' SEED HOUSE, MANHATTAN, KAN.

Both houses are equipped with the best of machinery for cleaning, grading and handling all kinds of field seeds and seed corn, and the firm is prepared to ship in small or in carload lots at any time. The seed corn elevator has 15,000 bushels' capacity and has a crib annex with capacity for 6,000 bushels in addition.

The Fieldings grow most of their seed corn on their own farms and take great pains in its selection at the proper time to secure the best quality, while that which is purchased from others is subjected to complete tests to secure pure strains and high germinating quality.

SOYA BEAN IN GERMANY.

Germany has removed the tariff on soya beans; and a recent importation of 4,823 tons of the beans (worth $166,600) by Stettin, direct from Vladivostock, is said to "mark the beginning of a new industry" at Stettin, towit, the crushing of the beans for oil, a local company having been organized with capital of $357,000 for this purpose. The price of beans at Stettin on April 10, 1911, was $16.42 per 100 kilos (220.4 pounds); of meal, $29.27 per 1.1 tons; cake, $28.08 per 1.1 tons. The new company at Stettin will have its products on the market shortly, which will compete with American cotton seed production.

The reasons that have induced the Germans to go into the soya bean pressing industry are (1) that as a competitor of linseed oil soya bean oil can be sold at a price one-third lower than the former; second, that soya bean oil is a valuable oil for soap manufacture, where such oils can be substituted; third, that for cattle feed purposes the residue remaining in the process of oil extraction can compete with the American cottonseed oil cake; fourth, that meal also can be produced therefrom which, when mixed in correct proportion with wheat flour, makes an edible bread or biscuit, provided the meal has been manufactured by the extraction process, which removes the 8 per cent of oil present in the ordinary meal.

Consul Heingartner reports from Batum, Russia, that the first crop of soya beans grown in the Caucasus has been sold to Hamburg. The amount to be shipped is 500 tons, and the price at Batum was $35.12 per metric ton. At this price the cultivation of the soya bean is very remunerative to the farmers; and it is estimated that this year's crop for export, judging by the quantity of seed beans retained for planting, will amount to 16,000 tons; and that, if the present demand continues, it is expected that in a few years the production of soya beans in the Caucasus will assume very large proportions.

THE GRAIN SORGHUMS.

In the West and Southwest a number of concerns have installed plants for thrashing and grinding the grain sorghums; and "Milo" and "Kafir" chops have become quite popular as commercial feeds. While there is a wide variation in their chemical content, the grain sorghums are all valuable as feeds, and average a little higher than corn in protein, but not so high in oil. The variation in the different grain sorghums, even of the same variety, shows that by selection the feeding value might easily be increased.

The grain sorghums are not only used as stock feed, but also as chicken feed. Meal made from them is not uncommonly used for making batter cakes; and there seems no reason why, when properly milled, the meal from these grain sorghums should not be used in much the same manner as corn meal. In parts of Africa and Asia, where these crops are largely grown, they are not only a common article of human food, but in some cases the chief article of diet.

Kansas and Oklahoma each devote over half a million acres to the grain sorghums. In the latter state the yield has averaged only from 10 to 16 bushels per acre. This is noteworthy, as it is these grain sorghums that have sometimes been exploited as new kinds of grain or wheat, with phenomenal yields. The principal groups of these sorghums are the "Milos," "Kafirs" and the white Durra, this last known as Jerusalem corn. The cut, which is taken from a bulletin of Carleton R. Ball, of the Department of Agriculture, an export in grain sorghums, gives the natural size of the seeds of six varieties. *A* shows the seeds of Milo; *B*, of White Durra; *C*, of Blackhull Kafir; *D*, of Red Kafir; *E*, of Brown Kowliang; *F*, of Shallu. This last is the grain which has been known as "Egyptian" wheat and has been fully described in a former issue of the "American Elevator and Grain Trade."

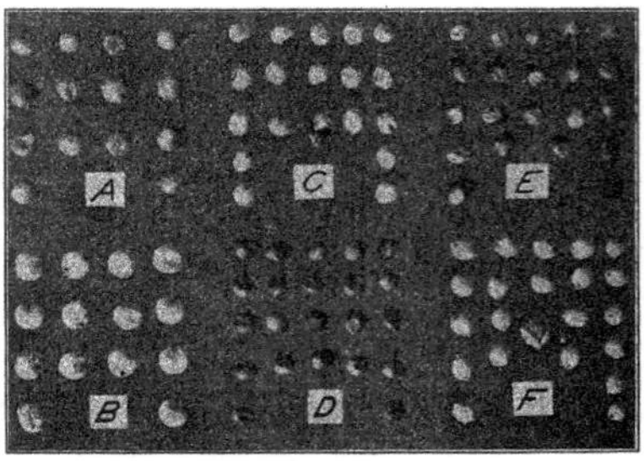

SEEDS OF GRAIN SORGHUM.
A, Milo; B, White Durra; C, Blackhull Kafir; D, Red Kafir; E, Brown Kowliang; F, Shallu—All Natural Size.

VARIETY TESTS OF OATS.

F. D. Gardner and J. A. Runk of the Pa. State College Exp. Sta., in Bulletin 108, report the results of a long series of tests of varieties of oats at that station, the object of the tests being to ascertain the relative productiveness of well-known varieties as well as those of recent introduction when grown under uniform conditions. The soil on which the trials are made is Hagerstown clay loam, and is typical of the soil of the station farms as well as the soil of the limestone valleys of Pennsylvania. For many years it has been devoted to a four years' rotation, consisting of clover and timothy, potatoes, oats, and wheat, each one year. The land is in four equal plats, so that the oats are on a different plat each year and always follow potatoes. Farm elevation, 1,200 feet above sea level.

"It is a well-known fact," the authors say, "that the relative productiveness of varieties of any crop cannot be determined from a trial of only one year. For reasons not usually understood, the highest yielding variety in any one year may be a relatively low yielding variety the next, and so a fair trial of a variety should usually comprise tests for a number of years."

"Japan," the variety longest grown at the station, is used as the standard by which to compare all varieties. All seed is treated with formalin for smut (1 pt. 40 per cent formalin in 30 gallons of water). The results of the tests are given as follows:

"In the group that has been tested for five years, none of the varieties has been equal to Japan, either in yield of grain or straw. Those most nearly approaching Japan in yield of grain are Long's White Tartar and Fourth of July. Of the next group, tested for four years, we find none that equals Japan in yield of grain and three that slightly exceed it in yield of straw. Those most nearly approaching Japan in yield of grain are Lincoln and Irish Victor. Of those tested for the four years, 1907-1910 inclusive, Sixty Day and Joanette have both outyielded Japan in grain, although they are below Japan in yield of straw. Sixty Day is a very early variety, with very short and light straw. As an average of the four years tested, it outclassed Japan by 6.1 bushels per acre, at the same time falling below Japan in average yield of straw to the amount of 726 pounds per acre. Japan gave two-thirds of a pound of grain for each pound of straw, while Sixty Day produced one pound of grain for each pound of straw.

"Kherson, which has been tested for only two years, is also an early variety and closely resembles Sixty Day in both straw and grain. During the two years it outyielded Japan by 7.6 bushels per acre. During the same two years, Sixty Day outyielded Japan by 10.3 bushels per acre. These are two very promising varieties. These two varieties are characterized by short, thin straw and small, medium long grains of yellow color. In 1910 they were less affected by rust, blade blight and blast than any other varieties.

"Of the medium maturing varieties, the following are recommended: Japan, Liberty, Heavy Weight Champion, Irish Victor, Silver Mine, White Maine, Fourth of July, Czar of Russia, Big Four and Joanette.

"As a general proposition, late varieties are not recommended."

For three years the station has been conducting tests, in co-operation with farmers, in growing winter oats; and finds that "the results indicate that winter oats are not adapted to Pennsylvania conditions, although in mild winters they may succeed in the southeastern portion of the state."

THAT WINNIPEG "SPREAD."

In the arguments that have been used to array the farmers against Canadian reciprocity, much has been made of the disparity between the price of wheat in Winnipeg and in Minneapolis and Duluth. It has been pointed out with great force that the primary markets in this state have been paying the farmers on the average ten cents more a bushel for their wheat than Winnipeg was paying the Canadian farmers. This difference, it has been strongly argued, would instantly disappear with the adoption of reciprocity, and the Minnesota price level would sink to that of Manitoba. The fact that wheat prices have of late been on the decline has been ascribed to the reciprocity agitation, and it has even been positively asserted that merely the threat of reciprocity had been sufficient to beat down prices on this side of the Line.

Professor James D. Boyle, of the University of North Dakota, in his evidence before the senate finance committee, gave a perfectly rational explanation of the difference in price level between Winnipeg and Duluth. These two markets should be on a parity, because each is a shipping point for export wheat, the Winnipeg quotations being for wheat ready to load at Port Arthur. The Minneapolis market is often forced to a higher point because of the strong local milling demand, millers being frequently willing to pay a premium for wheat in order to fill their contracts for flour. Professor Boyle pointed out that until the middle of 1908 Winnipeg and Duluth were actually on a parity, and that the "spread" between them has come entirely since that time.

What caused the change? Was it the American tariff on wheat, as the opponents of reciprocity argue? On the contrary, there was good reasons for the depression of prices at Winnipeg entirely apart from the question of the tariff. This reason was the passage of hostile legislation by the Manitoba Legislature. This legislation was directed against trading in futures, and it had the effect of disrupting entirely the Winnipeg Produce and Grain Exchange. It was forced out of business, and a voluntary organization known as the Winnipeg Grain Exchange took its place. Trading in futures was given up. Government elevators were also built in competition with the private ones.

The result of these changes was that Winnipeg grain dealers could no longer pay the prices they had hitherto paid. Elevators, which had been accustomed to "hedge" by selling in futures against what they bought for cash, had to give up this form of insurance against loss. They had to carry the risk themselves now, whereas formerly they had been able to protect themselves against it. Naturally that risk had to be paid for. It was paid for in lower prices for wheat. The Manitoba farmer is therefore paying insurance against loss to the agencies that gather and ship his wheat—an insurance that was before taken care of by the device of trading in futures.

The American tariff had nothing whatever to do with this depression of Canadian prices, in Professor Boyle's view. In fact, he produced a great mass of facts and figures to show that the American tariff has no effect whatever on the price of wheat on either side of the line, substantiating thereby Senator Nelson's declaration in May, 1909, that the wheat tariff is of no benefit to the American farmer.

The record of prices on the Winnipeg, Duluth and Minneapolis exchanges corroborates Professor Boyle's theory remarkably. Observe these prices, bearing in mind that the hostile legislation of the Manitoba Legislature was passed in 1908:

CASH WHEAT, NO. 1 NORTHERN.

	Mnpls.	Duluth.	Win'peg.
Dec. 22, 1906	$0.78⅝	$0.78½	$0.73⅝
Nov. 22, 1907	1.01⅞	1.00⅜	1.01½
Dec. 23, 1907	1.07½	1.06⅝	1.05¼
Jan. 15, 1908	1.09¼	1.07¼	1.08
Feb. 19, 1908	1.02¾	1.01⅞	1.03¾
March 15, 1908	1.07⅞	1.07	1.10
April 15, 1908	1.02½	.99½	1.02⅞
May 20, 1908	1.06⅞	1.06⅝	1.10⅝
June 17, 1908	1.09⅛	1.08⅜	1.06
July 1, 1908	1.07¾	1.09	1.00⅞
July 15, 1908	1.16⅝	1.13	1.04⅞
Aug. 18, 1908	1.24	1.17	1.10
Sept. 16, 1908	1.04	1.04¼	.99¾
Oct. 7, 1908	1.03	1.02½	.98
Nov. 18, 1908	1.07¼	1.07½	1.02¾
Dec. 16, 1908	1.08½	1.08½	.98¼
July 27, 1910	1.25¾	1.25¼	1.10⅜
Aug. 24, 1910	1.11½	1.12⅜	1.07½
Sept. 28, 1910	1.11	1.11⅝	.99
Oct. 26, 1910	1.05⅜	1.04¾	.93½
Nov. 23, 1910	1.05½	1.05¾	.98⅝
Dec. 28, 1910	1.02¾	1.02½	.90
Jan. 25, 1911	1.05⅞	1.05¾	.94¾
Feb. 21, 1911	.98¾	.96¼	.90¼
March 15, 1911	.98⅞	.98⅞	.90¼

—Minneapolis Journal.

A TYPOGRAPHICAL ERROR.

The substitution of a lower-case letter "c" for the letter "o" in an advertisement in the Sioux City, Omaha and local newspapers has caused all kinds of trouble to John C. Trothers, a grain merchant located at Neligh, Neb., by the New York World which tells the story.

Trothers, wishing to replenish his supply of oats, concluded to advertise. Writing his advertisement on a typewriter, he manifolded it and sent copies to the newspapers as follows:

"Wanted—Delivered on track at Neligh, 10,000 bushels of cats. Will pay highest market price."

Not noticing the error, he awaited results, which came sooner than he expected. Within a week cats of all kinds and descriptions commenced to arrive, consigned to Trothers. Some were sent prepaid and others collect. They came from the East, the West, the North and the South. The agent of the Northwestern road became alarmed. He was being swamped by cats and wired the superintendent for instructions. That official, not knowing what else to do, wired back:

"Release all cats not accepted."

Still cats continued to arrive, and still Trothers refused to accept the felines, but his troubles did not end there. Boys about town had learned that he was in the market for cats. They commenced to catch the strays and take them to his place of business. Some days last week he refused as many as 500 cats brought in by boys and three and four times as many coming in by rail.

It is estimated that fully 5,000 cats have been shipped into Neligh and the end is not yet. They are becoming a nuisance, and the City Council is about to take action and order a slaughter of the animals.

LATE PATENTS

Issued on May 9, 1911.

Alfalfa Mill.—Edward F. Rose, Fort Collins, Colo., assignor to Kansas City Feed Company, Ltd., Prescott, Ariz. Filed October 12, 1908. No. 991,893. See cut.

Car Mover.—Osman E. Hunt, Eagle Grove, Iowa. Filed October 17, 1910. No. 991,997.

Issued on May 16, 1911.

Door for Grain Cars.—Andrew Devan, Sandpoint, Idaho, assignor of one-half to Thomas R. Lynch, Drummond, Mont. Filed September 22, 1910. No. 992,710.

Dust Collector.—William E. Allington, Saginaw, Ill. Filed March 25, 1909. No. 992,531. See cut.

Issued on May 23, 1911.

Grain-Door for Cars.—John Henry, Grand Forks, N. D. Filed June 10, 1910. No. 993,250.

Grain Distributor.—Clarence E. Hoff, Rocklake, N. D. Filed August 19, 1910. No. 993,167. See cut.

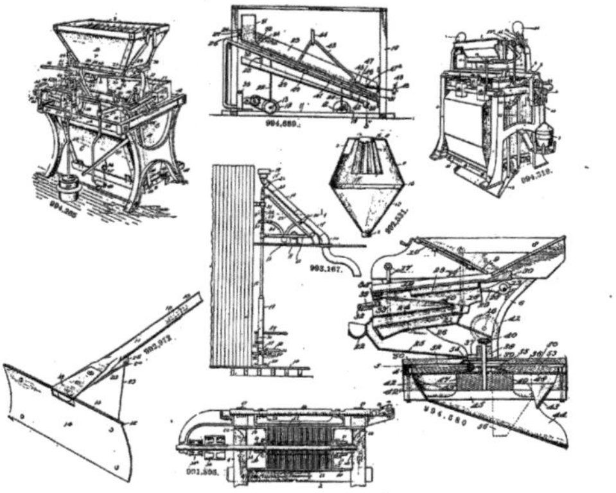

Grain Scoop.—Perry L. Meadows, Fairfield, Iowa, assignor of one-half to Walker H. Carnagey, Fairfield, Iowa. Filed September 6, 1910. No. 992,972. See cut.

Issued on May 30, 1911.

Grain-Car Door.—Joseph A. Richley, Minneapolis, Minn. Filed April 4, 1910. No. 993,876.

Issued on June 6, 1911.

Grain Cleaning Machine.—Oscar J. Erickson, Benson, Minn. Filed July 13, 1910. No. 994,580. See cut.

Grain Separator.—Samuel M. Schindel, Hagerstown, Md. Filed October 10, 1910. No. 994,659. See cut.

Automatic Scale.—John L. Jenkins, St. Johnsbury, Vt., assignor to E. and T. Fairbanks Company, St. Johnsbury, Vt. Filed December 19, 1907. No. 994,319. See cut.

Grain-Weighing Scale. Angus McLeod and Alexander T. McLeod, Bloomington, Ill. Filed June 14, 1909. No. 994,265. See cut.

SHRINKAGE OF CORN IN STORAGE.

To those engaged in the handling of grain the natural shrinkage of shelled corn while in storage and in transit is a matter of prime importance, and often a source of dispute because of shortage reported at time of receipt at warehouse, and a further loss at date of final sale.

In order to determine the amount of shrinkage, or loss of weight, occurring in shelled corn containing various percentages of moisture while in storage in elevators or during transit in cars, the Department of Agriculture, in co-operation with the Baltimore and Ohio Railroad Co. and the Baltimore Chamber of Commerce, has conducted an experiment with 500 bushels of shelled corn, the test beginning January 5, 1910 and lasting 147 days.

The corn used was taken from regular car receipts and was left in the wooden hopper of a 30,000-pound scale at Elevator B of the Baltimore and Ohio system at Locust Point, Baltimore. At the time of storage the moisture content was 18.8 per cent and at close of the test 14.7 per cent, or a loss of 4.1 per cent. The weight per bushel had decreased from 54.7 pounds to 50 pounds, and the total loss of weight was 1,970 pounds, or slightly more than 7 per cent.

The shrinkage was found not to be constant, as at certain periods there was a retardation in the rate of shrinkage or even a temporary increase in weight due to the absorption of moisture from the atmosphere. The average temperature of the corn and the temperature of the air was 20° F. The shrinkage during the first 105 days, while the corn remained in good condition, was approximately four-tenths of one per cent; while from April 21 to May 14, during which time the corn went out of condition, becoming sour and hot, with a maximum temperature on May 2 of 138° F, the shrinkage was 2.6 per cent. The shrinkage from May 14, after the corn had been cooled to 55° F, by three elevations to June 1, the end of the experiment, was 2.6 per cent.

While the corn was in good condition the rate of shrinkage was largely influenced by the weather conditions and by the relative humidity and temperature of the atmosphere, as shown by the data published in a pamphlet (Cir. No. 81, Bureau of Plant Industry) recently issued by the U. S. Department of Agriculture.

Peter A. Murphy of Chicago will become connected with the Simonds-Shields Grain Co. of Chicago and has applied for membership on the Kansas City Board of Trade.

E. E. Hovden has resigned his position as manager of the Bingham Brothers Elevator at Brookings, S. D., on account of ill health, and will be succeeded by Iver Dybdahl.

Bert Berkins, who formerly had charge of the Van Dusen Elevator at Chester, Minn., now has charge of that company's elevator at Rochester, Minn., in place of John Cohen.

George Devries, who for ten years has been grain buyer for the Western Elevator Co. at Alta, Iowa, has mysteriously disappeared. He left for Storm Lake on a fishing trip and has not been heard of since.

A. A. Hauge, who has assisted Mr. Henjum in the elevator at Hartford, S. D., for the last two years, has secured a position as manager of the newly organized Farmers' Elevator Co. at Dimock, S. D.

E. P. Jones, who represented the Southwestern Insurance Agency in the Southwest for several years, has resigned and will cover the Illinois territory for the Millers' National Insurance Co. His headquarters will probably be at St. Louis, Mo.

J. A. Heath, general manager of the Richmond Elevator Co. at New Haven, Mich., has just completed a handsome residence in Richmond, Mich., on land taken up by his grandfather Alex. Beebe, under the administration of President Van Buren.

BARLEY *and* MALT

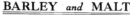

A steel malt elevator is being installed in the plant of Ballantine & Co. at Newark, N. J.

J. H. Kurth & Co., brewers of Columbus, Wis., are erecting a malt house at a cost of $100,000.

The old malt house of S. K. Nester at Geneva, N. Y., has been purchased by C. H. McLaughlin of Buffalo.

An addition will be built by the Star Malt & Grain Co. to its plant at Lomira, Wis. It will be 50x100 feet and four stories high.

The Cold Spring Malting Co. of Cold Spring, Minn., has been incorporated by John Oster, Ferdinand Peters and Eugene Hermanutz, all of Cold Springs, with a capital stock of $60,000.

The Colorado Malt & Barley Co. of Longmont, Colo., which was recently organized, is erecting a malt house. The structure will be of brick, 54x70 feet in diameter and will contain a kiln room 30x32 feet.

The Chicago Consolidated Brewing & Malting Co.'s plant in Chicago has been purchased by the Fleischmann Co. of Cincinnati. The plant consists of a large malt house, formerly owned by the American Malting Co.

"In the May issue I said that the visible supply would soon be under the million bushel mark, and on May 13 it was 961,000 bushels. After that, it increased a little and on June 1 was 1,066,000 bushels, but soon will go lower."

The Winnipeg Free Press in May distributed fifty sample lots of seed of a new strain of barley developed by Prof. C. A. Zantz at the Ontario Agricultural College, which is said to be strong in the straw, a good yielder, practically immune from rust, and a good malting barley and from which splendid results have been already obtained at Brandon experimental farm.

The Fleischmann Malting Co. has been chartered at Columbus, Ohio, with a capital stock of $2,000,000, by Julius Fleischmann, Casper H. Rowe, Charles J. Christie and others, for the purpose of taking over the malt house properties owned by the Fleischmann Co. The companies to go into the new corporation are the Riverside Malting & Elevator Co. in Sedamsville, which has a capacity of 600,000 bushels; the Griesback Malting Co. of Chicago, which has a capacity of 1,000,000 bushels, and Charles G. Curtis & Co.'s two malt houses at Buffalo, with a combined capacity of 1,500,000 bushels. The Fleischmann Malting Co. will now have an annual malting capacity of 3,100,000 bushels. Julius Fleischmann will be president. The plant of the Kentucky Malting & Elevator Co. at Louisville, Ky., which was recently purchased by Casper H. Rowe and Dr. Alois Zeckendorf from the estate of John Greisbach, the manager of the vinegar interests of the Fleischmann Co., will not be placed in the new corporation at present.

The mixing of all kinds of stuff with barley to gain barley prices, is still in full swing, says W. H. Prinz in "American Brewers' Review." "This practice should be strongly condemned, and the outcome will be that markets or shipping points that tolerate such a practice and ship out such mixed barley, will lose their prestige and also their trade. Another feature of the market which has appeared lately is the mixing of Coast malt with our malt. This malt will not alone crush unevenly, but also give a lower yield, and the practice should be condemned. Again, the same as last year where malting barleys were short, much barley has to be used that is really only feed barley and not malting barley; and it is certain we shall go into the new season with no stocks of barley on hand and new barley will have to be used before it is fit for malting, as new barley at the beginning of the season never malts as well as old barley. In former years maltsters always had a certain amount of old barley on hand to start their plants at the beginning of a new season, but this has not been the case in the last few seasons. So they will again have to start their houses with new barley. What this new barley will be is much of a question, as the harvest is about three months off and barley is never safe until it is harvested.

BARLEY AND MALT PRICES.

The range in prices between the different grades depends entirely upon the relative quantities produced of the various qualities during a crop year, and of course the relative demand for the better grades of malt, and is not arbitrarily fixed. With the exception of the crop of 1907, which was considerably short, prices of barley for a number of years have been largely regulated by the prices of oats and the demand for feeding and mixing barley. That is not true of this year's crop, which is reported about 20 per cent below normal in quantity, and so far barley prices have ruled relatively higher than corn and oats, owing to the urgent demand and light supply. The relative cleaned cost of barley has also been determined by the demand for barley screenings for feeding and oat mixing purposes. It is not strange that the superficial observer will not understand that the apparent spread between barley prices, as he sees them in market reports, and prices he pays, does not exist, because of the nature of the crop, which may mean a large percentage of screenings that may be sold at comparatively low prices, whereas in some other crop year it may cost little or no more than original cost to prepare barley for the steep, and that, after all, his maister is not getting more than a fair profit, if that.—Am. Brewers' Review.

WISCONSIN BARLEY.

In a recent bulletin (No. 212) by the University of Wisconsin Experiment Station, Prof. R. A. Moore says that:

"The Wisconsin barley crop comprises about one-eighth of all the barley grown in the United States, or approximately 25,000,000 bushels annually. The main barley growing section is in south and eastern Wisconsin, in Dodge, Washington, Ozaukee, Fond du Lac, Sheboygan, Manitowoc and Calumet Counties. However, the barley growing area is being extended and several western counties are producing considerable amounts.

"The classes of barley which have proved the best yielders in Wisconsin have been six-rowed varieties known as Oderbrucker, Manshury, Silver King and Golden Queen. The new Wisconsin pedigree varieties have demonstrated their superior value by returning higher average yields than the other sorts. The result of twelve years of barley experiments at this station has been the breeding and selection of a few reliable varieties to be multiplied in quantity for dissemination throughout the state.

"The dissemination of barley to most of the growers of the state has been made possible through co-operation with the members of the Wisconsin Agricultural Experiment Association over 1,200 of whom are growing barley and selling seeds of improved quality to their neighboring farmers. Tests by these growers have shown that the pedigree varieties are much superior in yield and quality to the common varieties grown in the community.

"The culture of barley needs to be improved along with the use of better seed. Careful seed testing followed by sowing on a well-prepared soil will aid in securing greater yields. Treatment of seed barley for smut by the hot water method has proved effective in keeping down losses from this cause. If this method is regularly practiced there will be no serious losses from smut."

For Sale

[Copy for notices under this head should reach us by the 12th of the month to insure insertion in the issue for that month.]

ELEVATORS AND MILLS

ELEVATOR IN CORN BELT FOR SALE.

Elevator in corn belt for sale. Easy terms. Address

COON BROS., Rantoul, Ill.

ELEVATORS AND MILLS

FOR SALE.

Elevators in Illinois and Indiana that handle from 150,000 bushels to 300,000 bushels annually. Good locations. Prices very reasonable. Address,

JAMES M. MAGUIRE, Campus, Ill.

KANSAS ELEVATOR FOR SALE.

Only elevator and grain business in a good grain and alfalfa locality is for sale. Bumper wheat crop now in sight. Address

J. JACOBSON, Formoso, Kan.

CHOICE MILLING PROPERTY FOR SALE.

One of the finest milling and grain shipping properties in fine grain section of Nebraska for sale, either as a property or a controlling interest in same. Address

M. C., Box 4, care of American Elevator & Grain Trade, Chicago, Ill.

LINE OF COUNTRY ELEVATORS FOR SALE

Line of 22 country elevators for sale, all located in good territories, 15 in Minnesota and 7 in North Dakota. Will sell as a line or singly. An excellent proposition. Address

ELEVATORS, Box 3, Care American Elevator & Grain Trade, Chicago, Ill.

IOWA ELEVATOR FOR SALE.

$5,000 cash will buy a modern elevator plant in the best corn and oat section of Iowa on the C., R. I. & P. Road. Station will handle 400,000 bushels, good competition. Address

IOWA, Box 5. Care of "American Elevator & Grain Trade," Chicago, Ill.

TO INVESTORS.

$100,000 new issue of capital stock of the Albion Milling Co., is offered for sale by single shares or in large blocks. It is purposed to increase the flouring and grain business. A fine property in a good grain section, and has been profitable to investors. Address,

ALBION MILLING CO., Albion, Nebr.

SOUTH DAKOTA ELEVATOR FOR SALE.

Elevator and coal business in South Dakota for sale. Elevator capacity 30,000 bushels, built 1908, modern and up to date. Doing a business of 125,000 bushels per year. Coal sheds have capacity of 80 tons. Coal sales from 1,000 to 1,200 tons annually. Address

LOCK BOX 96, Conde, S. D.

ELEVATOR NEAR CANADIAN LINE FOR SALE.

Elevator in Bottineau County, N. D., near Canadian boundary, for sale. Reciprocity will make a splendid market. Two hundred and ten acres for sale with elevator; farm buildings are forty rods from the elevator. An ideal opportunity for an industrious investor. Address

NORTH DAKOTA, Box 4, Care American Elevator & Grain Trade, Chicago, Ill.

WESTERN OHIO PLANT FOR SALE.

A 15,000 bushel elevator and 75-barrel flour mill, combined, with coal business, for sale. Well located in western Ohio, with no competition. Plant built six years ago, all new machinery, everything in first class shape and doing a good business. Reason for selling—too much other business. Price $7,500. Inspection solicited. Address

E. C. BRUNGARD, Big Springs, Ohio.

OHIO ELEVATOR FOR SALE.

A 6,000-bushel Ohio elevator for sale. Has good trade; is located on T. & O. C. Ry., in as good a farming section as there is in Ohio. Everything new and up-to-date; 12-h.p. St. Marys Engine, No. 4 Monitor Cleaner, 1,000-bushel Avery Automatic Scale. Good coal trade, no competition. Also handles hay, flour and mill feed. Price, $3,500. Address

BOX 51, Climax, Ohio.

MACHINERY

ENGINES FOR SALE.

Gasoline engines for sale; 5, 7, 10, 20, 30 and 45 horsepower.

TEMPLE PUMP CO., 15th Place, Chicago, Ill.

STEEL ELEVATOR BOOT TANKS FOR SALE.

Five large steel elevator boot tanks for sale. Good condition, water tight, low price. Address

R. E. JONES CO., Wabasha, Minn.

CORN SHELLER FOR SALE.

Marseilles Corn Sheller for sale. Absolutely new; never installed. Address

J. B. HORTON & CO., Memphis, Tenn.

GAS ENGINE FOR SALE.

A 20 H. P. Capital Gas Engine, as good as new, for sale. Price $300. Address

COLUMBIA FURNITURE MFG. CO., 1312 W. 22nd St., Chicago, Ill.

ENGINES FOR SALE.

We have for sale the following engines:
One 5 H. P. Fairbanks Morse.
One 9 H. P. Lauson.
One 12 H. P. Lauson.
One 30 H. P. McVicker.

and a great many other sizes and styles. We have what you need. State your requirements. Address

THE BADGER MOTOR CO., 917 Third St., Milwaukee, Wis.

MACHINERY BARGAINS.

Corliss, Automatic and Throttling Governor Steam Engines of all sizes.

Gas Engines—
1 25 H. P. Fairbanks & Morse.
1 25 H. P. Climax.
1 25 H. P. Walruth.
1 5 H. P. Pierce.

Belting, Shafting, Pulleys and Hangers. Address

CLEVELAND BELTING & MACHINERY CO., Cleveland, Ohio.

REBUILT MACHINERY FOR SALE.

List of rebuilt machinery standard makes, late designs, carefully overhauled, and shipped to responsible parties on open account.

ATTRITION MILLS.

One 18-in. Engelberg; one 24-in. Foos; one 24-in. Cogswell.

CYCLONE DUST COLLECTORS.

Three No. 5, 6 No. 6, 4 No. 7.

GRINDING MILLS.

One No. 10 Bowser grinder; one 9x18 three pair high Noye; one 9x14 three pair high Wolf; one 7x18 three pair high Bradford.

CORN SHELLERS.

One No. 1 and one No. 2½ Western.

SCALES.

One Howe Wagon Scale; Dormant scales, 100 to 1,000 pounds capacity.

SEPARATORS.

One No. 2½ B. & L. Warehouse; one No. 4 Monitor receiving separator; one No. 0 Richmond receiving separator.

SCOURERS.

Two No. 7 Eureka for elevator work, capacity 4 to 5 hundred bus. per hour.

GASOLINE ENGINE.

One 34 H. P. Miami, Gas or Gasoline Engine.

ORVILLE SIMPSON CO., Sucessors to The Straub Machinery Co., Station A., Cincinnati, Ohio.

MACHINERY

REBUILT MACHINERY FOR SALE.

FEED MILLS—7x14 Richmond, 9x14 Allis, 9x24 Barnard & Leas, all two pair high; 7x14 Richmond, 9x18 Noye, 9x18 Smith, 9x18 Nordyke & Marmon, 9x24 Alfree, 9x30 Wolf, all three pair high; No. O Willford, three roll two reduction, and many others.

ATTRITION MILLS—19-inch, 24-inch and 26-inch Foos, 30-inch American.

ROLLER MILLS—All sizes, 6x12 inch to 9x30 inch in all standard makes.

BUHR MILLS—Portable, iron or wood frame, all sizes.

Dust Collectors, Corn Shellers, Reels, Purifiers, Scourers, Separators, Belting, Pulleys, Shafting, Elevator Supplies.

Write for "Gump Bargains," giving complete list of all machinery in stock.

B. F. GUMP CO., 431-437 S. Clinton St., Chicago, Ill.

SCALES

SCALES FOR SALE.

Scales for elevators, mills, or for hay, grain or stock; new or second-hand at lowest prices. Lists free.

CHICAGO SCALE CO., 299 Jackson Boulevard, Chicago, Ill.

NEW AND SECOND HAND SCALES.

A 3,500-lb. refitted Fairbanks Dormant Scale, in first-class condition, for sale very cheap; also a 10 Ton refitted Fairbanks Wagon Scale, with compound beam, in first-class shape. This is an extra scale used by the Milwaukee Chamber of Commerce. Write for particulars on these bargains; also new scales. Address

MILWAUKEE SCALE CO., 134 Sycamore St., Milwaukee, Wis.

Miscellaneous Notices

[Copy for notices under this head should reach us by the 12th of the month to insure insertion in the issue for that month.]

ELEVATORS BOUGHT AND SOLD.

I have elevators for sale in all the grain belts, also buyers for all kinds of plants. Write me.

R. W. JETER, The Elevator Salesman, Ashton, Ill.

MOTOR WANTED.

Want a good second-hand 7 to 8 H. P. direct current electric motor, slow speed. Give particulars and lowest price. Address

J. ZIMMERN'S COMPANY, Mobile, Ala.

HELP WANTED

MEN WANTED.

One or two reliable and experienced men are wanted to run country elevators in Kansas. None but men of experience and with first-class references need apply. Address

A. B. C., Box 3, care American Elevator & Grain Trade, Chicago, Ill.

Grain and Seeds

SEEDS FOR SALE.

Whippoorwill Cow Pea, Fancy German Millet and Cane Seed for sale. Ask for samples and prices. Address

LOUISVILLE SEED CO., Louisville, Ky.

MAHOGANY CORN WANTED.

Can use up to 25,000 bushels of mahogany corn. Send samples and name lowest price. Address

C. C. LEWIS, Chamber of Commerce, Buffalo, N. Y.

FLOUR AND MILL FEEDS.

Mixed cars of flour and mill feeds in 100-pound sacks are our specialties. Would like to send you a trial order to convince you of the superiority of our products.

ANSTED & BURK CO., Springfield, Ohio.

PATENT FOR SALE

ROOFING AND SIDING

GRAIN RECEIVERS

PITTSBURG

CRAWFORDSVILLE, Ind.

CINCINNATI

ꟻCEIVERS

LANCASTER

NEW YORK CITY

MILWAUKEE

ST. LOUIS

BATTLE CREEK, Mich.

HAVANA, CUBA

GRAIN RECEIVERS

GRAIN RECEIVERS

CHICAGO

For Intelligent, Prompt and Efficient Service
Consign to
Rosenbaum Brothers
Commission Merchants
77 Board of Trade Chicago

H. M. PAYNTER
GRAIN COMMISSION
Special attention given consignments of grain and seeds. Orders in futures carefully executed
402-408 Western Union Bldg., Chicago
All business transacted through and confirmed by H. W. Rogers & Bro.

BOGERT, MALTBY & CO.
(INCORPORATED)
COMMISSION MERCHANTS
Correspondence and Consignments Solicited
Orders for futures delivery carefully executed.
Screenings and Mill Feed
306-308 Postal Telegraph Bldg., CHICAGO

J. K. HOOPER, President — E. G. BROWN, Secy-Treas.
HOOPER GRAIN CO.
OAT SHIPPERS
Postal Telegraph Bldg., Chicago
OPERATE ATLANTIC ELEVATOR AND GRAND TRUNK WESTERN ELEVATORS, CHICAGO

F. E. WINANS & CO.
GRAIN AND FIELD SEEDS
COMMISSION MERCHANTS
Barley, Oats, Wheat, Corn, Rye, Timothy, Clover, Flax, Hungarian Millet
98 BOARD OF TRADE, CHICAGO
Write us freely on all matters pertaining to grain and field seeds. Your questions fully and cheerfully answered; particular attention paid to timothy seed and grain by sample. Consignments and speculative orders receive our careful personal attention.

J. C. Shaffer & Co.
BUYERS AND SHIPPERS OF
GRAIN
234 S. La Salle St. Chicago

CHICAGO

GEO. S. DOLE, Pres. — H. N. SAGER, Sec.
J. H. DOLE & CO.
(Established 1852)
Commission Merchants, Grain and Seeds
We solicit your
CONSIGNMENTS
and orders in futures
226 La Salle Street. - - CHICAGO

HENRY H. FREEMAN & CO.
Hay, Straw and Grain
COMMISSION MERCHANTS
Correspondence and Consignments Solicited.
Market Reports on Application.
66 Board of Trade CHICAGO, ILL.

H. W. ROGERS, Pres. — J. C. ROGERS, Vice-Pres. — C. J. HURLBUT, Sec'y and Treas.
ROGERS GRAIN CO.
(Incorporated)
Buyers, Shippers and Exporters of
GRAIN
Elevator Proprietors on Illinois Central and other Railroad Systems
Main Office: 402-408 Western Union Building CHICAGO

DETROIT

A. S. DUMONT — R. C. ROBERTS — R. L. HUGHES
Dumont, Roberts & Co.
RECEIVERS GRAIN SHIPPERS
Chamber of Commerce DETROIT, MICH. — Merchants Exchange DECATUR, ILL.
Consignments Solicited. Ask for our bids and quotations.

CAUGHEY & CARRAN
DETROIT, MICH.
Grain and Seed Merchants and Commission
OUR SPECIALTY: OATS AND CLOVER SEED
We handle Beans, Barley, Rye, Corn, Wheat. Try us. Liberal advances.
OFFICES: 620 to 624 Chamber of Commerce
ELEVATOR and SEED HOUSE: Cor. 14th and Baker Sts.

BUFFALO

W. W. ALDER, Pres. — T. J. STOFER, Treas. — F. J. HEINMILLER, Secy.
ALDER GRAIN CO.
Consignments a Specialty
833 Chamber of Commerce, BUFFALO, N. Y.
Lahr Block, La Fayette, Ind.

L. S. CHURCHILL, President
G. W. BARTLETT, Treasurer
The Churchill Grain & Seed Co.
Commission Orders Executed. Grain and Seed Bought and Sold
Offices: Buffalo, N. Y. Toledo, Ohio
Seed Warehouse: Located at Toledo, Ohio
Members: New York Produce Exchange, Toledo Produce Exchange, Buffalo Corn Exchange

BASIL BURNS
GRAIN COMMISSION MERCHANT
CONSIGNMENTS SOLICITED
BUFFALO - - NEW YORK

A. W. HAROLD
GRAIN
BARLEY A SPECIALTY
717 Chamber of Commerce BUFFALO, N. Y.

PHILADELPHIA

L. F. MILLER & SONS,
Receivers and Shippers of
GRAIN, FEED, SEEDS, HAY, ETC.
OFFICE: 2931 N. BROAD ST., PHILADELPHIA, PA.
CONSIGNMENTS SOLICITED. Special attention given to the handling of CORN AND OATS.
REFERENCES: Manufacturers' National Bank, Philadelphia, Pa. Union National Bank, Westminster, Md.

E. E. DELP GRAIN CO.
GRAIN AND FEEDS
453 BOURSE PHILADELPHIA, PA
ELEVATOR, TRANSFER HOUSE AND MILLS: BOURBON, INDIANA

SEEDS THE ALBERT DICKINSON CO.
DEALERS IN
GRASS SEEDS, CLOVERS, FLAX SEED, LAWN GRASS, BEANS, PEAS, POPCORN, BIRD SEEDS, BUCKWHEAT, BAGS, ETC
CHICAGO, Ill. Branch: Minneapolis, Minn.

UNIVERSAL GRAIN CODE

(AND MILL FEED SUPPLEMENT)
Compiled for use of GRAIN AND MILLING TRADES
of the United States and Canada
SEND FOR A COPY NOW. PRICE $3.00.
MITCHELL BROS. & CO., 431 South Dearborn St., Chicago, Ill.

GRAIN RECEIVERS

TOLEDO

Born 1846

C. A. KING & CO.

FUTURES

Toledo and Chicago

Be Friendly. Write Occasionally.

JOHN WICKENHISER & CO,

Buyers and Shippers of Grain

We buy F. O. B. your station for direct shipment to interior points.

Personal attention to consignments.

TOLEDO, OHIO

ESTABLISHED 1868

SEEDS

We will buy or sell Red and Alsike Clover, also Timothy Seed. Try us.

S. W. FLOWER & CO., - Toledo, Ohio

WHY NOT RECEIVE

Our Daily Market Letter

IT COSTS YOU NAUGHT

SOUTHWORTH & COMPANY

Toledo, Ohio

National Milling Co.

Toledo, Ohio

Daily Flour Capacity 4,000 Barrels. Elevator Capacity 1,500,000 Bushels.

Always in the market for milling wheat; ask for our daily bids.

FRED MAYER FRED JAEGER

ESTABLISHED 1879.

J. F. ZAHM

& COMPANY

TOLEDO——OHIO

Specialists on handling consignments of grain and seeds and filling orders for futures.

Pay Drafts promptly on all consignments.

Our Daily Red Letter will be sent it. for the asking

MINNEAPOLIS

PV **F. H. PEAVEY & CO.**

MINNEAPOLIS,

GRAIN RECEIVERS MINN.

Consignments Solicited.

MILLING WHEAT A SPECIALITY

DECATUR

OFFER US GRAIN FOR ANY MARKET

ASK FOR CARD BIDS

C. A. BURKS & CO.

DECATUR, ILL.

GRAIN BROKERS

"LIVE WIRES"

WIRE, PHONE OR WRITE

WE REPRESENT RESPONSIBLE RECEIVERS

OUR

BIDS

ARE

GOOD

ONES

BALTIMORE

JOHN M. DENNIS, Pres't.
FERDINAND A. MEYER, V.-Pres't.
THOMAS C. CRAFT, JR., Treas.

LOUIS MÜLLER CO.

Grain Receivers and Exporters

BALTIMORE, MD

Members of the Baltimore Chamber of Commerce, Chicago Board of Trade, St. Louis Merchants' Exchange, Grain Dealers' National Association, Indiana Grain Dealers' Association.

CHAS. ENGLAND & CO.

RECEIVERS OF

GRAIN and HAY

308-310 Chamber of Commerce

BALTIMORE, MD.

DO YOU SELL OR CONSIGN?

KIRWAN BROS. GRAIN CO.

BALTIMORE, MD.

BUYERS, RECEIVERS AND SHIPPERS

THEY GET RESULTS

KANSAS CITY

R. J. THRESHER, Pres. L. A. FULLER, Sec'y

THRESHER-FULLER GRAIN CO.

Grain Commission Merchants

CONSIGNMENTS SOLICITED

Grain Bought and Sold for Future Delivery

311-14 Board of Trade KANSAS CITY, Mo.

OMAHA

HOLMQUIST ELEVATOR CO.

OMAHA, NEBRASKA

Receivers and Shippers of Grain

Sacked Corn and Oats a Specialty

Consignments Solicited

CAVERS ELEVATOR CO.

OMAHA

Receivers and Shippers of Grain

SACKED CORN AND OATS

Members: Omaha Grain Exchange Chicago Board of Trade.

MEMPHIS

J. B. HORTON & CO.

Consolidated with and Successors to

J. C. WEST & CO.

HAY = MILL FEED = GRAIN

BROKERAGE & COMMISSION

CONSIGNMENT SPECIALISTS

MEMBERS: Memphis Merch'ts Exch'ge, Various Associations | MEMPHIS | REFERENCES: The Mercantile Agencies, Central Bank & Trust Co.

CLEVELAND

The Union Elevator Co.

BUYERS AND SHIPPERS

Wheat, Corn, Oats, Hay and Straw

Our Speciality: Recleaned Illinois Shelled Corn

CLEVELAND, O.

E. F. SHEPARD O. W. TRAPP CHAS. G. CLARK

Shepard Clark & Co.

WHOLESALE GRAIN, HAY, FEED

SPECIALTY: Split Cars of Grain and Mill Feed. O. P. Oil Meal and Cotton Seed Meal, Distillers Dried Grains.

218 The Columbia Block, Cleveland, Ohio

Chas. G. Clark, formerly with The Union Elevator Co.
O. W. Trapp, formerly with The Union Elevator Co.

INDIANAPOLIS

JOE F. COPPOCK

DEALER IN

Grain and Hay

CAR LOTS

621 Board of Trade INDIANAPOLIS, IND.

The

Bassett Grain Co.

INDIANAPOLIS

Telephones 80 615-616 Board of Trade

Our name is conspicuous by its absence.
See Page 666.

ELEVATOR

Engineers and Builders
CHICAGO

LOOK—LISTEN—TAKE HEED

Your business is not our business. Our business is to Build Elevators and your business is to want the best you can get for the money.

And that is just what we give you.

We build the best and ask for a chance to prove it to you

PEERLESS CONSTRUCTION CO.
WICHITA, KANSAS
Long Distance Phone—Market 2380

L. O. Hickok & Son
Engineers and Contractors for
Elevators
AND
Fireproof Storage
Minneapolis, Minn.

SHREWD calculators know that renewals, repairs, and maintenance of grain spouts are expenses, NOT INVESTMENTS. But added together at the end of the year, the amount is considerable, and is all a LOSS, and this is the SMALLEST loss occasioned by their use.

The Hall Signaling Distributor is an investment. It is property. Instead of a loss, it brings revenue, year in and year out, greater than any other investment in grain business. Any person who bought one over ten years ago has it now as good as new, and it will be just as good for his grand children.

HALL DISTRIBUTOR CO.,
506 Ramge Bldg., Omaha, Nebr.

G. H. BIRCHARD
Contractor of
Grain Elevators
Especially Designed for Economy of Operation and Maintenance
LINCOLN, NEB.

I BUILD
Modern Grain Elevators
COMPLETE

Do all kinds of **repairing and remodeling**, sell and install all kinds of **mill and elevator machinery, gasoline and steam engines.**

Don't let your contract until you get my price. Plans and estimates furnished free. Write for reference.

R. M. VAN NESS, Fairbury, Neb.

The P. H. Pelkey Construction Co.
Contractors and Builders
Grain Elevators, Mills, Warehouses, etc.
Also Mill and Elevator Supplies.
Wichita - - Kansas

HODGMAN & BROWN
DWIGHT, ILL.
Designers and Builders of Elevators and Mills
Write for Plans and Estimates.
(We designed and built the Angola (Ind.) Elevator, illustrated on page 557 of the April "American Elevator and Grain Trade".)

Elevator Machinery and Supplies

FLOUR AND FEED MILL MACHINERY
STEAM AND GAS ENGINES
Pulleys, Shafting, General Power Transmission Machinery, Roll Grinding and Corrugating
Largest Factory and Stock in Western Country
SEND FOR 450-PAGE CATALOG

GREAT WESTERN MFG. CO.

General Office and Factory
LEAVENWORTH, KAN.

Warehouse and Salesrooms
1221-1223 Union Ave.
KANSAS CITY, MO.

YOUR ELEVATOR

Should be the best that money can buy.
It will be if IBBERSON builds it.
Get a price from me before you build.

T. E. IBBERSON, 300 Corn Exchange Bldg. **Minneapolis, Minn.**

Reliance Construction Company

Furnish Plans, Estimates and Build
COUNTRY GRAIN ELEVATORS
Our long experience as a builder of elevators insures you an up-to-date house. Write today.
625 Board of Trade Building, - INDIANAPOLIS, IND.

DUST! DUST! GIBBS PATENT DUST PROTECTOR is invaluable to operatives in every industry where dust is troublesome. It has been thoroughly tested for many years in every kind of dust, and is the most reliable protector known. Perfect Ventilation. Nickel-plated protector, $1, postpaid. Circular free. Agents wanted. GIBBS RESPIRATOR CO., "B" 124 East Ave., Oak Park (Chicago), Ill.

Triumph Power Corn Sheller
C. O. Bartlett & Co.
Cleveland, O.

The "NEW ERA" Manlift
is the
EASIEST RUNNING
SAFEST
BEST
We make Hand Elevators and Dumbwaiters of all kinds.
Write today.

Sidney Elevator Mfg. Co.
SIDNEY, OHIO.

Fire Proof Steel Grain Elevators and Storage Tanks

Almost anywhere between the Mississippi and the Pacific Coast, you will find elevators like these that we have built.

WE ARE DESIGNERS AND BUILDERS

MINNEAPOLIS STEEL & MACHINERY CO.
MINNEAPOLIS, MINN.
Denver, Colo. Seattle, Wash. Spokane, Wash. Salt Lake City, Utah Butte, Mont.

KENNEDY CAR LINERS

are the modern, sure and cheap way of avoiding losses and troubles occasioned by leakage in transit. Made by

FRED W. KENNEDY
SHELBYVILLE, IND.

1879—LAUSON "FROST KING"—1911

The engine of quality. Not how cheap, but HOW GOOD. Used exclusively by the leading Grain Elevator Companies for nearly 15 years. 1 to 25 H. P.

THE JOHN LAUSON MFG. CO.
59 Monroe Street New Holstein Wis.

Robinson Telegraphic Cipher
Revised Edition

Cloth Binding $1.50
Leather Binding 2.00

MITCHELL BROS. & CO.
431 S. Dearborn St., Chicago

MILLERS' MUTUAL FIRE INSURANCE ASSOCIATION OF ILLINOIS

Established 1878. Alton, Illinois

Insurance on Flour Mills and Elevator Properties.
Grain Insurance for short terms a Specialty.

CASH ASSETS - $376,783.32
G. A. McKINNEY, Sec'y

Grain Dealers Everywhere are Using

The Automatic Dump Controller

Entirely under the driveway floor and takes up no room.

Easily attached to a rail, platform or dump scale.

Has control of the dump from the time that the trigger is pulled and causes it to settle down easily and without the least jerk or jar.

Shipped on 30 or 60 days' trial

Also build
Grain Elevators
Write for plans and estimates.

L. J. McMILLIN
627 Board of Trade Building
INDIANAPOLIS, IND.

Millers' National Insurance Co.

137 S. LA SALLE ST.

CHICAGO - - ILL.

CHARTERED 1865

Insurance with a maximum of security at a minimum of cost for ELEVATORS, WAREHOUSES and CONTENTS, on the Mutual Plan

Five-Year Policies or short term policies on grain, if required.

Semi-Annual Assessments costing about one-half Stock Company Rates.

Gross Cash Assets............ $1,645,117.45
Net Cash Surplus and Permanent Fund.................. $966,846.27
Losses Paid Since Organization.... $7,108,022.20

The Jeffrey Mfg. Co.

We design and build Labor Saving Machinery for Grain Elevators.

Elevator Buckets	Shafting
Spiral Conveyers	Pulleys
Belt Conveyers	Elevator Boots
Link Belting	Gears
Sprocket Wheels	Chains, all kinds
Friction Clutches	Take-ups

Write for Catalog and let us figure with you.

Columbus, Ohio

Want ads. in this paper bring results. Rates on application.

Every Policyholder is a Stockholder in the

Michigan Millers Mutual Fire Insurance Company

of Lansing, Michigan

Therefore every policyholder is vitally interested in the size of his dividend (deducted every six months from the assessment levied.) These dividends may be increased by

THE PREVENTION OF FIRES

All fires are the same size at the start.
70% of them are preventable. 90% are extinguishable.

DIXON'S SILICA-GRAPHITE PAINT

THE PROVEN SHIELD FOR IRON AND STEEL. INERT PIGMENTS, GOOD COVERING CAPACITY, DURABILITY RECORDS IN ALL CLIMATES. Write for Booklet 17-B.
JOSEPH DIXON CRUCIBLE COMPANY, JERSEY CITY, N. J.

THE RAYMOND P. LIPE CO.
SHIPPERS OF GRAIN AND HAY
1330-1333 Nicholas Building
ROBINSON CODE
TOLEDO, O. April 22, 1911.

The American Elevator & Grain Trade,
Chicago, Ill.

Gentlemen:

Please discontinue our elevator advertisement, as it is sold. Your paper did the work.

Yours truly,
THE RAYMOND P. LIPE CO.

WE CAN DO THE SAME FOR YOU.

SEE THAT YOUR CONTRACT CALLS FOR THE

CUTLER STEAM DRYER

SOLD BY ALL MILL FURNISHERS

Not an Experiment. In successful use 30 years drying

CORN MEAL AND HOMINY,
BREWERS' GRITS AND MEAL,
BUCKWHEAT, RICE AND
ALL CEREAL PRODUCTS.

ALSO SAND, COAL DUST, GRAPHITE, CLAY AND ORES

Automatic in operation, requiring no attention.

THE CUTLER CO., North Wilbraham, Mass.
CATALOG ON REQUEST

Don't Buy Gasoline Engines

until you investigate "The Master Workman," a two-cylinder gasoline, kerosene or alcohol engine, superior to any one-cylinder engine; revolutionizing power. Its weight and bulk are half that of single-cylinder engines, with greater durability. Endorsed by the Board of Underwriters. Especially adapted for grain elevator work, owing to steady pull, quick and easy starting, small space occupied and practical overcoming of vibrations. Costs less to buy—less to run. Send for Catalogue. This is our 56th year.

THE TEMPLE PUMP COMPANY, Manufacturers, - - - Meagher and 15th Streets, CHICAGO

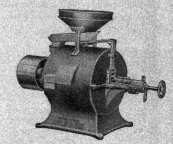

Lightning Source UK Ltd.
Milton Keynes UK
UKHW010631161218
333983UK00010B/1151/P

9 780331 434682